Applied Psychoanalysis: Explorations and Excursions
by David S. Werman

IPBOOKS.net
International Psychoanalytic Books

International Psychoanalytic Books (IPBooks),
New York   http://www.IPBooks.net

Offered in tribute to David S. Werman

Dedication

We dedicate this book posthumously to our father David S. Werman (January 1, 1922–June 3, 2014).

He instilled in us his love of art and the written word, he encouraged our intellectual exploration and he taught us to always look deeper.

—*Marco Werman and Claudia Werman Connor*

Applied Psychoanalysis: Explorations and Excursions

by David S. Werman

Contents

INTRODUCTION

David Werman: Setting the Agenda

by Claudia Heilbrunn

What is the role of the psychoanalyst in contemporary life? What is at stake if the psychoanalyst does not actually and actively define or embrace this mission? These two questions were central to David S. Werman's life and work, and they are explored and answered with insight in the papers which appear in this volume. This introduction highlights the overarching concern of Werman's articles, a concern that Werman shared not only with Freud, but also with so many others who care deeply about the continued welfare of humankind. This concern is most apparent in Werman's "reappraisal" of Freud's *Civilization and its Discontents* (chapter 10), but it is also evident throughout his other works. Werman notes that the "life Freud himself lived is a superb model of devotion to the individual, to a search for truth, and to the duty of being human" (p. 159): Werman's activities as presented in this volume show all too clearly that he too was devoted to these same principles—that his preoccupying concern, in effect, was with the same ideals.

David Werman's wide-ranging interests and traits are amply displayed in this volume of fifteen essays. Werman valued authenticity, believing that "there is no more worthy effort than to help relieve a little human misery" (Werman, 1984a). His book, *The Practice of Supportive Psychotherapy* (1984), focuses on the topic of providing quality therapeutic care for patients with more severe psychological deficits, a topic which had received little attention before 1984. Werman was a much sought-after supervisor throughout his career because "he was such a kind, thoughtful and often hilarious observer of the human condition" (*New York Times* Obituary, 2014). An exceptional speaker and brilliant discussant, Werman enjoyed asking incisive questions which often resulted in "spirited debates between fine minds" (Mayer, 2015). Werman prized developments in psychoanalysis that brought about theoretical and technical departures from the mainstream. He held that "the consequence of [an] open ambience has been that innovators have been given the opportunity to be heard and to influence conventional thinking;" only in such an environment, he believed, would intellectual growth and change generally occur (Werman, 1984b). Upon retirement, Werman's thirst for knowledge was still not sated: he continued to explore and enjoy his many subjects of interest, including literature, music, languages and applied psychoanalysis, and he studied piano up to his death in 2014.

In this introduction I try to articulate how Werman used both applied and theoretical psychoanalysis to elucidate important subjects, including friendship, aggression, attachment, and revenge. To this end, I first highlight key points in his article, "Freud's Civilization and its Discontents—A Reappraisal" (chapter 10). Thereafter, I demonstrate how his other chapters explore elements fundamental both to Freud's book and to Werman's seminal article on it. At every stage along the way, we shall observe Werman's belief in the necessity of free, thorough and honest inquiry, of using the creative arts and culture as tools to help people attain greater happiness and understanding, and of dedicating one's talents to the welfare of humankind more generally.

Like Freud and many others, Werman sought to show how aspects of the human unconscious and of childhood experiences are expressed in human behavior in a wide variety of ways. By looking at art, literature, and friendship through the lens of psychoanalytic theory, he broadens our understanding of important present-day cultural phenomena, and of humanity itself. Werman approached applied psychoanalysis with care: he believed that "superior" studies had to be based in the "plausibility and firmness of interpretation" rather than in "weak" conjecture (Werman, 1989), and that art must be viewed experientially, so that the psychoanalytic critic's own experience is usefully considered (Werman, 1998). In "Methodological Problems in the Psychoanalytic Interpretation of Literature: A Review of Studies on Sophocles' *Antigone*" (chapter 12), Werman cautions readers to approach all works of art as they would patients, namely with as few a priori ideas as possible: "We must turn to the text . . . as the source best embodying the data to be studied" (p. 182). He believed that great works of art have multiple levels of meaning and are open to multiple interpretations, all of which are not just valuable, relevant and true, but also corroborate, demonstrate and advance psychoanalytic theory.

I. "FREUD'S *CIVILIZATION AND ITS DISCONTENTS*—A REAPPRAISAL" (CHAPTER 10)

In his reappraisal of Freud's *Civilization and its Discontents*, Werman makes clear the urgent crisis facing our contemporary world:

> *If the increase in violent crime, terrorism, and hijackings constitutes some sort of benchmark, if the anecdotal observations about a "narcissistic" era have any basis in reality, then it is clear that civilization—at least as it exists in many countries today—is barely succeeding in fulfilling its raison d'être* (p. 157).

> *How comforting it would be if we could only ascribe this nightmare [World War II] to a given nation or a particular people; and that indeed has been attempted. But the daily newspaper ceaselessly demonstrates that no given society has a monopoly on aggression, and I speak not only of individual acts of violence but especially of national policies* (p. 154).

> *Has society improved the mutual relations between individuals in the past 50 years? It is not possible to answer in the affirmative. As I noted in regard to nations, where aggression has not abated, there does not seem to be a more effective control of individual aggression* (p. 157).

To re-examine Freud's book with the knowledge gleaned and gained since it was written is, for Werman, urgent because the destructive nature of man continually and increasingly threatens to destroy civilization. In his analysis, Werman briefly summarizes Freud's main propositions, but pays particular attention to Freud's primary theme: the unresolvable conflict between the individual and civilization, brought about by the demands and frustrations civilization imposes on man and by man's intrinsic aggression. While Werman disputes that man suffers because of societal restrictions placed on libidinal and aggressive drives, claiming instead that "human misery appears to be . . . the bitter fruit of object loss, disease, death, war, and poverty—what Freud called the unhappiness of everyday life" (p. 158), he supports the contention that aggression—whether inborn or acquired—can be attenuated if frustration is lessened or if individuals are able to modify hostile responses by strengthening intrapsychic defenses. Indeed, Werman, like Freud, saw that the modalities by which drive-frustration is mitigated, including art and other cultural pursuits, play a significant role in lessening unhappiness; and yet for Werman the additional significance of these modalities lies in their role of providing human beings with direct gratification, even joy. Cultural pursuits and their products—art, literature, theater, and more—thereby become essential mechanisms by which aggression and self-destruction can be subdued.

II. JAMES ENSOR, EDGAR ALLEN POE & ARTHUR RIMBAUD (CHAPTERS 1, 2, 3 & 4)

The psychoanalytic study of art takes as a premise (1) that human behavior and activity originate in the human unconscious, and (2) that the application of psychoanalytic theory to various art forms increases understanding of the human unconscious and how it expresses itself in so many aspects of human life and culture. These two factors crucially condition Werman's approach in "James Ensor, and the Attachment to Place" (chapter 1), an essay which draws welcome attention to the inner world of this distinguished Belgian artist (1860–1919). By reference to Ensor, Werman explores the psychological factors which create human bonds with and devotion to physical places: "from Homer to the poets of our time, many have evoked the joys of home and homeland, and have lamented the sorrow of separation" (p. 10). Werman looks to Ensor's life, writings and work to explain the artist's deep attachment to his seacoast town despite the conflict-riddled home within which he lived. Ensor's attachment to his home and the sea had specific psychodynamic meanings that were often painfully related to his early experiences. For Ensor, the sea represented a much-needed antidote to the critical world, which rejected him and his art, and a necessary solace from a dominating, intrusive, and humiliating mother, who never appreciated Ensor's talent. Unlike his actual mother, the sea represented (as Werman puts it) "a beautiful, virginal mother, who was always available to him, offering calm and consolation, who never reproached him and never sought to intrude in his life" (p. 4). Ensor's strong attachment to his home and the sea was an adaptive mechanism, Werman argues, that enabled him to withstand his extreme isolation and torment.

Ensor's paintings and etchings bear witness, of course, to his emotional experiences and conflicts. Several works (e.g., *The Tower of Lisserweghe*, 1888; *Christ Calming the Sea*, 1891) show his devotion and attachment to the sea, and they no doubt offered him solace in the act of painting the place that offered him warmth and consolation. Yet Ensor also used painting to communicate his experience of reality and conflicts directly. In "James Ensor and the Mask of Reality" (chapter 2), Werman demonstrates how Ensor used the painting of masks to lay bare the true selves of those he disdained, and as a vengeful weapon against (and a blatant provocation of) his enemies. Paintings such as *Scandalized Masks* (1883), *The Entry of Christ into Brussels* (1889), and *Self Portrait Surrounded by Masks* (1899) were meant to strip away people's benevolent pretenses and to reveal their hypocritical, detestable natures. Ensor was well aware of the purposes his mask paintings served: "I took some pleasure in painting masks," he wrote. "In this way I was able to make a study of the hypocritical, secretive, and selfish faces of the cowardly scoundrels whom I crushed by my progress! It was a happy choice . . . it reflected the self-serving criticism of my colleagues—their ignorance and dishonesty. The clumsiness of the critics, the vile and mean-spirited attacks of erstwhile imitators, forcefully kept me on this singular path" (p. 21). Far from hiding his enemies, Ensor's masks were meant (ironically) to expose them, and because his paintings directly attacked his enemies, who responded with their own virulent counterattacks, Ensor merely ensured the repetition of the vicious, cyclical conflict and repeatedly confirmed his self-conception as a victim and martyr. Ensor's mask paintings also served as a means by which he could both displace the rage he felt toward his family and project his own rage on to others; and yet the rage he felt from both internal and external sources became all-consuming and, eventually, self-destructive. Ultimately, it consumed him and his work and negatively impacted his creative abilities and his life down to his death in 1949 (see chapters 3 & 4).

Werman extends his discussion of the impact of vengefulness in two other articles: "Edgar Allan Poe, James Ensor, and the Psychology of Revenge" (chapter 3) considers how the power of vengeful feelings can alternately destroy or stimulate creativity; and "The Passing of Creativity: Two Histories: James Ensor and Arthur Rimbaud" (chapter 4) explores how two artistic geniuses dealt with the vengefulness that motivated their respective art forms. In these two articles, Werman stresses that the subject of revenge, to which there have been few psychoanalytic contributions, should command interest and concern because it impacts not only individual behavior, but also the behavior of religious sects, races, nations and other powerful groups. Both Ensor and Poe, whose childhood suffering had never been adequately resolved, explicitly expressed their vindictiveness in their work; yet while Ensor's work was gradually overtaken by his need for revenge so that his creativity deteriorated to such a degree that he primarily "fire[d] off verbal and pictorial broadsides," Poe's vengeful desires became the "controlled motor force" of many of his best stories. While neither extinguished his desire for revenge, Poe's creativity and expertise remained untouched by his anger.

Like Ensor, Arthur Rimbaud's work was dominated by vengeful feelings and emotional needs rather than by purely "aesthetic considerations." His poetry served as a vehicle through which he could voice his intense rage, pain, scorn, and vindictiveness, but once he expressed all the venom within him, he was seemingly exhausted, as if there was nothing left to say. Though the creativity of both Ensor and Rimbaud was strangled by their needs for revenge, Rimbaud exorcized his rage through poetry until, it seems, the poetry was no longer needed; but Ensor's vengeful feelings never abated, and he became an "embittered, bombastic, envious buffoon, given to making angry speeches." Through his combined studies of Ensor, Poe and Rimbaud, Werman surely offers good advice for the modern world in highlighting the danger that the desire for revenge poses not just for the individual, but also for humanity as a whole: "it leads people, individually and in groups, to the very heights of destructiveness and remains virtually untouched by reason or the lessons of history" (p. 44). A voice of sanity in the darkness.

III. FAUST, *THE WELL BELOVED* & ANTIGONE (CHAPTERS 12, 13 & 14)

In "The Faust Legend Seen in the Light of an Analytic Case" (chapter 15), Werman explores a psychological phenomenon that widely affects human contentment in legend, literature and actual lives. By describing a patient who suffers from the "Faust complex," defined by Werman as "a distorted and maladaptive hypertrophy of the more normative and ubiquitous strivings of human beings for strength, knowledge, wisdom, and gratification of the sexual drive" (p. 221), Werman increases our understanding both of Faust and of the Faust legend's sustained appeal down to the present day. While Werman notes that the psychogenetic development of people who suffer from the Faust Complex shows wide degrees of variation, his description of a patient who made magical pacts with supernatural beings (usually god) in order to attain great power, knowledge, and freedom from sexual anxiety and guilt adds to the understanding of both the Faust figure and those who suffer from the Faust complex.

Werman again usefully combines his analyses of literature and clinical work to elucidate the theme of infatuation. "Thomas Hardy's '*The Well-Beloved*' and the Nature of Infatuation" (chapter 13) gives an account of the inherent features of infatuation, which are vividly and thoroughly described in Hardy's novel about a man who repeatedly feels he has fallen in love. Werman contends that, in Hardy's novel, infatuation is experienced because of an unconscious need to establish intrapsychically an idealized self-object that will counter the protagonist's feelings of guilt and depression, which accompany his incessant conflicts over aggression. Yet infatuation is not simply a "happy" emotion. Hardy describes it as "insanity", "madness" and "folly," and Werman designates it as "intense, irrational . . . intoxicating and painful" (p. 198). The infatuated person aims to merge with the object of desire (the ideal mother) in order to feel complete. Yet because merger is prohibited by both the incest taboo and the adult ego, the infatuated person is fated to feel not only thrilled, but also anxious and depressed. The infatuation felt by Hardy's protagonist is a "life-long characterological compulsion," unlike the "contingent" infatuation experienced by the patient described in the article.

A recurrent feature in Werman's psychoanalytic studies of art and literature is his explication of a psychic need—whether for a protective sanctum, revenge, omnipotence, or merger—which can wreak havoc on oneself and others if it is not better understood, managed and mitigated. "Methodological Problems in the Psychoanalytic Interpretation of Literature: A Review of Studies on Sophocles' *Antigone*" (chapter 12) offers a contrasting case in point: Werman focuses on the methodology of applied psychoanalysis, suggesting techniques of literary interpretation that adhere to and are supported by the text of the work, rather than by the preconceived notions that an analyst seeks to find confirmed within the text. He also stresses the importance of considering the subjective experiences of the spectator when s/he forms a critical response to a work. Another primary concern of this article is to emphasize the many ways in which theatrical performances and other cultural products communicate with people on conscious and unconscious levels, thereby helping people to negotiate their own unconscious fantasies, feelings and conflicts.

IV. SIGMUND FREUD, ROMAIN ROLLAND, YVETTE GUILBERT, JAMES JACKSON PUTNAM & THE "OCEANIC EXPERIENCE" (CHAPTERS 7, 8, 9 & 14)

In two articles, "Freud, Yvette Guilbert, and the Psychology of Performance: A Biographical Note" (chapter 9) and "Sigmund Freud and Romain Rolland" (chapter 8), Werman delineates the ties that bring and hold people together, even when those people differ in important ways. The article about Guilbert and Freud also broaches the question of whether conscious or unconscious dynamics enable the creative process to occur—a question that Werman closely relates to a more controversial debate: which holds sway, free will or psychic determinism? In both articles, Werman explores the varying needs that cause people to connect and become friends even when they disagree about important matters.

In chapter 8, Werman contends that Freud and Rolland's remarkable friendship was based on a mutual concern for the direction of humanity and civilization in a time of unrest and war. Their reciprocal admiration began before they met: Rolland characterized Freud as the "Christopher Columbus of a new continent, the mind" (p. 103), and Freud revered Rolland as "an artist and apostle of love for mankind" (p. 118). Though both men found fault in each other's belief systems, their reverence for the rewards of human creativity and intellect, and their mutual horror in the face of man's destructiveness, drew them together. It also seems that Freud admired in Rolland something he himself lacked. Freud believed love for mankind was essential "because in the face of our instinctual drives [Freud was] compelled to consider this love as indispensable for the preservation of the human species" (p. 119). In contrast, Rolland held a deep belief in spirituality and embodied a strength, energy and power that Freud held in high esteem. Rolland also committed himself to utopian goals, despite their unrealistic nature, a commitment which Freud, the "self-styled . . . terrestrial animal," could not match.

Two other subjects that are explored in Werman's articles about Freud's friendships (chapters 8 and 9) are considered in greater depth in individual articles, "On the Nature of the Oceanic Experience" (chapter 7) and "James Jackson Putnam: Philosophy and Psychoanalysis" (chapter 14). Freud began his exploration of the "oceanic experience" because of Rolland's response to *The Future of Illusion* (1927): Rolland remarked in a letter to Freud that he wished Freud had analyzed "spontaneous religious feeling," which is described as "a feeling of something limitless, unbounded—as if it were "oceanic" (p. 124). This feeling, for Rolland, is a subjective fact, not an article of faith; but, for Freud, it results from the "melting" of ego boundaries with the external world. In his article, Werman demonstrates the impact that a person's values and culture have on the oceanic experience, and he argues that the oceanic experience, like other states of consciousness, is a complex phenomenon born from all aspects of the psyche. Like Freud, Werman believes that the oceanic feeling can be an individual's defensive attempt to achieve union with the universe in order to avoid feeling the "painful limitations of oneness" (p. 87).

Werman first mentions James Jackson Putnam in his article (chapter 9) about Freud and Guilbert's friendship in his discussion about the controversy over free will versus psychic determinism. Putnam brought this controversy to the forefront of psychoanalysis in 1911, when he claimed the necessity of "ennobling" patients' minds by bringing into psychoanalysis a particular philosophical outlook and ethical viewpoint. Although Freud agreed with Putnam's own moral standards, he believed that urging a patient to adhere to a particular philosophy in order to ennoble his mind was a form of violence. Freud asserted that "it was not moral estimates that were needed for solving the problems of human life and motives, but more knowledge" (p. 215). Werman uses the example of Putnam to call attention to the danger posed (as perhaps in our own day) when science is invaded by cultural bias: he points to the intertwining of value-systems with observational methods, the destructive vogue of anti-reason, and the populism and relativism within psychiatry as examples of alarming trends. Werman warns that the more distant inferences remain from clinical data, the more likely they are to reflect cultural biases, and so to be harmfully applied.

V. NOSTALGIA, CHANCE & THE "NARCISSISM OF MINOR DIFFERENCES" (CHAPTERS 5, 6 & 11)

In the three remaining chapters of Werman's book, he touches upon themes already mentioned in the articles discussed so far: attachment to a particular place, people's desire for control and their unease in the face of powerlessness, and the dangers of human aggression and self-destruction. "Normal and Pathological Nostalgia" (chapter 6), written almost a decade before he wrote "Ensor, and the Attachment to Place," explores the feeling of nostalgia, the "bittersweet" affect which is associated with specific memories of a distinct setting at a particular time. Although often a "normal" occurrence, a longing for a time in the past which a person relishes without wishing to actually return to it, nostalgia can become pathological; this is especially so when it becomes a substitute for mourning, when it seeks to idealize and displace the reality of a painful past, and when it is used as resistance or to distort rather than illuminate the past in the psychoanalytic setting.

Like feelings of nostalgia, the inability to believe in chance occurrences and an intolerance of ambiguity, discussed in "Chance, Ambiguity and Psychological Mindedness" (chapter 5), also have an impact on psychoanalytic treatment: they are often outward displays of "poor psychological mindedness," in particular, of difficulties with introspective thinking. In this chapter, Werman suggests that an individual's belief in chance occurrences should be evaluated when s/he is considered for psychoanalytic treatment, not least because it relays information about the individual's failure to develop secondary process thinking. The ability to believe in chance attests to a person's awareness of life's unpredictability and one's lack of control over so many events; it also demonstrates the capacity to tolerate ambiguity, which is essential for the creation and appreciation of great art because great art is open to multiple interpretations and communicates to us on several psychical levels. The belief in magical thinking can be related to growing trends in mysticism, irrationalism, anti-intellectualism, and the rejection of psychic determinism, all of which run counter (Werman asserts) to scientific inquiry and progress.

Werman's concern for destructive psychological tendencies is re-emphasized in "Freud's 'Narcissism of Minor Differences': A Review and Reassessment" (chapter 11). While Werman's paper explores the impact that the narcissism of minor differences has in psychoanalytic organizations and treatment, he pays particular attention to the potential harm that the narcissism of minor differences can bring about. Freud used the term 'the narcissism of minor differences' to refer to the use of minor differences, by both groups and individuals, as rationalizations for a hostility that has no objective base; in *Civilization and its Discontents* (1930) Freud writes that the "narcissism of minor differences" is a "convenient and relatively harmless satisfaction of the inclination to aggression, by means of which cohesion between the members of the community is made easier." In the psychoanalytic establishment, this can be seen when trivial matters become invested with an importance that they hardly warrant; it can also be seen in psychoanalytic treatments in which either the patient or the analyst has a vested interest in remaining distinct from the other. Werman strongly rejects Freud's supposition that the narcissism of minor differences is harmless. Indeed, he declares that "the history of the last half-century, if not of preceding millennia, suggests that the narcissism of minor difference has a malignant potential to erupt in vast bloodbaths which have even reached the level of genocide" (p. 166).

Werman strongly believed that it was our responsibility to understand and tame human aggression, and to spurn the notion that aggression is an essential and inescapable element of the human condition. This collection of essays amply testifies to his commitment to this cause. His tireless exploration of mind-impacting conditions and his ceaseless ambition to elucidate and mitigate psychic pain and the destructive action it can spur amount to an important contribution toward the controlling and sublimation of aggression, in all its various forms. He believed that the narcissism of minor differences was so deeply entrenched in human relations because it enhances self- and group-esteem and permits a socially acceptable discharge of aggression. It may not be a far leap to imagine that the more self-esteem individuals (and groups) possess, and the more individuals are able to sublimate their aggression through cultural endeavors, the less need there would be to create discord in the guise of truth. Perhaps the lessons contained in Werman's volume are self-evident and, in a way, even relatively simplistic truths: the more people can connect despite their differences, the greater our ability to sublimate and derive satisfaction from the fruits of culture, and the better able we are to tolerate ambiguity and modify our aggressive responses, the better chance humanity has of appreciating itself and of valuing its continued existence. Such, at least, is the hopeful vision that Werman holds out to (and for) us in this outstanding collection of essays.

REFERENCES

WERMAN, D.S. (1984a). *The Practice of Supportive Psychotherapy.* New York: Routledge.

———— (1984b), review of R. Schafer, *The Analytic Attitude* (New York, 1983). *Psychoanalytic Review* 73C: 398–403.

———— (1989). Book review of: *Virginia Woolf and the "Lust of Creation" a Psychoanalytic Exploration*: By Shirley Panken. Albany: State University of New York Press, 1987, 336 pp. *Psychoanalytic Quarterly* 58:131–134.

————— (1998). Film Reviews Guest Editorial. *International Journal of Psycho-Analysis* 79:387–388.

OBITUARY of D.S. Werman (2014). *New York Times,* June 11.

MAYER, B. (2014). Comment on D.S. Werman obituary. International Psychoanalysis.net, June 15, online at:
http://internationalpsychoanalysis.net/2014/06/14/david-s-werman-1922-2014/#comment-341781.

CHAPTER 1

James Ensor, and the Attachment to Place

[Werman, D.S. (1989). *International Review of Psycho-Analysis,* 16:287–295.]

One of the remarkable aspects of the long and singular life of the Belgian painter, James Ensor, was his tenacious attachment to the North Sea and his home in Ostend, the city of his birth, where he lived almost without interruption for eighty-nine years.

Attachments to place are complex phenomena, into which psycho-dynamic, developmental, and socio-cultural strands interweave, and, more than likely, constitutional factors play a role, since for most people a certain propensity for attachment to place exists. For James Ensor, from what we know of his life, his works and his writings, I believe that his attachment to home and to the sea largely represented a multiply-determined adaptive process.

When Ensor was born in 1860, Ostend was a provincial city on the North Sea, 75 miles west of Brussels; it was still surrounded by ramparts, and boasted of some sixteen thousand inhabitants. During the long bleak winter Ostend was principally a sleepy, provincial city of fishermen and shopkeepers. In the summer months, however, its beaches swarmed with holiday-makers from England and the Continent, who, Ensor felt, desecrated his beautiful sea and its shores. (*The Beach, Ostend,* c. 1910.)

Manifestly, there was little in Ostend to anchor a young *avantgarde* painter working during the last quarter of the nineteenth century—a revolutionary time for an artist. The barrenness of Ostend—worse still, the hostility of the Ostenders toward the Ensor family—was not lost on James, and yet it was here that he spent most of his life, 'nailed to the sea', as he put it, with the exception of two years spent at the Art Academy in Brussels.

Ensor's parents owned a souvenir shop, the sort that, to this day, can be seen in any seaside resort. James' father, James Frederic Ensor, was born in Brussels of well-to-do English parents who generally spent a part of each year on the Continent. He had started studying medicine in Bonn and Heidelberg, but abandoned it and returned to England where he was employed by a civil engineer. It was on a holiday in Ostend with his parents that he met his future wife, the daughter of Flemish lace merchants, and they entered into what has been described as a 'horrendous' marriage; he was then 23 and she a year older. They were mismatched in almost every way, and what brought them together can only be conjectured. His parents reacted by disinheriting him.

Ensor described his father as an 'intellectual', fond of music and art, sensitive and gentle, but haughty in his dealings with some people. He felt out of place in Ostend, and shortly before James' birth, set out for the United States to look for work; within months of his arrival the Civil War broke out, and he returned to his young family. He appeared depressed, 'life seemed to have virtually gone out of him' (Van Gindertael, 1965, p. 13) ; although at first he helped out in the shop his interest waned, and 'he finally preferred to drink rather than to be like the rest of us' (Ensor, 1974, p. 205). Although Ensor never wrote a critical or angry word about his father, he acknowledged that the family had suffered from his drinking. (*Scandalized Masks*, 1883.) Gradually he grew totally dependent on his 'authoritarian' wife and her shrewish unmarried sister, and became the laughing stock of the townspeople who delighted in getting him drunk and depositing his unconscious body at the door to the shop. When James had a modest success with his paintings, some people took revenge and shaved off half of his father's beard and moustache. He finally died in the street of alcoholism and exposure when James was 27 years old.

Ensor's mother was a good manager—shrewd and controlling; she held the family together, emotionally and financially, although frequently ill. A description he gave of his maternal grandmother seems equally appropriate to her: 'She was an expert business woman and good with money. As she grew old she grew hard ...'

By all counts, as a child Ensor was, at least materially, over-indulged. 'My mother nourished me on pralines and sugared almonds, and a good Aunt puffed me up on over-sweetened milk.' Despite the family's relatively modest means James was tutored at home until he was 13 when he began to attend school; however, he left after two years—the same length of time he was later able to tolerate in art school.

He grew up surrounded by the bizarre objects found in his parents' shop: apart from the usual things such as toy shovels and pails, sea-shells, fishing nets, dried sea plants and stuffed animals, there were the grotesque masks and costumes that the Ostenders wore during their annual carnival.

James spent many hours amid the jumble of even stranger objects stored in the attic, where, he later claimed, there were dried monkeys, skeletons, turtles, mermaids and a 'stuffed Chinaman'. To add to this Gothic setting, an elderly Flemish servant relished telling him mysterious tales of fairies and wicked giants; all of this dream-like, if not nightmarish material later found its way into Ensor's paintings, at first as 'found' objects for still lifes but later taking on more symbolic meanings.

As a boy he wandered off and made sketches of the villages, the dunes and beaches that lay outside Ostend. Recognizing the boy's talent, his father secretly encouraged his work and arranged for James to take lessons from two local painters. Their limitations eventually led to James' attending the Art Academy in Brussels. Although his mother apparently did not overtly disapprove of her son's vocation, she never seemed to understand either his precocity or the nature of his work; in fact, later on, she was mostly interested in selling his 'hand-painted' pictures of local scenes in the souvenir shop and urging her son to earn a proper living.

Ensor was 17 when he went to the Academy; it was to be his only major absence from Ostend. He soon dealt with the separation from home by, in effect, adopting a new family and home. Not only were the Rousseaus a substitute family, but they embodied the fantasy of the family romance in so far as they were, by most criteria, 'ideal'. Ernest Rousseau, a warm and erudite man, was a professor of physics and the Rector of the University of Brussels. His wife, Mariette, nineteen years his junior, and so much closer to Ensor's age, and by coincidence having the same name and nickname as his sister, was a botanist and lover of art. Their son Ernest, a medical student, became Ensor's closest friend during this period. The Rousseau home was a gathering place for many of the intellectuals of Brussels; although they themselves were socialists and atheists, their home was open to people of every conviction. A greater contrast to James' home in Ostend would be hard to imagine, and, not surprisingly, he flourished in this environment.

Mariette Rousseau occupied a central place in Ensor's life at this time. A condensation of mother, sister and an object of affection—if not of deeper and more ambivalent feelings—she became, in effect, his muse: she approved of his work, encouraged him, gently scolded him when he was lazy, and bought some of his early paintings. This pattern of dependency on a woman, in many ways repeated—without her intrusiveness— his relationship with his mother, and prefigured that which he was to develop with Augusta Boogaerts.

However, despite the advantages that life in Brussels offered, after two years at the academy, with one more year left, he dropped it all and returned home. It is true that from the outset he found the professors at the Art Academy intolerable. That institution for the 'near blind' drove him to despair, and he was to ridicule it throughout his life. Still, he might have left the Academy and remained in Brussels where there was an important circle of *avant-garde* artists, where he had friends and a stimulating home that was always open to him.

Many years later he wrote that in his return to Ostend he was 'guided by a secret instinct, a feeling for the atmosphere of the seacoast which I [had] imbibed with the breeze, inhaled with the pearly mists, soaked up in the waves, heard in the wind' (Haesarts, p. 50). This description of his return, and not withstanding his escape from the academy, is consistent with his subsequent attachment to the sea and to Ostend. However, it does not touch on what, I believe, the sea principally represented to him; a beautiful, virginal mother, who was always available to him, offering calm and consolation, who never reproached him and never sought to intrude in his life. He wrote that he was born on a Friday, the day of Venus: 'At my birth, Venus came toward me, smiling, and we looked long into each other's eyes. What beautiful sea-green, blue-green eyes . . . Venus was blonde and beautiful, all covered with foam. She smelt pleasantly of salt water' (Ensor, 1974, p. 73).

Once back in Ostend, Ensor set up a studio in the attic of his parents' house. From its windows he could look out from one side over the city, and from the other toward the sea. From this attic, during the next fourteen or fifteen years, until about 1895, he created the masterworks on which his reputation rests.

His parents' home continued to be a domestic hothouse, with his resolute mother, assisted by her unmarried sister, in opposition to Ensor's defeated, passive and alienated father. In the dark rooms only a thin light was allowed to penetrate. The interiors Ensor painted in 1881, the year after his return from Brussels (*Afternoon at Ostend*, 1881; *Woman in Distress*, 1882; *Russian Music*, 1881) convey an airless world—genteel, static and provincial. So too are the portraits of his parents: joyless and sombre (*Portrait of the Artist's Father*, 1881; *Portrait of the Artist's Mother*, 1881; *A Cross Face*, 1890). For eight months of the year the inhabitants of these rooms hibernated, literally napping throughout the day, waiting for the vacation season to erupt. In this dull, shadowy but often acerbic atmosphere, arguments frequently burst forth. Ensor's mother had a ready store of recriminations. Madame Ensor 'distrusted everything and every-one, and did her best to set son against husband. The latter, an essentially frustrated and unhappy man, rebelled in vain, lashed about like a wild beast in a cage. James' sister [one year his junior] got away from the house at every opportunity. His aunt was given to highly vocal self-pity. Even the moments of relative calm were heavy with the boredom peculiar to provincial life' (Haesarts, p. 65). The appeal of such a home, to young Ensor, is not immediately apparent.

The critical points in the family's subsequent chronology can be briefly stated. Against the entire family's opposition, his sister, always looking for an escape, married a Chinese merchant and ran off to Germany. After a short marriage her husband left her and she returned with her baby. She became dependent on the family, remaining a particular source of worry and aggravation for Ensor. In 1887, at the age of 52, his father died under the circumstances I described earlier. His mother lived on until 1915, his aunt died a year later, and Mariette died in 1945.

In 1917 Ensor moved, with his sister, niece and two servants, to a house he inherited from an uncle, scarcely a stone's throw from his parents' house. Again, on the ground floor was a souvenir shop, which Ensor left intact even though it was never to be opened again. He set up living quarters above the store, as his parents had done, a studio on the floor above that, and here he remained until his death in 1949. Although during World War I a German shell landed next to his house, and during the Second World War the Nazis occupied Ostend and built a blockhouse that cut off his view of the sea, he refused to move. 'All my works are there; how could I go elsewhere?' he exclaimed, as if those works were as attached to Ostend as he himself was.

During the four years following his flight from the Academy, Ensor had a few occasions when he was able to exhibit his work; but from 1884 onwards he was increasingly attacked by the critics; even the contempo-rary artists rejected his paintings and refused to show them with theirs. This only fuelled his desire to avoid Brussels—indeed, the outside world altogether—and entrenched him in his isolation and growing bitterness. Despite these feelings and the attitude of the critics, he continued to work productively until about 35 when his creative powers began to wane.

After the years of rejection, gradual acceptance finally followed. In 1896 he had his first one-man show; that year also marked the first major purchase by a museum of one of his works, the *Lamp Boy*, painted 16 years earlier. Appreciative studies began to appear and in 1903 he was made a Knight of the Order of Leopold. In 1929, after much string pulling by Ensor himself, King Albert named him a Baron—obliging him finally to give up his British citizenship, a connexion to which he had clung since it seemed to confer on him some social superiority and to legitimize his social image as one who is 'different'. On a deeper level, it had probably represented another aspect of his identification with his father, an 'English gentleman'. Understandably, prior to receiving the baronetcy, Ensor withdrew the plates for a print he had done in 1889 called *Doctrinal Nourishment*. Literally scatological, and typical of many others, it depicts King Leopold and his retinue sitting on the edge of a wall and defaecating into the eager faces of the populace below.

'Different', superior and eccentric was the *persona* he adopted, and it was a means to depreciate, to mock and manipulate the world. Thus, with honours came visitors from all walks of life, who made the pilgrimage to Ostend. The guest was obliged to traverse a particular ritual: he would be admitted by Augusta, Ensor's male servant, wearing a blue apron and a red fez. The presentation to the Master took place while he was seated by the window. His pink skin and soft white hair and beard were set off by an elegant blue suit, a flowing bow tie, and a black Homburg hat which he wore indoors, much like the farmers in the surrounding countryside. The visitors were then led upstairs to admire his paintings, especially the *Entry into Brussels of Christ*, a variety of masks, sea shells and the other iconographic images that appear in his work. When Ensor died, in 1949, all of Ostend and dignitaries from many countries marched in the funeral procession. Since his death, his reputation as one of the most influential innovators of modern art has only continued to grow.

When Ensor wrote, as I mentioned earlier, that he quit the Academy because he was guided back to Ostend by a 'secret instinct', he was, as he had repeatedly done, giving voice to a driven attachment to home and the sea. This theme recurs repeatedly in his writings and speeches, and although he tended to mythologize and falsify his past, there is little doubt that the return home and his staying on arose from an extraordinary intensity of feeling. The inanimate presence of home was, on a conscious level, at least as important to Ensor as the people there. Home usually connotes safety—a safety afforded the small child by a familiar environment, both human and inanimate, in which the child's anxiety can remain within tolerable limits. This general experience of home is obviously subject to numerous vicissitudes, and consequently to a spectrum of attitudes ranging from pathological homesickness and the house-bound 'phobic', through various degrees of nostalgia (Werman, 1977), to a compulsive urge to escape. For Ensor, home and the sea had specific psychodynamic meanings that influenced his intense attachments to them.

Of paramount importance in these relationships were his earliest experiences with his mother. Although she 'over-indulged' him, the emphasis, in his memories, is on the *things* that she gave him. It is also evident that as long as she lived she attempted to control his life, and at the same time failed to appreciate his genius. When he wanted to marry Augusta Boogaerts, she 'harshly rebuked' him; she even forbade him to paint nudes; and generally she made him feel inadequate and marginal (*Ensor and His Family*, 1886). One is hardly surprised to learn that not only did Ensor never marry, but there is scant evidence that he ever had a significant intimate or erotic relationship with man or woman. Years later he wrote that in the 1890s, when he suffered from rejection by the critics, he turned to 'the charnel spirit of women' but soon moved away from this 'mask of flesh'. Throughout his life he demonstrated both a dread of and repugnance for women. When he was 25, as I mentioned earlier, he met Augusta Boogaerts, who worked in the Ensors' shop, and in this way she virtually fell into his arms. She was almost 10 years younger than him. Although she wanted to marry him, his parents opposed the marriage, and Ensor, somewhat indifferently, let them and Miss Boogaerts struggle over him, with the result that the couple never married, and for a considerable time met secretly and only intermittently; their relationship lasted until Ensor's death.

In 1905 he painted *Our Two Portraits*, depicting Miss Boogaerts and himself during a brief visit to Paris. The ambiguity of the scene is almost provocatively enigmatic to the observer. The two figures are not only distant, and look away from each other, but Ensor himself is represented by his reflection in a mirror. He sits with thumb hooked in his vest, a somewhat cocky pose, while Miss Boogaerts, whom he had ironically nicknamed 'the Siren', gazes towards the window of the hotel room, with a faint trace of a smile. Her gloved hand holds a drooping flower, and several others, straggly, lie on the floor. Draped across her knees is a brown fur scarf almost the same colour as her hair. Although the picture ambiguously deals with their sexual relationship, it vividly communicates an absence of intimacy and warmth, not to speak of passion. Indeed, one of the qualities of Miss Boogaerts that pleased Ensor was that like him she had a caustic wit and was as quick in repartee. Nevertheless, he still disparaged her. (*The Call of the Siren*, 1883).

Indeed, although he sang the praises of the sea and art as embodiments of woman, these did not refer to actual women, but rather representations of an idealized pre-oedipal mother. Compare such adulation with a poem about women that he wrote in 1925: 'Deceiving sex, respecter neither of law nor religion, heartless and devoid of honor/Sink of hypocrisy/Hotbed of lies and dissimulation/Mud-pit of malice', and so on for 22 lines, concluding with: 'Constant mask and endless smile' (Haesarts, p. 360). The sense of deception, fear and disappointment that pervades his references to women, suggests an early time in childhood when his mother was at least adequately, if not richly responsive to his needs, but that at some point that phase came to an end, to be followed by a mode of mothering more characterized by attention to his physical rather than his emotional needs and by control and intrusion. In particular, although his home was a sanctuary where his material requirements were attended to, it clearly was not where he could find the solace and calm that he required in the face of a critical world that rejected him.

For that fulfilment he turned to the sea, which had already served him in his youth. In writing about *Cabin on the Beach* (1877), which he painted when he was 16, he recalled 'I was becoming melancholic and wanted to live in a large cabin in front of the sea. I would cover it with pearly shells and sleep there, ideally soothed by the sound of the sea' (Legrand, 1971, p. 16). Now, as an adult, it became the means of dealing with an insistent need for a soothing which he could find nowhere else. His perorations to the sea represent a total idealization: the sea is never cruel—indeed, 'we have all come from the sea, and we're drunk on her foam'. Ensor's sea is not only a beautiful woman, a muse, but it is 'chaste', 'virginal', it has been 'washed clean', it is flawless, it is a goddess. 'Night and morning', he exclaims, 'I embrace . . . my beloved'. The sea also embodies light that sweeps away the gloom and shadows from his lugubrious home; it is this light that for a few years floods his work (*The Tower of Lisserweghe*, 1888; *Christ Calming the Sea*, 1891). The sea becomes a metaphor, a condensation of the consoling pre-oedipal mother, the sensual oedipal mother, whose sexuality he denies, and a muse towards whom he turns for reassurance in his work. Not only is the pathetic fallacy adored, but the beaches and dunes that adjoin the sea are apostrophized as a woman with entrancing 'buttocks' and 'breasts'. For the artist, increasingly isolated and denigrated, the sea becomes his salvation and he worships it in almost religious terms. Repeatedly he plays on the word, 'la mer', the sea, which is a homonym in French for the mother, 'la mère'.

At the same time, living at home, he increasingly identified with his father: with his father's intellectual and artistic aptitudes, his snobbish views of other people, his passivity and utter dependency on his wife. His father sought refuge from his wife, himself and a world that derided him as much as he despised it, in self-isolation, immersion in books, music and alcohol. Ensor found his path through his art and the sea.

After his father's death his mother increasingly nagged him to earn more money, but at best he helped out in the shop in the same lackadaisical way as his father had done. Five years after his father's death he went to London for four days, where he visited his father's mother, now a widow; what his aim was in taking this trip, what fantasies he had consciously or unconsciously entertained, is unknown. Perhaps it was a last attempt to break out of his bondage to Ostend and his mother. In any event, in London he found an old woman who was polite but cool; he returned home 'sullen and tired'. This event coincidentally occurred with the onset of the waning of his creativity; the failure to escape from his dependency on his mother seems to have represented a final capitulation and identification with his father.

Increasingly Ensor saw himself as a martyr. (*The Good Judges*, 1891.) Bitterly he dipped his brush in acid, and mercilessly caricatured his enemies. His rage was progressively directed toward a variety of targets: vivisection, urban developers, vacationers, other artists, doctors, the critics and eventually a good part of man and woman-kind. (*Death Chasing the Flock of Mortals*, 1896.)

Throughout his artistic life Ensor chose himself as a subject. Either as the principle figure in a painting or drawing, or as a secondary one, he is present in over one hundred of his works. Although some of these may be seen as narcissistic displays, more frequently they convey their subject's fear, self mockery, and perhaps a groping for self-discovery. Increasingly he represented himself as tortured by devils (chiefly critics and women) (*Demons Teasing Me*, 1895; *Christ Mocked*, 1886), impotent, derisory, and skeletal, if not already dead. It was almost inevitable that he would finally experience and pictorially represent himself as Christ—at first only by an affinity of attitude, and later explicitly by using his own features. (*Man of Sorrows*, 1891; *Calvary*, 1886.) Ensor as Christ did not see himself as a God-like figure (although he increasingly wrapped himself in a messianic cloak) but as the Christ on Golgotha: mocked, crowned in thorns, mutilated and crucified. The more he felt besieged by the world outside, the more he rebuffed the world and clung to the sea and his home.

DISCUSSION

Attachment to place is not behaviour restricted to man: most animals manifest some form of attachment. Ethological studies have provided a wealth of data demonstrating how animals mark off and attach to their territory generally with the principle aim of survival by ensuring their food supply and regulating the conditions for mating and species continuity. In non-human animals this behaviour has a significant genetic basis, even though it often requires specific stimuli, during critical phases of development, to bring the inborn potentials to full functional realization. To what extent man possesses such an hereditary predisposition to attach to place is not known, but in the light of the ubiquity of such tendencies in other species, it would be best not to dismiss, out of hand, such a possibility for man.

In one of the few psychoanalytic case studies on attachment to place, Edith Sterba (1940) referred to the 'millions of human beings torn against their will from the soil to which they are bound' during the 1930s. She observed that the loss of country is generally experienced as the loss of the mother; indeed, this has so often been observed and 'sung by so many poets that it has almost become a platitude' (p. 701). She described a 5-year-old girl whose development was unremarkable until, along with her family and nurse, she was forced to leave her country. The little girl developed a 'severe depression' and regressed to a stage where she had to be soothed by having a particular cloth, an earlier transitional object, placed next to her. Such attachments, Sterba writes, have made it 'impossible for many to leave their home country although they may often be obliged to live there under wretched conditions and may come near to starving' (p. 707).

As Sterba remarked, poets and folksingers have long been aware of man's attachment to places: from Homer to the poets of our time, many have evoked the joys of home and homeland, and have lamented the sorrow of separation. Wanderers like Ulysses and emigrés like Ruth conjure up for us the suffering of those who are far from home. Even the nomadic Bedouins follow more or less well-travelled routes, camp in well-known places, and carry their tents and belongings with them.

Unlike Sterba's little patient, Ensor was not forced to leave his home, but leaving, for him too, seems to have represented a painful separation from the protective pre-oedipal mother. To remain at home was a conflict-ridden enterprise: it required a loss of independence, humiliating submission and daily compliance. Ensor worked out a solution of sorts by maintaining a fairly superficial relationship with his mother, accepting her help and financial support, but turning to the sea for warmth and consolation.

Such a solution to Ensor's conflict is a dramatic contrast to that of Arthur Rimbaud, a fellow-Belgian, who also attempted to deal with an intensely hostile and dependent relationship with his mother. Whereas Ensor remained attached to Ostend, Rimbaud fled from Charlesville, a city that was culturally similar to Ostend. Living at the same time as Ensor, the poet cried out: 'I am dying, rotting away in all this platitude, stink and colourlessness ...' (Carré, 1926, p. 41). Escaping from his home at 17, he spent the rest of his short life in one move after another, criss-crossing half the world. Not only did he flee from his mother and home, but from his mother tongue as well, abandoning poetry for commerce, and steeping himself in half a dozen foreign languages. For Rimbaud, home, city, country, language and mother, became condensed into one repugnant entity. Ensor dealt with his hostility by spewing it out on canvas and in words. (*Wizards in a Squall*, 1888.)

Piron (1968), in a psychoanalytic study which focuses principally on Ensor's loss of creativity, argues that for Ensor the sea symbolized the erotic oedipal mother. He states that the intensity of Ensor's repressed sexual desire, and the powerful associated guilt and fear of reprisals from his father, precluded an adult heterosexual relationship. The death of Ensor's father in 1887, he believes, permitted a fresh creative phase, but within five years, guilt over his death wishes towards the father led him to sacrifice his life symbolically through a loss of artistic creativity, and caused an (hypothesized) impotence. Although Piron offers many valuable perceptions, his thesis is chiefly theoretical; his only evidence is Ensor's well-known 'recollection' (or fantasy) that he had as an adult. In this memory, a huge black sea bird, attracted by the light, flew into his room while he lay in his crib. Piron posits that the bird represents Ensor's terror in the face of a castrating father. However, aside from this 'memory' there is nothing to support such intense anxiety in regard to his father. Nor is there anything that suggests that Ensor nursed an 'exorbitant incestuous passion' for his mother, as Piron argues. What *is* well documented is his suffering from rejection, his bitterness and anger, his material dependency on his mother and his emotional dependency on the sea.

Even if Ensor had experienced his earliest years as idyllic, those pre-oedipal years were, in fact, transcended by the reality of a gloomy frightening home and by parents who were embittered by their mutual contempt, by his mother's grim domination and his father's passivity. Disappointment was heightened when he discovered that his masters at the Academy were inept and foolish, and disappointment reached its height when he found himself the butt of mockery by the art critics that has rarely been surpassed in critical invective. These deceptions, along with other more formal considerations, undoubtedly contributed to Ensor's painting of masked figures, masks which, I believe, reveal rather than conceal the truth about the wearer. (*Masks and Death*, 1897; *Self Portrait Surrounded by Masks*, 1897; *The Entry of Christ into Brussels*, 1888.) Ensor undoubtedly had more or less unresolved oedipal wishes; nevertheless, it was probably not these which kept him 'nailed to the sea'. Moreover, although Piron states that Ensor sacrificed his art in atonement for presumed death wishes toward his father, it is more plausible that with the loss of this only reliable mentor, and bedevilled by detractors and revilers, he did not possess an adequate reservoir of confidence and self-esteem to sustain him in the face of these attacks. Like his father he abhorred the petty-bourgeois Ostenders, who, like his mother, were insensitive to his work; indeed, even when his fame grew, few in the town knew who he was. When his work was rejected, like his father he turned his back on the world and looked to the sea and art for unambiguous solace; indeed, before art he could kneel freely with neither fear, rage nor malice, but only in profound humility. (*The Consoling Virgin*, 1892.)

In view of Ensor's tenacious attachment to home, we may ask if that did not instead, or also, represent a phobic fear of places away from home, a form of agoraphobia. Some authors have observed that agoraphobia at times 'serves to protect the [mother-child dyad] at the expense of creating a dangerous outside world' (Frances & Dunn, 1975, p. 437). But despite Ensor's rare absences from Ostend, nothing suggests that he experienced any anxiety in leaving his home unaccompanied. In fact, weather permitting, he walked alone along the piers of Ostend every day of the year. Later in the day he would sit in a café for two hours by the clock, speaking to no one. similarly, in the evening, he repaired to the Falstaff café where he remained until closing time. What is prominent in Ensor is not some unidentified phobic anxiety, but his attachments and displacements.

Human beings experience places in an astonishing variety of ways, and the psychological manifestations of such relationships are equally varied. This potentially rich lode of human behaviour has been only barely explored by psychoanalysts. Aside from Sterba, Searles (1960) wrote about the 'non-human environment'. The oceanic experience, as it has been described (Werman, 1986), frequently relates to wide vistas such as of mountains, the sea and broad fields with and through which individuals experience a sense of fusion with the universe and all humanity. In the same way that experience cannot be reduced to some universal meaning, but is specific to each individual, so all attachment to places—as well as the severing or avoidance of attachment—can only be understood in the context of its meaning to a given individual.

SUMMARY

James Ensor (1860–1949), the Belgian painter, lived most of his long life in Ostend, the city of his birth. During that time he showed a remarkable attachment to his home and the sea. Based on what is known of Ensor's life, his work and his writing, I suggest that his home provided him with a material sanctuary from a rejecting world and that the sea served him as maternal source of consolation and calm. In exploring his attachments to place I have sought to cast some light on one aspect of Ensor's life. At the same time, this exploration draws attention to the profound meanings places may have in our intrapsychic world.

REFERENCES

CARR, J.M. (1926). *La vie aventureuse de Jean-Arthur Rimbaud*. Paris: Plon.

CROQUEZ, R. (1917). *L'Oeuvre grav de James Ensor.* Genve-Bruxelles: Editions Pierre Cailler.

———— (1970). *Ensor en son temps.* Ostend: Erel.

ENSOR, J. (1974). *Mes ecrits*. Lige: Editions Nationales.

FARMER, J.D. (1976*). Ensor.* New York: Braziller.

FRANCES, R. & DUNN, P. (1975). The attachment autonomy conflict in agoraphobia. *Int. J. Psychoanal* 56:435–439.

HAESART, P. (n.d.). *Ensor.* London: Thames & Hudson.

JANSSENS, J. (1978). *James Ensor.* Naefels: Bonfini Press.

LEGAND, F.C. (1971). *Ensor, cet inconnu*. Bruxelles: Collection Renaissance-Art.

LESKO, D. (1985). *James Ensor.* Princeton: Princeton University Press.

OLLINGUER-ZINQUE, G. (1976). *Ensor by Himself.* A. Kennedy (Trans). Brussels: Laconti.

PIRON, H.T. (1968). *Ensor: Een Psychoanalytische Studie.* Antwerp: Uitgerverij, de Nederlansche Boekhandel.

SEARLES, H. (1960). *The non-human environment.* New York: Int. Univ.

Press.

STERBA, E. (1940). Homesickness and the mother's breast. *Psychoanal. Q.* 14:701–707.

STEVO, J. (1960). Ensor lui-meme. *Rev. Gn. Belge* 6:91–102.

VAN GINDERTAEL, R. (1965*). Ensor*, V. Menkes (Trans.). Boston: New York Graphic Society.

WERMAN, D.S. (1977). Normal and pathological nostalgia. *Psychoanal. Q.* 25:387–398.

———— (1985). On the nature of the oceanic experience. *J. Am. Psychoanal. Assoc.* 34:123–139.

CHAPTER 2

James Ensor and the Mask of Reality

[Werman, D.S. (2003). James Ensor, and the Mask of Reality. *Journal of Applied Psychoanalysis Studies* 5 (3):335–348.]

James Ensor (1860–1914), the Belgian painter, in his 23rd year, began to represent subjects wearing masks, and he continued to do so until the end of his life. Beyond the primarily formal use to which Ensor originally put the mask, it soon also became a means of representing his perception of the true selves of people. Thus, for Ensor, the visible face itself was a mask, a persona, concealing a subject's true self In a brief discussion, the mask is situated in a broader, historical and psychosocial context, and Ensor's use of the mask is related to his early life and later experiences.

In 1883, in his twenty-third year, Ensor painted Scandalized Masks, a work that was to be followed by a series of paintings and graphic works, unique in the history of Western art by the presence of masked figures, which appeared in hundreds of his works. The meanings of the Ensorien masks were overdetermined, and they evolved during his life. The singular feature of the mask in, Ensor's work is that instead of concealing the wearer's identity or representing another, among the characteristic and virtually universal functions of the mask, Ensor's masks were ultimately created to reveal the true self, the hypocritical face behind the mask. Thus, to an important extent, Ensor's masks were intended to tear away the wearer's benign persona and expose his or her hidden self. Moreover, by their very inanimateness, masks dehumanize the wearers, and so further devalue them. But finally, in heaping scorn on his enemies through his pictures, Ensor ensured that the people he savaged would respond with vitriolic counterattacks. further validating his view of himself as a victim and martyr.

Ironically, pathetically, and perhaps inevitably, over the years, Ensor, the maker of masks of reality, was to create a false face for himself that not only stamped his physiognomy and general appearance but pervaded his demeanor: his speech, writing, manner of living, and the

Professor Emeritus of Psychiatry, Duke University Medical Center, Durham, NC.

An earlier version of this paper was presented at the Annual Meeting of the American Psychoaralytic Association, New York, December 16, 2000.

personal mythology he devised; in short, he himself assumed a mask which served both as a defensive shield against despair and resignation, and as a sword with which to attack and provoke the "demons" of the world who beset him. From a perplexed, uncertain, rather passive, young man, seemingly experiencing feelings of shame, he became a self-styled giant and precursor in art, a bitter iconoclastic buffoon-self-inflating, jeering at the world, mocking his contemporaries and demeaning the artists who came after him; thus he became the very windbag of which he had accused his enemies of being. Tragically, in some ways Ensor was a genuine precursor although one whose influence was less than he urged people to believe.

From early childhood, circumstances naturally led him to regard the people around him as different from what they were "supposed" to be: loving parents could be hateful, neighbors were often cruel, and as a young avant-garde artist he found that the critics and even his fellow artists could be spiteful and humiliating.

Ensor was born into a family that was almost ostentatiously "different" in the provincial seaside city of Ostend. His mother, the daughter of Flemish lace merchants and small shopkeepers, was an able manager, and despite her litany of complaints, she held the family together by a powerful sense of responsibility and industriousness. As viewed through the lens of the adult, Ensor's memories of his early childhood, his mother and her maiden sister who lived with the family were, perhaps, more lavish in providing James with "pralines and sugared almonds" than with the kind of attention that fosters the development of a sense of self-worth and self-confidence. He described his maternal grandmother in terms probably befitting his own mother. "She was an expert business woman and good with money. As she grew old she grew hard" (Stevo, 1960). By all accounts his mother was barely literate and thoroughly petit-bourgeois in outlook; she never quite grasped her son's genius and railed at his inability to earn a living, and when he persisted in painting, she urged him to at least paint some local scenes that she could sell in the family's shop as genuine "hand painted" pictures.

Although Ensor was never publicly critical of her, he never spoke of her in loving terms. Instead, from an early age he turned to the North sea for soothing, the sea that he "adored" as a consoling "virginal mother" (Werman, 1989). Indeed, until his death he scarcely missed a day for his long walks along the sea, and he ridiculed the vacationers who swarmed over his beaches.

Reliable information on his earliest years is scanty. We do know, however, that he became a life-long misogynist; that he had only one long relationship with a woman, allegedly unconsummated, and whom he mocked; and that he possessed little self-confidence.

In sharp contrast to Ensor's mother, his father was the only child of well-to-do English parents. He had started studying medicine in Bonn, switched to Heidelberg, and then characteristically threw it over and returned to England where he worked for a while for a civil engineer. While on vacation in Ostend, he met his wife-to-be; he was then 23 and she a year older when they entered into what has been described as a "horrendous" marriage. Ensor described his father as an "intellectual" who was fond of music, art, and literature. He was also an alcoholic, living off the income from the shop that was managed by his wife and sister-in-law. Early in the marriage, feeling totally alienated in Ostend, he left shortly before James' birth and set out for the United States to create a new life; within months of his arrival, the Civil War broke out, and, presumably because of the war, he returned to his young family. He appeared depressed, "the life seemed to have virtually gone out of him" (Van Gindertael, p. 13). Although at first he helped out in the shop, his interest waned, and " . . . he finally preferred to drink rather than to be like the rest of us" (Ensor, p. 205).

Gradually he grew totally dependent on his "authoritarian" wife and settled down to a life of hard drinking and indolence. He became the laughing stock of the townspeople who delighted in getting him drunk and dropping his stuporous body at the door to the shop. During the Carnival, masked revelers stood under his window and mockingly serenaded him, proclaiming that he was "mad." When James succeeded in having a few paintings exhibited, some envious Ostenders shaved off half his father's beard and mustache. In a vain attempt to control his drinking, his wife would doubly lock the doors to keep him from going out. Despite her efforts, he finally died in the street of alcoholism and exposure when James was 27 years old.

Despite everything, Ensor always spoke highly of him and in many obvious and more subtle ways developed a profound identification with him, perhaps most striking in his aloof and patronizing attitude toward the people of Ostend. He seemed to feel that his English lineage conferred superiority and distinction on him, and he maintained his British citizenship until 1929 when he was obliged to renounce it in order for King Albert to make him a Baron. But until belated recognition came to him, Ensor, like his father, was regarded as an outsider, a view that at times was colored by suspicion, open hostility or, at the least, patronizing tolerance, feelings that were more than reciprocated by their scorned and contemptuous subject. Even as a child he was aloof and usually alone; except for a year or so at school, he was tutored at home. The Ostenders mockingly called this tall thin man, unfailingly alone and dressed in black, the "Grim Reaper."

When James was still a child he began to draw during his solitary walks along the coast; an understandable pastime for a youth little given to intimate relationships. Wandering along the North Sea beaches he sketched the dunes and outlying villages. In early adolescence with his father's encouragement he took lessons from two Ostend painters whose limitations were to lead, finally, to the decision to send him to the Royal Academy of Art in Brussels. Although the course of study was of three years' duration, at the end of the second year-despite an affectionate relationship with the Rousseaux, a distinguished and caring family, Ensor walked out of this "institution for the near-blind" and returned to Ostend. There, in 1880, at the age of twenty, we find him settled in his family's apartment above their shop, with a studio in the attic; he was to remain in Ostend, in fact, in the same neighborhood, with the exception of a few short absences, until his death almost 70 years later.

For the two to three years after his return, Ensor's paintings show only glimpses of the eruption of light and color that would soon flood his canvasses. During this early period his colors are generally somber, muted by earth tones, and the subjects are frequently family members in domestic scenes, such as *Lady in Distress* (1881): views from the attic windows, *Rue deFlandre* (1880); and paintings of working people, *The Lamp Boy* (1880; *Tramps Trying to Get Warm,* 1882, *The Oarsman,* 1883).

Typically, these paintings are imbued with an aura of loneliness, malaise or, as in the so-called intimist paintings, a subdued dread of a dramatic situation about to occur. The more tranquil interiors, such as *Russian Music* and *Afternoon in Ostend,* evoke the provincial dullness and emotional stasis that characterized the long somnolent afternoons his family spent during the winter months waiting for the summer season to arrive and bring with it the usual horde of holiday-makers. But always, lurking behind the stolid petit-bourgeois stillness were the outbursts, the bitter fights that rent the heavy silence of Ensor's home.

Some of the paintings executed during this "dark" period already show hints of the coloristic brilliance that was to dominate Ensor's palette: *The Colorist, Lady with a Fan,* (all done in 1880), and the *Woman Eating Oysters* (1882) mark critical steps in Ensor's subsequent unremitting fascination with light and color and precede his "discovery" of the mask. Although there is some truth in Ensor's assertion, in 1911, that" . . . Thirty years ago I pointed the way to all the modern experiments, to the whole idea of the influence of light and freedom of vision, long before Vuillard, Bonnard and the Luministe painters" (Ensor, p. 17) such defensive expressions of self-aggrandizement were to become increasingly frequent from the turn of the century onwards.

From 1883 Ensor moves from a clearly realistic vision in his work to one in which the data of the real world begin to crumble, where hostility and even cruelty begin to dominate his canvas. It becomes an arena where light and harsh color clash and compete. Although the changes in Ensor's style surely owe much to Turner, Whistler, and the early French impressionists, we may also speculate that this exuberance of light and color served him, in part, as a shield against deepening dark moods. Indeed, during most of this decade Ensor was to undergo the harsh experiences not only of the rejection of his work, but subjection to personal calumny and humiliation. Although he was able to exhibit a few of his paintings in 1880 and 1881, repeatedly he began to find much of his work rejected in one Salon after another. In 1883, *l'Essor,* a group of artists in Brussels, accepted five paintings but refused his *Woman Eating Oysters* and, in succession, *Afternoon in Ostend, Cabbage,* and *Scandalized Masks,* all among his most powerful early paintings. De Ridder (1930) noted that "The public . . . was alarmed and promptly turned away from him; the critics, whose preconceived ideas and safe doctrines were shattered by his work, were hostile; and, what is worse, was the hostility of his fellow-artists at whose side he was struggling" (p. 32).

Defensively, Ensor joined a group of young artists who had also felt the sting of the critics' abuse and had organized *Les XX,* a group of independents. But by 1888, a clique within *Les XX* forced him to withdraw all of his paintings from an exhibit even though they had already been listed in the catalogue. Two years later the paintings he submitted for another show were accepted by only one vote-rumored to have been his own. When these paintings, again including some of Ensor's finest work, were finally exhibited, the critics were unsparing in their invective:

he was berated as illiterate and decadent, his artistic vision deemed "ridiculous," his imagination "sick," and the paintings dismissed as "trash." In this war of words, which was waged furiously from 1887 until at least 1892, Ensor responded by isolating himself from the art world and viciously caricaturing his tormentors, provocatively throwing oil on the fire. Not surprisingly, there are some suggestions that during this decisive time he suffered periods of depression alternating with bouts of rage, as well as a number of unspecified physical illnesses.

His bitterness and impotent hatred grew, unabated, along with a grinding feeling of having been abandoned, of being uncared for and cast off as unworthy. Even as late as 1909 he would still write Emma Labotte, a patron and admirer, that "At times when I think of my misery, a hideous despair comes over me, and I curse many people." The next year he once again complained to her that he was "still waiting for a word of sympathy or interest from you" (Legrand, p. 22). Despite her considerable help and warm generosity, he dismissed her as nothing but a "blue stocking."

It was three years after his return to Ostend that Ensor painted the *Scandalized Masks* (1883), marking the beginning of his use of masks as something other than an object chiefly suitable for a still-life-as it had been, essentially, in the *Mask Gazing at a Negro Mountebank* (1878) or much later in the *Attributes of the Artist's Studio* (1889). The spread of these dates demonstrates that Ensor never abandoned the purely decorative value of the mask.

We need not wonder that Ensor first began to use masks in his paintings; they were familiar objects from his earliest childhood. In his parents' shop, a veritable world of wonders, were all manner of astonishing things for a child. The store was the sort of souvenir shop that is still to be found in seaside towns. But in addition to the usual toy shovels and pails, sea-shells, fishing nets, dried sea plants, and stuffed animals, it had an array of the grotesque masks that Ostenders wear during their annual Carnival when these usually stolid people don strange costumes and bizarre masks and under the cover of anonymity permit themselves to engage in whatever behavior their fantasies stimulated and circumstances permitted.

By the time Ensor paints the *Scandalized Masks,* the mask has transcended the merely "found object" and assumes a more complex existence in his work. This painting strikes the observer like a photograph taken by flash exposure. An elderly woman has just come through a door surprising a masked man; he sits hunched over a simple table, a half-filled bottle before him. His hands rest awkwardly, embarassedly on the table. His slightly turned-in feet suggest a guilty boy and brings to mind a portrait of Ensor's father painted the year before, *(Portrait of the Artist's Father* (1881). The woman wears a grotesque mask and holds an elongated horn or noisemaker in a vaguely threatening manner. The two figures confront each other in a mysterious frozen silence.

There is little agreement as to what this painting represents. Many years later Ensor wrote that on occasion his maternal grandmother would don a mask and costume and participate in the Carnival. Here, perhaps, it is she who has stumbled into this sordid room and discovered her boozing son-in-law. The pig-like mask that covers the man's face, the grimly leering mask on the woman, and the blotchy yellow light cast on the far wall evoke an atmosphere of degradation, shame, suspicion, and despair. Whoever the figures represent, the masks conceal their identity and, for the first time in Ensor's work, provide the spectator with information about the subjects that would not be visible in their faces.

From this time on the mask "stuck" with him, as he said some years later. Although his comments on the mask, made in later years, are often contradictory, rationalizing and vague, his work shows that after 1883 his use of the mask closely coincided with his discovery of light and brilliant, often brutal color, and simultaneously with his counterattacks of the critics. His first and most lucid statement on his use of masks was in 1899. In a letter (to Dujardin) he wrote, ". . . surrounded by hostility . . . and relentlessly criticized . . . I took some pleasure in painting masks. . . . In this way I was able to make a study of the hypocritical, secretive, and selfish faces of the cowardly scoundrels whom I crushed by my progress! It was a happy choice: it naturally brought out violent and intense colors, it reflected the self-serving criticism of my colleagues-their ignorance and dishonesty. The clumsiness of the critics, the vile and mean-spirited attacks of erstwhile imitators, forcefully kept me on this singular path" (Legrand, pp. 78–79).

Demolder observed that when Ensor saw himself surrounded by "the hostility and jeering-that base jeering that the typical Belgian critic gives off like spittle on whatever he doesn't understand-in feeling himself abandoned even by those whom he had inspired, he imagined himself surrounded by the masks of the Carnival of life: it was then that he delighted in painting masks and throwing them, helter-skelter, in the face of the public" (Legrand, p. 79).

"From 1883 onwards," Ensor wrote, "masks had a profound effect on me. . . . With my pursuers close upon my heels, I joyfully closed myself up in the solitary world where the mask occupies a place of honor, [where] masks, wholly made up of violence, light, and brilliance, hold sway. The mask speaks to me of freshness of tone, sharpness of expression, sumptuous decoration, sweeping and startling gestures, disordered movement, and an exquisite turbulence" (Ensor, p. 164).

During the late 1880's and 1890's, Ensor was strikingly original and richly productive; in addition to his paintings, he completed over three hundred etchings and dry points that stand in the front rank of graphic art. But in his loudly trumpeted independence, his allegiance to no school, his irreligious posturing, his acidulous caricatures and his haughty aloofness from the art world, he managed to alienate almost everyone. His work was described as hideous and distasteful. "A hail of cruel comments is falling on my head," he complained. "They are abusing me, insulting me; I am [said to be] crazy, stupid, wicked, evil, incapable and ignorant!" (Ensor, p. 76), and he struck back in a series of paintings that, in turn, ridiculed and mocked his adversaries.

Although similar critical attacks had been meted out to many other artists, such as Pissarro, Renoir, and Van Gogh, among others, who were also treated as clowns, decadents, neurotics, or ignored, they managed to pursue their work, which was generally free from critical polemics. However, they usually enjoyed some understanding and support from fellow-artists or, as with Van Gogh, from a supremely loyal, generous and knowledgeable brother. In Ostend, Ensor was professionally isolated, and even the townspeople mocked the "splenetic Pierrot" who walked their streets. With no regular occupation. sitting for hours alone in his favorite café, speaking with no one, he ensured his isolation which was further fueled by his father's open disdain for the people of Ostend and by his frequent bouts of drunkenness.

Ensor then let loose a stream of pictorial invective. These graphic representations of his rage and bitterness were not limited to the critics; his misanthropy splattered over the clergy, physicians, the police and the military, women. holiday makers-indeed, virtually all of mankind; (see *The Good Judges. Wizards in a Squall*). And it was to a large extent through his use of masks and caricatures that he heaped scorn and contempt on his "demons." Although these multiple vendettas led to many paintings and drawings that are barely above the comic-strip level, some were, at times, saved by Ensor's sense of humor, his clowning, in making visual puns and jokes.

As mentioned earlier, Ensor's first use of the mask was primarily, and at least consciously, a more or less neutral and decorative element in a still life, a use which he never completely abandoned. However, in the *Scandalized Masks* and *The Astonishment of the Mask Wouse* the mask takes on manifestly personal, often arcane meanings. Ensor was well aware that masks with their savage colors provided him with a powerful icon. Eventually, however, the mask became a major weapon that he used against his enemies to flay the skin and reveal the horror beneath. Additionally, it is likely that projective elements entered many of these works.

The most extraordinary and surely the best known of Ensor's paintings with masks is *The Entry of Christ into Brussels.* This massive canvas was not to leave his studio, to be publicly exhibited, until 1929. Vanbeselaere, (in Van Gindertael, 1975) writing of *The Entry,* concisely characterized Ensor's general use of masks:

> *The Entry of Christ* not only represents the greatest triumph to Ensor's luminous palette, it also represents and indeed this is its chief importance, the transformation of light and full coloring into a whole series of shrill and discordant chords, which are coarse and brutal. yet genuinely exciting. With them he was able to demonstrate his own highly imaginary and personal view of the world of masks, in which men's feelings are deliberately and fully laid bare (p. 79).

In retrospect, we can now see that this huge work—some 9 by 14 feet—represents nothing less than a revolutionary moment for Ensor—a critical break with his past. And in some more or less obscure manner, Ensor himself realized the historic importance of *The Entry,* both in the world of art and in his own creative odyssey, and even though only many years later he finally agreed to sell it, the buyer was obliged to acquiesce to a stipulation that he would receive the painting only after Ensor's death. Thus the masterpiece hung in his living room, dragging on the floor in back of his harmonium until his death.

Much has been written about *The Entry of Christ into Brussels,* in particular its social and political implications, and these are evident. But relevant to this essay are the representations of the hundreds of masked figures streaming out of the frame towards the observer. While many are clearly masked, others have faces that are so grotesque as to suggest either a mask or a caricature. Stamped on these faces is every form and manner of human folly, while almost lost in this hallucinatory tragi-comic carnival is Christ, resembling Ensor himself, haloed, astride an ass, one arm outstretched blessing a mob oblivious to his presence. This is, by the way, but one among the many times that Ensor depicted the Christ figure-tortured, humiliated, mocked and crucified-in representations that became increasingly explicit in suggesting his identification with Christ; ultimately he simply inscribed the name Ensor on top of the cross on which Christ is nailed in *Calvary.*

In *The Entry of Christ,* the seething crowd is nothing less than mankind itself. Singled out once again for his contempt is the church, physicians, the military, the court, the bourgeoisie and the aristocracy, on whom he heaps ridicule and to whom he assigns almost every imaginable egregious trait. Not that the painting is without humor; the unrelenting bitterness that at times deadens some of his work-representing, I suggest, a loss of artistic control is not present here. Instead, we relish a robust Brueghelesque scene of the human comedy.

In contrast, *The Intrigue* (1890) lacks such boisterous buffoonery. Here the faces, less obviously masked, only ambiguously represent masks. Nine figures, one holding a baby, are aligned on both sides of a joyless bride and bridegroom. The latter, with Asian features, suggests the Chinese merchant who married Ensor's sister against his bitter opposition, and who abandoned her not long after.[1] A usually joyous occasion is turned on its head: the bride, apparently past her youth (actually his sister was then only 30 years old) simpers inanely; the bridegroom is impassive, his head, like a turtle, is sunk deeply into the shell of his fur collar. The other faces appear sly, horrified, or hypocritically beatific; one is a death's head, another is of a woman, her mouth open, holding the baby-more like a rag doll-pointing accusingly to the inscrutable groom. The harsh greens, yellows and slate blue colors, splashed with a brutal red, convey Ensor's total mockery of the wedding ceremony and his hostility towards the people who attended it. The presence of the baby is a mute accusation of at least one possible motivation for the marriage. The picture may also allude to his own parents' marriage and his conception.

Also explicit is the *Self Portrait Surrounded by Masks* (1899) 34) in which Ensor, in a parody of Ruben's self-portrait wearing a plumed hat, is surrounded by about 30 masks and skulls. As the masks recede towards the background (perhaps further back in time) they become increasingly grotesque and frightening. Ensor's face might almost be lost in this sea of masks, but it is saved by its somewhat larger size and by his theatrical plumed hat bedecked with flowers. Although the surrounding masks seem indifferent to Ensor, he represents himself as anxious, suspicious, vulnerable and perplexed amid these bizarre faces. Even though this self-portrait presents Ensor as less obviously a victim than he is in the earlier *Demons Tormenting Me* (1895) it shows him engulfed in a world of figures who are variously cruel, ferocious, inane, mendacious or leering, and although they are all around him, they seem oblivious of him. Ensor's experience of the world could not be represented more graphically.

DISCUSSION

Not surprisingly, Ensor's uses of the mask resonate with those that man has employed over millennia. A detailed account of the history of the mask is beyond the scope and aim of this essay, but in order to situate Ensor in the context of that history, a brief survey may be useful. Masks have appeared in almost every society known, and their ancestry has been traced as far back as the Stone Age. In the rare instances where a people, such as the Australian aborigines, did not use masks as such, they employed paint, scarification, or adornments to transform the human face into a mask. Indeed, throughout history cosmetic make-up itself, as Burand wrote, may well represent a "vestige of the mask" (Burand, 1961).

In cultures dominated by an animistic world view, the spirit of the totemic ancestor—usually an animal—is protected, worshipped and honored in a variety of ways, not the least of which is in materializing the spirit in a mask that houses the spirit of the totem (Freud, 1913). In this way masks could be assigned many roles: exorcism of evil spirits, cure of disease, success in hunting and warfare, human and crop fertility, protection of the dead, and clan cohesion and order. The erotic and frightening uses of masks are almost universal.

From its early use in ritual and story-telling, the mask underwent a lengthy evolution. Bihalji-Merin (1970) noted that "when the wearer ceases to identify himself with the mask, when he overcomes its magic power, the mask becomes a means of disguise and self-adornment" (p.9). With the realization that man can "only change his outward appearance, [and] not his true self . . . ritual ceremonies and mythical actions become theatrical plays. And thus arises the Attic tragedy, with its human heroes" (ibid., p. 71). Accordingly, in ancient Greek drama masks-the *personae-became* the means of impersonating both gods and men alike.

Under the dominant influence of Christianity, the original demonic and erotic ·nature of the mask was recognized only too clearly by the Church Fathers, and it was no longer tolerated. Although the mask was banned from Asia Minor to Rome, it managed to survive at the outer boundaries of Christendom—particularly England and Germany, and by the 16th century it had suddenly taken on a new life, crossing the Alps "into the heart of its old anti-Christian domain" (Gregor, 1937).

However, despite its disfavor in the eyes of the church, throughout the Middle ages the mask was freely used in mystery plays where it typically represented one or another of the seven deadly sins, or devils and demons. In secular representations, stock characters such as Harlequin, Columbine, the Dottore, Captain Cocodrillo, etc., evolved, who were readily identified by recognizable masks worn by actors in the *comedia dell'arte*. Indeed, the use of the mask in the theater continues to this day in the traditional Japanese Noh dramas and Chinese theater and opera where the actors may apply make-up to simulate masks. In the 20th century, in the West, masks have been used by Hauptmann, Yeats and O'Neil, among others.

As a psychosocial appurtenance, use of the mask reached its height in 18th century Venice where it represented a breakdown of social restraints at least for affluent Venetians. It was simple to "slip into the ample cloak of invisibility, to don the three-cornered hat, and to poise the [mask] in front of one's nose in order to become unseeable and uncontrollable" (Gregor, p. 19). Masks were worn by both men and women who went abroad at night in search of pleasure. Paintings by Tiepelo and Longhi capture the demonic nature of these masks which bring to mind a mischievous bird such as a raven.

In Isak Dinesen's "The Deluge at Norderney" (1934), a character relates that a witty woman "chooses for her carnival costume one which ingeniously reveals something in her spirit or heart which the conventions of her everyday life conceal; and when she puts on the hideous long-nosed Venetian mask, she tells us, not only that she has a classic nose behind it, but that she has much more, and may well be adored for things other than her mere beauty. So speaketh the Arbiter of the masquerade: 'By thy mask shall I know thee' " (p. 26).

The rise of rationalism in the Western world was accompanied by the waning of the mask as a demonic device. By the 19th century it was generally relegated to the familiar and relatively benign means of disguise with which we are familiar: the bizarre false-face of Halloween and the half-mask or domino, often worn during Carnivals and other festivities, where the anonymity it imparts loosens social taboos against casual sexual encounters and sanctions buffoonery.

Situated in the context of this long history of the mask as *disguise,* Ensor was perhaps the most prominent and consistent artist who used the mask. Ensor was not, however, especially interested, if at all, in abstract issues pertaining to the persona and the true self. What patently did concern him throughout his life, almost obsessively, were the dismissive and humiliating views of the critics who, just at the dawn of his career, cast him into a dismal obscurity; and, beyond the critics, were still others who stoked the flames of his bitterness, his disdain, and his belligerence. In this respect we have only to recall the scornful Ostenders and his expulsion from groups of his contemporary fellow artists. Even long after most of these detractors were dead, he continued to pillory them in his paintings, drawings and speeches. He seemed unable to give up this melange of rage and buffoonery that carried malicious echoes of that other Fleming, the mythic trickster Tyl Eulenspiegel, celebrated by Da Coster and Richard Strauss.

As previously mentioned, some of the determinants of Ensor's particular uses of the mask were: At first he used masks, the commonplace objects in his parent's shop, seen all over Ostend during the annual Carnival, primarily as colorful and exotic objects for a still life. Subsequently, in the mid 1880's, three critical events converged: the first was Ensor's discovery of luminism, the power and beauty of light, that was henceforth to infuse his paintings and etchings. Second, was his genial recognition that the garish masks fairly burst with brilliant, often crude, color. And. finally, his discovery that the mask provided him with a spectacularly suitable weapon that he could use to satirize and excoriate the "demons who tormented" him.

It is plausible that the external circumstances described are sufficient to explain his tenacious use of the masks in the service of not only aesthetic purposes, but, progressively, out of a desire for revenge against his contemporaries. However, I believe we can discern deeper and earlier influences that may have fostered his wish for revenge. We recall how his father became the town drunk, a laughing stock of the Ostenders. A failure by any standards, (he brings to mind the more endearing and comical Mr. Micawber) he had haughtily seized the moral high ground and regarded the townspeople as provincial boors worthy only of disdain, and this was precisely the path that his son was to follow-not the least of the ways in which he identified with his father-for like the latter, he too remained a sneering outsider to his neighbors, passive, clinging to family and home, hostile and yet remaining dependent.

Some observers have regarded the death of Ensor's father as playing a critical role in his artistic deterioration. That surely must have been significant for Ensor, not in the least because it deprived him of the one person whose support he had always enjoyed. However, the death occurred when Ensor was 27 years old, and for the next eight to ten years he produced many of his finest works. Ultimately, the importance of his father's death remains unclear.

Ensor left little information regarding his earliest childhood; there is, however, enough to suggest that his mother had not fostered in him a strong and resilient sense of his worth. Indeed, this overburdened woman, stuck in a miserable marriage with her increasingly dependent and alcoholic husband, could hardly be expected to have been able to provide her son with joyous nurturance; apparently she was, at best, able to provide him with material care. The halcyon days of Ensor's infancy waned; a sister was born before he was two, and life became somber and oppressive. His mother grew hypochondriacal and seemingly chronically depressed. With time she grew hard and embittered, and after vain attempts to mobilize James' father, she gave up trying, undoubtedly realizing the hopelessness of the task. To her horror, she observed her son following in his father's path-becoming "idle," passive and dependent. Like his father, his help in the shop was never more than a token effort, and as she had nagged her husband to do some work, so she began to nag her son to "earn a living"-something he never managed to do during her lifetime. In fact, the first major purchase of a painting, *The Lamp Boy,* by the State was in 1896 when Ensor was already thirty-six years old.

Ensor was simply not prepared to receive and endure the impact of critical and humiliating rejection. How it happened that he had failed to receive from his family what may have given him the strength to hold on to an inner awareness of his genius, can only be conjectured. Ultimately, what is relevant, is that he was unable to transcend his demons. He was badly bruised: he felt, and in fact received, little or no encouragement; his creative energies declined and he sought refuge in graphic invective, in lampooning the critics. What bitterness and rancor he felt towards his family was modulated and expressed in a tame and polite aloofness, and his anger was displaced to the outside world. In so doing he created a vicious circle of attack and counterattack.

Finally, as mentioned earlier, the most poignant mask Ensor created was of the face and demeanor of a grandiloquent guru of art, the precursor, the martyr, the Christ, and the clown-savant. But beneath this often jocular mask was a bitter, thwarted genius whose artistic trajectory soared for little more than fifteen years and then all too rapidly fell to earth. But in those few years he put together an artistic legacy of such originality and power as to secure a secure place for himself in the history of art.

REFERENCES

BIHALJI-MERIN. O. (1970). *Great Masks.* New York: Harry Abrams, Inc.

BURAND. G. (1961). *Les Masques.* Paris: Club des Editeurs.

DINESEN, I. (1934). The Deluge at Norderney, in *Seven Gothic Tales.* New York: Vintage Books. 1972.

ENSOR, J. (1974). *Mes Ecrits. Liege:* Editions Natonales. 5th edition.

FREUD, S. (1913). Totem and Taboo. *Standard Edition*: 1–131. London: Hogarth Press, 1959.

GREGOR. J. (1973). *Masks of the World.* New York, B. Blom, Inc. 1988.

LEGRAND, F.C. (1971). *Ensor cet inconnu.* Bruxelles. Collection Renaissance-Art.

STEVO. J. (1960). Ensor, lui-meme. *Rev. Gen. Beige.* Mar–Apr.

VAN GINDERTAEL, R. (1975). *Ensor, trans.* V. Menkes. Boston: New York Graphic Society.

WERMAN, D.S. (1989). James Ensor and the Attachment to Place. *International Review of Psychoanalysis.* 16:287–295.

——— (1993). Edgar Allan Poe, James Ensor. and the Psychology of Revenge. *The Annals of Psychoanalysis.* 21:301–314.

——— (2000). The passing of Creativity: Two Histories: James Ensor and Arthur Rimbaud. *Journal of Applied Psychoanalytic Studies.* 2(I):65–80, 2000.

CHAPTER 3

Edgar Allan Poe, James Ensor, and the Psychology of Revenge

[Werman, D.S. (1993). *Annual of Psychoanalysis,* 21:301–314.]

The desire for revenge can so pervade the inner world of an individual as to become an obsessive and destructive force in that person's life. For a creative artist, such an idée fixe can go so far as to totally dominate his or her work, with ruinous results. Although both Edgar Allan Poe (1809–1849) and James Ensor (1860–1949) were under the sway of such imperatives, Poe's urge for revenge was, for the most part, kept under control and was subject to his critical self-scrutiny and demanding aesthetic standards; in contrast, Ensor's thirst for vengeance so egregiously permeated his work that it evolved from a possibly stimulating influence to a straitjacket that finally contributed to choking off his creativity.

AIn addition to their revengeful propensities, Poe and Ensor were directly linked by the influence Poe's tales had on Ensor, who claimed to have "devoured" them. Indeed, he made etchings illustrating two of these stories, "King Pest" and "Hop Frog".

The former tale takes place in England during a time of wide-spread plague. Two drunken sailors have left the Thames-side Inn, where they have been carousing, and are headed back to their ship. Losing their way, they find themselves in an area that has been placed "under ban" because of a plague. Inadvertently, they stumble into an undertaker's shop, and lifting a trap door to the basement, they descend only to discover an extraordinary assembly: Seated around a huge "punch bowl" are six bizarre individuals, presided over by a man identified as King Pest (or plague); the others in his retinue are the Arch Duke Pest-Iferous, the Duke Pest-Ilential, the Duke Tem-Pest, and so forth

Suspended over the bowl is a skeleton, hanging by one leg. King Pest stirs the bowl with a human femur while the sailors, along with the others, quaff the wine from human skulls. King Pest demands a "humiliating submission" from the seamen, who, if they do not obey, are to be drowned in a hogshead of ale. When the smaller of the two sailors is, in fact, dropped into the barrel, the other strikes out with the skeleton; he brings down King Pest, overturns both punch bowl and hogshead, and in the turmoil the sailors make their escape, taking with them two women.

Ensor's etching *King Plague* illustrates the gruesome scene of the people seated around the punch bowl. We must suppose that his illustration of the story represents a particular interest that it held for him. Although Bonaparte (1933) plausibly interprets the denouement of the story as an act of parricide "that goes unpunished," I believe we can more parsimonously and more broadly affirm that "King Pest" is a story of revenge drawing from several developmental levels.

Ensor's interest in the motif of revenge is again brought home by his illustration for Poe's story. "Hop Frog," which he pointedly reentitled "Hop Frog's Revenge." The story relates how a crippled dwarf, Hop Frog, and a beautifully proportioned midget, Tripetta, are enslaved and brought to the court of a "corpulent, oily" king for his and his courtiers' entertainment. At one point, the king insists that Hop Frog swallow a bumper of wine, but Hop Frog is loath to drink because even one glass of wine "excited the poor cripple almost to madness" (like Poe himself). When the king demands that he drink a second glass, Tripetta begs for mercy on Hop Frog's behalf, leading the king to thrust her violently from him and dash the contents of the brimming goblet in her face.

Having planned a grand fete, the king calls on Hop Frog to organize the entertainment. By an "association of idea" Hop Frog recommends that the king and seven of his ministers should be dressed as "Ourang-Outangs" and chained together, as if they were wild animals that had escaped from their keeper. Thus, at the fete, in this guise, they actually terrify and astonish all the guests who at first take them for savage beasts. At the height of the ensuing hilarity, a chain descends from the overhead chandelier and Hop Frog attaches it to the chain linking the eight "apes" who are pulled up above the crowd, with Hop Frog clinging just above the king and his ministers. Amid the astonishment of the revelers, Hop Frog sets on fire the eight men, who are quickly burned to charcoal: "The eight corpses swing in their chains, a fetid, blackened, hideous and indistinguishable mass" (Poe, 1946, p. 183). Hop Frog then leisurely clambers to the ceiling and disappears through a skylight, and he and Tripetta effect their escape to their own country.

As with "King Pest," Bonaparte narrowly interprets "Hop Frog" as an oedipal triumph in which Tripetta represents Poe's dead mother, the actress Elizabeth Arnold, and the king symbolizes John Allan, Poe's hated foster father. Although her interpretation is credible, the more persuasive theme is one of revenge. The issue I am advancing is that although the oedipal interpretations of "Hop Frog" and "King Pest" are plausible and indisputably partially correct, they disregard the layering of experiences of abandonment, depreciation, and humiliation at different periods in the lives of Poe and Ensor, experiences that cannot simply be reduced to unresolved oedipal conflicts.

Ensor's colored etching *Hop Frog's Revenge,* in contrast to the black and white King Pest, graphically expresses his glee over the denouement of the story. We see the huge ballroom filled with hundreds of masqueraders staring up at the king and his ministers—a flaming ball of fire—above whom, holding his torch, sits Hop Frog. Prominent among the guests are two whose backs are towards the observer: One wears a robe on which a large simpering face has been drawn; on the other is draped a sash on which is printed "ENSOR."

The obsession of Poe and Ensor with revenge is hardly limited to the two stories and the respective illustrations I have described. The theme of revenge appears elsewhere in Poe's tales, and nowhere is it so manifest as in the well-known "The Cask of Amontillado" (Poe, 1846). The idea for the story was in part derived from a review Poe had written, some years earlier, of Frederick Chamier's *The Spitfire.* He wrote at that time that he himself would have liked to see "the success of an impudent rogue" (in the story), who would not "meet with punishment and shame" (Poe, 1846). The year he wrote "The Cask of Amontillado," he had been engaged in his own (verbal) feud with Hiram Fuller and T. D. English, two of his many literary enemies. In the story, the narrator, Montresor, plans his revenge: Not only must it eliminate his victim, but the avenger must "punish with impunity. A wrong is unredressed when retribution overtakes its redresser" (Poe, 1846). We never learn the nature of the "thousand injuries" he has received from his enemy, Fortunato, or when these took place. Indeed, we learn virtually nothing of the two protagonists, the epoch, or the place, other than that the tale takes place somewhere in Italy during "the carnival season"; in this way, it takes on the allure of a mythic revenge. At the end of the story, with Fortunato immured, Montresor cynically observes that his "heart grew sick—on account of the dampness in the catacombs" (p. 174); he hears no further sounds from the ironically named Fortunato.

Although Poe's poetry, in contrast to some of his stories, was generally free of themes of revenge, his literary criticism was marked by not only its brilliance but, as James Russell Lowell put it, by Poe mistaking "his phial of prussic-acid for his inkstand" (Quinn, 1942, p. 432). He berated other critics for being "Titmice" and "Tittle-bats," referred to Margaret Fuller as "grossly dishonest" and a "detestable old maid"; called Lowell a "fool"; and dismissed New England, with its abolitionist intellectuals, as "Frogpodium." He was especially scathing toward Longfellow, whom he repeatedly and unjustifiably accused of plagiarism. These attacks were particularly inappropriate because many of their intended victims had been generous and complimentary of him. Indeed, after Poe's death, Longfellow, with insight and kindness wrote that "The harshness of his [Poe's] criticisms, I have never attributed to anything but the irritation of a sensitive nature, chafed by some indefinite sense of wrong" (Quinn, p. 655).

From his mid-30s onward, that is, from about 1895, Ensor's work took on an increasingly polemical, caricatural, and abrasive character. As Haesaerts (n.d.) noted, it "mingled sarcasm, indifference, revenge, and sadness" (p. 66). As early as 1888 he had begun to produce works such as *Devils Thrashing Angels and Archangels,* and by 1896, with his powerful misanthropic etching *Death Chasing the Flock of Mortals,* he reached the height of his rejection of humanity, coinciding with the waning of his creative talent. In this painting, which reminds us of his great *Entry of Christ in Brussels* (1888), we see a horde of people fleeing through a narrow street, approaching the observer. In the mob are people from every walk of life: men and women, young and old, infants, priests, noblemen, prostitutes, and drunkards. Soaring overhead is a huge black insectlike skeleton, wielding a massive scythe. Smaller skeletons, also brandishing scythes, assist Death in his implacable task of extermination. Panic and bewilderment are written on the victims' faces while high in the sky, bathed in the light of a brilliant sun, bizarre angellike figures radiantly bestow their approbation upon Death's enterprise.

Although Ensor did little formal art criticism, in later years he gave many speeches in which he roundly deprecated other artists and art critics, and gave vent to his intense misanthropy. These talks were rife with neologisms, stunning insults and name calling, paranoiac allusions, and often plain gibberish. They were so self-congratulatory that he progressively grew to see himself as *the* precursor of all painting from the impressionists onwards. Rodin, he stated, was but an "incorrigible amputator," and "thirty years ago I laid out the path for Vuillard, Bonnard and Van Gogh" (Ensor, 1974, p. 17); Monet and Manet simply opened up a few "obtuse sensations"; the public are just "sheep"; one artist "revolts" [me], and one has the "gleaming eye of a rat nestled in a piece of cheese." His fulminations far exceed any criticism he himself had received. Moreover, his vituperations are often grossly misogynist and not without a hint of anti-semitism. Although he can find a little praise for some of his contemporaries, he is most comfortable in praising those who are dead: Rembrandt, Rubens, Breughel, and even Turner, to whom his debt is far greater than he ever allowed himself to acknowledge in public.

To the very end of his life he hungered for fame and honors. His intense string-pulling to be awarded a baronetcy by King Albert in 1929 led to behavior which he would have mocked had anyone else gone to such lengths. When recognition did come, not surprisingly, it did not assuage his bitterness nor his revengeful strivings. His dream of happiness, he wrote in 1921 in response to a questionnaire, would be to "wound the Philistines with the jaw-bone of a camel" (Ensor, 1974, p. 70).

Although both Poe and Ensor tenaciously harbored revengeful feelings throughout their lives, the respective psychogeneses of these feelings were different. Furthermore, not only were their ways of discharging these feelings dissimilar, but the effects of their attitudes on their lives and, in particular, on their creative work, were substantially different.

Poe's early childhood was stamped with death and abandonment, but the limitations of space preclude anything beyond sketching out some of the major traumatic events. He was born in 1809 of parents who were both well-respected actors, although his father, the son of a general in the revolutionary army, had the reputation of being unreliable and possibly an alcoholic. Before Poe was two years old, his father mysteriously disappeared. Whether or not he simply abandoned his family and died shortly thereafter, as it is believed, he was never heard from again. He left his wife, Elizabeth Arnold Poe, then three months pregnant, and two sons, Edgar and his older brother William.

Elizabeth Poe was virtually destitute and probably already suffering from tuberculosis. She was obliged to give William to his paternal grandparents for adoption, and she, Edgar, and the new baby, Rosalie, were kept alive only by the generous help of neighbors. Thus Elizabeth lived out the remainder of her short life with her two children, in a mean furnished room. She died in her twenties, when Edgar was three years old. The memory and sight of his mother's pitiable, slow death was never to leave him; he never transcended that loss, which was undoubtedly the wellspring of a series of intense, romantic but platonic attachments he was to make with older, maternal women in attempts, we can assume, to replace his mother.

After their mother's death, Rosalie was placed in one foster home and Edgar in another, further fragmenting the already splintered family. Edgar entered the home of Frances and John Allan, a well-to-do childless couple, who christened him Edgar Allan Poe. They would never formally adopt him.

Although John Allan seemed at first to be attached to Edgar, by the time the youngster was about 11 or 12, Allan's caring became more focused on Edgar's misbehavior. The boy was deemed to be "difficult"; although he could be sociable, he often was "savage," enjoying roaming the countryside by himself, picking flowers, daydreaming, drawing, and writing in secret. He was easily angered by criticism and tended "indeed to believe that the world owed him a living, at least an indulgence with his whims" (Allen, 1934, p. 36). John Allan reacted to such behavior by whipping the boy.

In contrast, Frances Allan was everything the motherless child could wish for. She adored Edgar much as he grew deeply attached to her, and John Allan's extramarital affairs only reinforced the relationship between her and the boy, perhaps kindling latent oedipal desires. Another woman who, at this time, took Edgar under her wing and whose love he would never forget, was Mrs. Jane Stanard. Unfortunately, this kind and generous woman was to die when Edgar was 15 years old.

Taking Edgar out of school in Richmond, Virginia, the Allans moved to England in 1815, where John Allan set up a branch of his business. Edgar attended schools there during the next five years until business reverses obliged the family to return to Virginia. Thus Edgar, now 11 years old, was yet again taken out of school. During the next six years he attended private schools in Richmond. These years are not well documented, but it is known that he suffered from frequent nightmares, was moody, rebellious, and was believed by his foster father to possess "not a spark of affection for us, not a particle of gratitude for all my care and kindness towards him" (Quinn, 1942, p. 89).

Around 1825 he fell in love with Elmira Royster, who many years later described him as a "beautiful boy," "generous," hating "anything coarse and unrefined," "warm and zealous in any cause he was interested in, very enthusiastic and impulsive." Elmira was "about 15 or 16" when she and Edgar became secretly engaged. Their relationship was curtailed when John Allan enrolled Edgar at the University of Virginia, and it was brought to a decisive end when Edgar's letters to Elmira were intercepted by her father, who hastened to have her engaged to a more acceptable man, whom she married the following year.

Poe's career at the University of Virginia lasted but 10 months. Despite controversy over many aspects of the time he spent there, it is likely that he did drink more than he could hold. He also gambled and ran up a debt which has been claimed to be as high as $2500. In a poignant letter to John Allan some five years later, he records in precise detail his expenses and Allan's unwillingness to adequately provide for even his minimal needs; he describes his "mortification" at having been "regarded in the light of a beggar." He felt obliged, he wrote, to borrow money to make ends meet, and to gamble in an attempt to pay his debts. His drinking, he rationalized, grew out of feelings of "desperation."

Allan brought Edgar back to Richmond and refused to let him return to the university. After four months working as a clerk, following a violent quarrel with Allan, Edgar ran off and soon landed in Boston—the city, incidentally, where his mother had given birth to him. There he joined the U.S. Army and published his first book of poetry, *Tamerlane and Other Poems,* presented as written "by a Bostonian." After rising rapidly to the highest rank of a noncommissioned officer, Sergeant Major, he wrote to Allan on at least three occasions, asking for help in obtaining a discharge from the service and an appointment to West Point. Before he was to leave the army, however, his beloved foster mother, Frances Allan, died.

In September 1830, Poe entered West Point, and the next month John Allan remarried. Although Poe did well in his courses, he began again to drink and to chafe under the discipline at the academy. By the new year he was writing Allan that he intended to leave West Point, pointing out that Allan had sent him there like a beggar. "The same difficulties are threatening me as before at Charlottesville—and I must resign" (Quinn, 1942, p. 172). As Quinn observed, Poe's accusation is "again a half truth." In his letter to Allan, Poe wrote that if he did not obtain Allan's written consent for his resignation, he would "neglect [his] studies and duties" and subject himself to dismissal. Allan did not answer his letters; Poe carried out his threat and was court-martialed in January 1831. Despite all of this, during his short stay at West Point he still managed to complete a third book of poetry, which was published a few months after his discharge. The month after he left West Point, his brother William died at the age of 24.

Edgar's relationship with John Allan remained acrimonious. Contact between them was limited and usually abrasive, and relations between the new Mrs Allan and Poe were cool; she generally seemed to have been unfriencly if not downright hostile toward her husband's foster son. John Allan died in 1835, and although he provided for his illegitimate children, his will made no mention of Edgar.

From the time Poe left West Point until his death almost twenty years later, he ranged up and down the Eastern seaboard holding editorial positions on magazines and newspapers in most of the larger cities. He was prolific and creative to the end of his life, writing poetry, stories, a novel, and considerable literary criticism. His earnings were always meager, he continued to be in debt frequently, and he probably drank excessively at times, but clearly not to such an extent that it interfered with his prodigious creative efforts.

In 1835 his paternal grandmother died, leaving a widowed daughter, Maria Clemm, and her daughter, Virginia, virtually penniless. For Poe, it was the loss of yet one more loving person. Earlier he had lived with his grandmother and the Clemms, and after his grandmother's death he helped the Clemms as best as he could. The next year he married his cousin, Virginia Clemm, who was then not quite 14 years old; the age difference was ill regarded. For Poe, his mother-in-law became a new mother. From all reports the marriage was a loving and happy one for the couple, despite the poverty that dogged them.

Contemporaries described Edgar and Virginia's devotion to each other, although some authors have suggested that the marriage was never consummated (Castelnau, 1945, pp. 161–169). Virginia was in precarious health from at least 1841 and finally died in January 1847. It took Poe almost a year to recover from the profound grief into which this new loss threw him—to the point, he related, of attempting suicide. He gradually resumed his former rhythm of work and in the next two years, until his own death, produced such important poems as "Ulalume," "Eureka," and "Annabel Lee," and powerful tales such as "Hop Frog," as well as perceptive, albeit often abrasive, criticism.

Poe was respected and often praised as a writer, but he was not well liked. Although he held many editorial positions on prominent literary journals, he achieved neither the recognition nor position he desired, nor any financial well-being. To no small extent, this was due to the nature of his writing, which was decades before its time. But Poe was also able to turn friends into enemies and was self-destructive in wrecking his own chances for success. One telling anecdote chillingly describes such behavior: In 1843, friends were attempting to obtain a position for him in the government, to which end they arranged a meeting with President Tyler. Poe arrived in Washington "sick," that is to say intoxicated, as he readily became after even "one glass of weak wine or beer or cider" (Quinn, 1942, p. 381), again suggesting a propensity to "pathologic intoxication," rather than excessive drinking. Thus, he arrived, to all observers, drunk. "Mr. Poe, as usual,' wrote Hervey Allen describing the scene, "wore a Spanish-looking cloak and it was his peccadillo while in Washington to insist upon wearing it wrong-side out, an eccentricity that certainly did cause somewhat of a sensation ..." (Allen, 1934, pp. 444–447). The meeting with the president never took place.

His final and perhaps most self-destructive act was to desecrate his own name after his death, by having named Rufus W. Griswold, a free-lance writer, as his literary executor. From numerous indications, Poe surely knew that Griswold would betray him and falsify his life. Indeed, Griswold was perhaps the major source of the slanders that Poe was: addicted to drugs, philandering, dishonest, dissipated, and more. Griswold's obituary for Poe, in the *New York Tribune* on October 9, 1846, laid bare his feelings. He wrote that "announcement [of Poe's death] will startle many, but few will be grieved by it. The poet was known, personally or by reputation in all this country; he had readers in England, and in several of the states of Continental Europe; but he had few or no friends; and the regrets for his death will be suggested principally by the consideration that in him literary art has lost one of its most brilliant but erratic stars" (Quinn, 1942, p. 646).

Whereas dramatic and obvious are the losses and deprivations in Poe's life, the deepest sources of James Ensor's misanthropy, implacable bitterness, and thirst for revenge remain obscure. Without reasoning backwards toward some unidentifiable pathogenic influences, the behavior Ensor exhibited during his adult years is striking and cannot be shrugged off as trivial quirks of character. One need only recall his compulsive attachment to the North Sea, his loss of creativity by the age of 35, the bombastic and grandiose clowning he engaged in during the last decade of his life, and his mean-spirited misogyny. Not only did he never marry, but the relationships that he did have with women were few and shallow. The only long relationship he had was with Augusta Boogaerts, whom he sarcastically called "The Siren" and caricatured in the *Call of the Siren* (1883).

Although Ensor's family remained intact (his father died when James was 27, his mother when he was 55), it was a family that was lacerated by conflict. Moreover, his family, and his father in particular, was regarded as bizarre, indeed ludicrous, by the people of Ostend.

The child of his parents' misalliance, Ensor never seemed to establish an identity as an Ostender, although it was his birthplace. He never made friends there; he spoke mostly French in a city in which, although bilingual, Flemish was the common language; and he typically kept aloof from the townspeople. His father, from an upper middle-class English family and possessing many intellectual interests, somehow found himself married to the daughter of Flemish shopkeepers. It was a position he was never able to adapt to, much as his wife was never able to accept his passivity, his unwillingness to help out in the family shop, and, above all, his alcoholism. It was his drinking that made him the laughingstock of the Ostenders, who delighted in plying him with drink until he was thoroughly intoxicated, and then dropping his inert body at the door to the shop. He died of alcoholism and exposure in the streets of Ostend. Ensor recalled that when he was a child, his mother and aunt spoiled him with sweets; his other references to his mother, however, were never more than respectful. What is indisputable is that regardless of what early care his mother gave him, he developed a contempt and disdain for women. He recognized his mother's ability to hold the family together and her managerial skills, but the pictures he painted of her (for example, *Portrait of the Artist's Mother,* 1881) portray a somber, possibly depressed woman. That this was so does not surprise us in view of the life she led with her husband, for their home was frequently the scene of acerbic quarrels that ripped through the provincial dullness. Perhaps Ensor's first "loss" occurred when, at the age of 18 months, his sister was born. Now in addition to devoting herself to the arduous tasks of keeping her family from falling apart, bearing the scorn of the townspeople toward her husband, and managing their shop, his mother had another child to care for. I speculate that it was from this time that Ensor's bitter misanthropy developed.

As I said, Ensor's relationships with women were few and seemingly shallow. He never married, and the long relationship he had with Augusta Boogaerts may never have been consummated. (This brings to mind Poe's numerous platonic relationships and the reports that his marriage had been without sex. Auden caustically, said that Poe made a mockery of sex, "crying in laps and playing house with his lady friends" [Bradley, 1973, p. 8].

As a child Ensor was a "loner," given to long walks along the North Sea beaches and surrounding villages, which he began to sketch. He had no playmates, and except for a two-year period at school, he was tutored at home. It was during these early years that he developed the intense attachment to the sea that remained with him until his death (Werman, 1989). Throughout his long life, he routinely walked by the sea each day- the sea that he experienced as a woman, "chaste," "virginal," "washed clean," a goddess whom he "embraced," "my beloved." Even when his mother was still alive, the sea seemed to have become the idealized, desexualized mother of his early, preoedipal years, his principal source of solace. With no friends among the mocking Ostenders, he had no other place to go when he suffered.

And he was to suffer intensely when his paintings were refused by exhibitors, when the critics not only were contemptuous of his work, but treated him as "degenerate," "neurotic," and "inept." Whatever bitterness, feelings of abandonment, and desire for retaliation he had stored up as a child because of the lack of a secure, caring home and sense of belonging to a community, now found a fertile ground for expression and were displaced onto the art world. His subsequent work bore witness to both his sense of martyrdom and his compulsion to revenge himself on those whom he regarded as his oppressors and "torturers."

DISCUSSION

Revenge is as ancient as written history and is as banal as it is regarded abhorrent-abhorrent, that is, unless the seeker of revenge has been identified as a noble person whose injuries received are recognized as dastardly and unforgivable. The concept of revenge contains the idea that an injury must be inflicted in return for one received. The idea of "paying back," returning like for like, "getting even," settling "accounts" or "the score," is etymologically embodied in such reflexive words as *re*taliation, *re*venge, and *re*tribution. Not generally described are the emotions of rage and hatred that usually accompany the desire for revenge. Deeply enmeshed in the wreaking of revenge is a need to retrieve a sense of control over one's destiny, to regulate one's injured self-esteem, to restitute feelings of strength—to reestablish the supremacy of the ego over the pain of feeling controlled, passive, castrated, impotent, and childlike. To carry out the revenge fills the perpetrator with a sense of triumph, control, and grandeur—of having seized the high moral ground.

There have been few psychoanalytic contributions to this subject, which should command our interest and concern, because it bears not only on much individual behavior, but on that of religious sects, races, and nations. Freud's comments on the phenomenon of revenge were few but trenchant. As early as the "Studies in Hysteria" (1895), he observed:

> The instinct of revenge, which is so powerful in the natural man and is disguised rather than repressed by civilization, is nothing but the excitation of a reflex that has not been released. To defend oneself against the injury in a fight and, in doing so, to injure one's opponent is the adequate and preformed psychic reflex. If it has been carried out insufficiently or not at all, it is constantly released again by recollection, and the 'instinct of revenge' comes into being as an irrational volitional impulse, just as all the other "instincts" [pp. 205–206].

Freud added little to the foregoing other than locating the origins of the desire for revenge in childhood, describing how Little Hans (1909) repeatedly took revenge on his father for leading him astray with the story of the stork. Similarly, in "Family Romances" (1908), Freud noted that children who were punished for "sexual naughtiness ... revenge themselves on their parents by means of phantasies" (p. 240) in which, for example, the mother is engaged in secret love affairs.

In 1923, citing Rank, he observed that just as erotic impulses show an indifference in regard to the object, "so neurotic acts of revenge may be directed against the wrong people." "Punishment," he observed, "must be exacted even if it does not fall upon the guilty" (Freud, 1923, p. 45). In all of these acts lies the magical assumption by the revenger "that the original act of aggression can be undone" (Freud, 1895, p. 380).

Kohut (1972), echoing Freud, regarded revenge as a compulsive need to right a wrong stemming from an early narcissistic injury and the ensuing narcissistic rage to which it gave rise. It is precisely such injured individuals, Kohut observed, who respond "to actual (or anticipated) narcissistic injury either with shamefaced withdrawal (flight) or with narcissistic rage (fight)" (Kohut, 1972, p. 379). This formulation reminds us of Ensor's childhood and youth, where ridicule and contempt were common. With Poe, the critical events were more heavily weighted on the side of actual losses, with the humiliating experiences not substantially intruding on his life until early adolescence. But for both men, there seems to have been an imperative need to turn passive experiences into active ones, as Freud (1920) described (p. 16), and perhaps, for both, a need to identify with the aggressor. The pain and rage, when the object fails to live up to the child's "absolutarian expectations," as Kohut wrote, signifies a significant loss of control over the environment, leading at a later time to strident demands for an "absolute control" over "an archaic environment," which is indispensable in order to maintain self-esteem.

Castelnuovo-Tedesco (1974) dealt with revenge in exploring the "Monte Cristo Complex." His paper focused principally on the hero's stealing as an act of revenge and restitution. The Count of Monte Cristo, Castelnuovo-Tedesco noted, saw himself as having suffered "a cruel, unwarranted and unfair deprivation; this in turn had given rise to a sense of uniqueness and to a conviction of being entitled to reparations for 'damages'" (p. 175). Thus Dumas's hero can "give back measure for measure," can carry out virtually any deed with impunity.

Neither Poe nor Ensor was able to satisfactorily exorcise the ghosts of their past. In their private lives as in their creative work, the pressures of their childhood suffering was never adequately modulated, never sufficiently neutralized. For both men, the people on whom they sought to take revenge-the critics, writers, and painters whom they pilloried without mercy-had, in some instances, indeed been hostile to them, but others had merely been convenient targets for the blistering chronic resentment and rage that Ensor and Poe harbored from their previous losses, disappointments, humiliations, and misery that fate had dealt them.

We also see that both men had developed idiosyncratic attitudes toward women: Poe passionately idealized and became infatuated with a series of mother surrogates. Ensor, as far as it is known, never had a satisfactory relationship with a woman; his attitude towards women was, at best, scornful. In a "poem" he wrote in 1925, he described women as "Deceiving sex, respecter of neither law nor religion, heartless and devoid of honor/Sink of hypocrisy/Hot bed of lies and dissimulation/Mud-pit of malice," and so on for 22 lines, concluding with "constant mask and endless smile" (Haesaerts, p. 360). But this hostility toward women was equally directed toward his fellow townspeople, critics, painters, and ultimately, in a festering misanthropy, to all people. This undeclared vendetta progressively pervaded his work and, if not in itself responsible for his early loss of creativity, could not but contribute to the deterioration of his work, to the compulsive production of the pictorial and verbal broadsides he fired off.

In contrast, Poe's creative life, if not the content of his work, was not significantly affected by his desire for revenge. Indeed, those desires became the controlled motor force of some of his finest tales, although in his literary criticism he often skated too close to the edge of what was appropriate and acceptable in the literary milieu of his time. Not surprisingly, this alienated him from people who had lauded his work and been kind to him; ultimately it was self-defeating.

CONCLUSION

The desire for revenge is one of the most powerful, irrational, and tenacious emotions. It leads people, individually and in groups, to the very heights of destructiveness and remains virtually untouched by reason or the lessons of history–personal or social. The revenge seeker deals with the pain of an injury he or she has experienced by harboring a fantasy organized around the perception of the original injury (or the epigenesis of that injury over time). This fantasy assumes the quality of a myth, which may be shared by a revenge-seeking family, caste, class, or nation. Although many such fantasies for revenge are not translated into action, many unfortunately are. For Ensor and Poe, as for many others, even the activation of the fantasy does not adequately moderate the desire for actual revenge that, like many neurotic trends, seems incapable of being subdued.

The origins of these implacable wishes for retaliation are diverse, revenge being but a final common pathway; the perception and experience of a humiliating injury, however, in whatever form it takes, seems to be its most prominent source. Ultimately, regardless of its genesis, unless revenge is worked through and laid to rest, it can lead to the "basest things [for] Revenge, at first though sweet/Bitter are long, back on itself recoils..." (Milton, p. 239).

REFERENCES

ALLEN, H. (1934). *Israfel: The Life and Times of Edgar Allan Poe*. New York: Farrar and Rinehart.
BONAPARTE, M. (1933). *Edgar Poe*. Paris: Les Editions. Denolët Steele.
BRADLEY, H. (1973). *Three Dimensional Poe*. El Paso, TX: Western Press.

CASTELNAU, J. (1945*). Edgar Poe*. Paris: Tallandier.

CASTELNUOVO-TEDESCO, P. (1974). Stealing, revenge and the Monte Cristo complex. *Int. J. Psycho-Anal.* 55:169–177.

ENSOR, J. (1974). *Mes Ecrits*. Liege: Editions Nationales.

FREUD, S. (1895). Studies on hysteria. *Standard Edition,* 2. London: Hogarth Press, 1955.

——— (1908). Family romances. *Standard Edition.* 9:237–24–1. London: Hogarth Press, 1959.

——— (1909). Analysis of a phobia in a five-year-old boy. *Standard Edition.* 10:5–149. London: Hogarth Press, 1955.

——— (1920), Beyond the pleasure principle. *Standard Edition* 18:7–64. London: Hogarth Press, 1950.

——— (1923), The ego and the id. *Standard Edition*, 19:12–59. London: Hogarth Press, 1961.

HAESAERTS, P. (n.d.). *Ensor*. London: Thames and Hudson,.

KOHUT, H. (1972). Thoughts on narcissism and narcissistic rage. *Psychoanal. Study Child* 27:360–400.

MILTON, J. (1667). *Paradise Lost*. New York: Leavitt & Allen.

POE, E.A. (1846). *The Annotated Tales of Edgar Allan Poe*, S. Peithman (Ed.). New York: Avemel Books..

QUINN, A.H. (1942). *Edgar Allan Poe: A Critical Biography*. New York: D. Appleton-Century.

WERMAN, D.S. (1989). James Ensor, and the Attachment to Place. *Int. R. Psycho-Anal.* 16:287–295.

CHAPTER 4

The Passing of Creativity: Two Histories: James Ensor and Arthur Rimbaud

[Werman, D.S. (2000). *Journal of Applied Psychoanalytic Studies* 1:65–80.]

ABSTRACT:

This essay explores the "passing of creativity" in James Ensor, the artist and Arthur Rimbaud, the poet. The former was burnt out by his thirty-fifth year. The latter abandoned poetry at age nineteen. I argue that in both men, their art was driven by revengeful needs; Ensor never transcended that imperative; Rimbaud had said it all and quit the field.

INTRODUCTION

Although there are certainly many reasons why an artist's creativity may come to an end, I will describe but two of them, and illustrate these with the examples of James Ensor (1860–1949) the Belgian artist, and Arthur Rimbaud (1854–1891) the French poet. Disparate as these two men were in many ways, they embody my point of view which relates to the subordination and devaluation of aesthetic goals to matters of an essentially nonaesthetic nature to the detriment of the former.

Perhaps almost as astonishing as the fertility of a creative artist is the ebb, or even the abrupt cessation, of his or her prodigious and yet mysterious gifts—a fate of many creative individuals: Marcel Duchamp, for example, who abruptly stopped painting at the age of 36 to devote himself to "ready-mades," multimedia *Etant Donne's* and chess; Whistler, whose later years were mired in controversies, and grew increasingly sterile; Utrillo, who spent his last years plagiarizing himself.

Ensor was such an artist, whose creative life declined dramatically over a few short years. Living at the same time as Ensor, Arthur Rimbaud, in his early twenties, deliberately and definitively abandoned poetry after having produced a body of masterpieces.

The nature of creativity itself is so poorly understood, and the voluminous literature pertaining to it so full of conflicting views, that, for the purpose of this essay, I shall arbitrarily take it to mean the production of a body of artistic work that has generally been accepted as of

high value, and that judgment has stood a "reasonable"test of time—
which for both Ensor and Rimbaud represents a period of over one
hundred years. The defects in this description of creativity are obvious;
it will, however, support the following exploration.

I.

The proximal influence on Ensor that disrupted his precocious and stunning accomplishment, was the bruising assaults he incurred from the critics at a time when he had barely begun to exhibit his work. Prematurely
leaving the Acade´ mie Royale des Beaux Arts, in Brussels, in 1879,
he returned directly to Ostend and his parents' home, where he set up a
studio in the attic. He was then nineteen years old. During the next two
or three years he was able to exhibit a few of his paintings, but beginning
in 1882, with the rejection of *Woman Eating Oysters* (1882) by the
Antwerp Salon, he was to find his work increasingly unacceptable.

Over the next decade he was able to show some of his work; however, in 1884, for instance, everything he submitted to the Brussels Salon
was rejected; the following year only six of his paintings were exhibited
by the independent group, *Les Vingt,* and six the following year. In the
ensuing years only very few were accepted; many of his best works were
refused. The sales were so poor that in 1893 he offered to sell everything
in his studio for 8300 Belgian francs—but no buyer came forward. Still
more painful were the harsh comments of the critics, some of whom,
although having earlier praised his work, now began to disparage it. His
paintings were described as "lacking form," others were characterized as
"street-fair art,' "ignoble sights," "sickening studio rubbish," "garbage."
Ensor himself was sorely treated: "A hail of cruel comments is falling on
my head," he wrote. "They are abusing me, insulting me; I am [presumed
to be] mad, stupid, wicked, bad, incapable, ignorant!" (Ensor, 1974).

To this barrage of invective Ensor replied in kind through words
and pictures, which in turn led to even more devastating criticism.
The most powerful and successful expression of his resentful misanthropy, still well under artistic control, was the huge *Entry of Christ
into Brussels* (1888). There, Christ, seated on a donkey, is almost lost
in a sea of bloated, cruel, imbecilic faces, representing people from
all stations and walks of life.

The tension between his revengeful impulse to lash out at those he
experienced and called his "persecutors," and his artistic vocation was

never to be satisfactorily resolved. At times his obsession with retaliation crudely overwhelms his painting. In *Dangerous Cooks* (1896), essentially a cartoon, two men attired as cooks, are serving human heads, on platters, to a group of men (critics) seated at a table; two of them are already vomiting. One of the heads is inscribed "Art Ensor."

Similarly unsubtle is *Doctrinal Nourishment* (1889): sitting on a balustrade, their backs to the viewer, are a king, a priest, a teacher, a judge and an army officer, all of whom are defecating into the mouths of a happy throng below. Not to let it remain ambiguous, the defecators are holding signs such as "Universal Suffrage" and "Obligatory Education." In 1929, Ensor destroyed this picture in order to facilitate his being named a Baron by King Albert. There were many of these baldly polemical drawings, interspersed, rarely, with relatively "conflict-free" work.

The ebb and flow of his conflict is strikingly embodied in the brilliant series of graphic works, chiefly etchings, mostly of the North Sea beaches and villages he had sketched as an adolescent. Lamentably, he did not pursue this over the following years.

The tendentious works are in marked contrast to the paintings he made after returning to Ostend from the Acade´ mie. These do not suggest the road Ensor was to take: many of them are "intimist" scenes in the Ensor home. In *Afternoon at Ostend* (1881) a younger woman and an older woman are sitting at a table having tea; the younger faces the viewer the older faces away, a scowl marking her face. The colors are muted earth tones; the women seem to be frozen for all eternity. *Russian Music* (1881) appears to be in the same room. A young woman, her back to the viewer, is seated at a piano, while a formally dressed genteleman, expressionless, is presumably listening to the music. The air is thick and motionless.

These were among the paintings that were rejected by the salons, as well as *Woman Eating Oysters* (1882), later to be considered one of Ensor's major works. The former two pictures convey a sense of the stasis and loneliness that characterize one of Ensor's first painings, dating from his sixteenth year: *A Cabin on the Beach* (1876). Standing on a totally deserted beach, is a modest beach cabin, on four shaky wheels. Behind it is the sea and sky. At the horizon one can see faint streaks of smoke from two ships. That is the only sign of life present. An atmosphere of isolation and detachment pervades the scene.

At the same time as the "cartoons" began to become prominent in his work, Ensor discovered light. Already in *Woman Eating Oysters* (1882) his palette had begun to lighten. In *The Tower at Lisserwegh* (1988) and *Christ Calming the Sea* (1891) he reached his full coloristic expression. At least in part derivative of J. M. W. Turner, and contemporaneous with the French impressionist school, this new departure coincided with his occupation with masks, which stayed with him for the rest of his life. It served him well. "From 1883," he wrote, "masks had a profound effect on me . . . With my pursuers close upon my heels I joyfully closed myself up in the solitary world where the mask occupies a place of honor, (where) those masks, wholly made up of violence, light, and brilliance, hold sway. The mask speaks to me of freshness of tone, sharpness of expression, sumptuous decoration, sweeping and startling gestures, disordered movement, and an exquisate turbulence" (Ensor, p. 164). They also provided him with the opportunity to represent the true face of hypocrisy and venality, to reveal the true person in the form of the mask.

In *The Intrigue* (1890) stand nine figures, one of whom holds a baby. They surround a joyless bride and a simpering bridegroom; the latter, with Asian features, portrays the Chinese merchant who married Ensor's sister, against his bitter wishes, and who abandoned her and their baby. Ensor's repugnance for his family is eloquently, if harshly represented.

His rageful feelings towards the critics and his sad and angry disappointment with his family coalesced and spread until it became a misanthropy that had no limits. Perhaps it is in *Death Pursuing a Flock of Mortals* (1896) that it reaches its culmination: A horde of panic-stricken people are fleeing through a narrow street towards the viewer. Overhead soars a gruesome, grinning skeleton brandishing a scythe, while a beatific face in the sun above, smiles down on the horrifying scene.

Ensor's mother was undoubtedly devoted to her children, but it seems that within a year or so of James' birth, perhaps coinciding with the birth of his sister, she began to limit her mothering to the provision of what was necessary, and sweets, all the while proccupied with the Herculean task of holding her family together.

In 1881 Ensor painted portraits of his parents. *Portrait of the Artist's Mother* shows a somber, possibly depressed woman. *Portrait of the Artist's Father* reveals a seated man, hunched over a book, his toes pointed in; clearly a man of no great strength. In neither of these joyless portraits, however, is there any sense of unkindness towards his subjects.

Within its walls the chronic dullness of the Ensor home was punctured by frequent acerbic quarrels, while from the outside world the family was subjected to the derision of their "fellow" townsmen. The elder Ensor had the sad distinction of being the town drunk. He ultimately died in the street of alcoholism and exposure. As for James, throughout his life, he kept aloof from the Ostenders, among whom he had no enduring friendships. Shy and diffident as a child, he was given to long solitary walks along the North Sea coast, to places which he began to sketch. Except for two years at a local school, he was tutored at home, further isolating him.

Nor was his budding artistic vocation, although encouraged by his father, ever understood or taken seriously by his mother, who saw it as a poor way of earning a living. Although he was dutiful towards her, it was not to her that he turned for soothing or affection, but to the sea which he explicitly and repeatedly apostrophized as his chief source of solace, "a virginal, consoling mother."

His feelings of marginality at home and in the city converged with his "persecution" by the critics, and he withdrew progressively into himself. Finally, under the sway of feelings of martyrdom he began to consciously identify himself with Christ, not as a God so much as a humiliated, uncared for, misunderstood and tortured man. In addition to *Entry in Brussels of Christ,* there were several scenes of the crucifixion, in one of which the Christ figure is wearing a sign: ENSOR. His creativity was ransomed to an implacable obsession with a need for retaliation. Even though this need did not at all times dominate his work, it powerfully contributed to suffocating his creative *e'lan,* and until his death in 1949, at the age of 89, he was never truly able to declare a truce in the war he waged against his "enemies"—many of whom were already long dead. During the last fifty years of his career he did, in fact, produce some valuable works, but many others were simply self-plagiarisms, some more or less unwitty caricatures, while still others just carelessly executed. From the courageous, brilliant young experimenter of the 1880s, he became an embittered, bombastic, envious buffoon, given to making angry speeches. Recognition, when it came, did little to soothe his resentful feelings, underscoring the intrapsychic nature of those conflicts.

His self-inflation even blinded him to the historic achievements of the great artists who had grown to prominence between 1885 and 1940, for whom, he insisted, he had been the precursor.

II.

In dramatic contrast to the relatively slow deterioration of Ensor's creative forces was Arthur Rimbaud's sudden decision to irrevocably abandon his vocation of poet. After a few years of fertility, perhaps unsurpassed in the history of poetry, this adolescent prodigy decided, at the very peak of his powers, to chuck literature, even to ignore the fate, indeed the success, of what he had already written, and to turn his back forever on his creative past and on literature altogether.

Virtually a contemporary of Ensor, Rimbaud was born in 1854, in Charleville, a city in the north of France, only too similar in its provinciality to Ostend. The epic of the poet's tumultuous short life—he died in 1891 at the age of 37—does not lend itself well to condensation. His father, who came from a family of small-town artisans, rose through the ranks to become a decorated captain in the French Army. He married Rimbaud's mother, the daughter of farmers in Roche, a town near Charleville. Their "conjugal life" was limited to his furloughs, which tended to be followed by pregnancies of Madame Rimbaud, and during the first seven years of their marriage she gave birth to five children, of which Arthur was the second. When Captain Rimbaud retired from the army he settled in Dijon—several hundred miles from Charleville, where his wife remained, clinging to the family farm which she managed until her death. Although Captain Rimbaud lived for fourteen years after his retirement, he apparently never had any contact with his family after the fifth child had been conceived. For all practical purposes he had abandoned his wife and children. Although Arthur was almost six years old at the time, he rarely alluded to him, other than recalling disputes between his parents. In the year of his father's departure, the Rimbauds first born child died. Madame Rimbaud forbade the children to speak of their father or to mention his name; he was to be regarded as worse than dead—as if he had never existed.

As a woman deserted by her husband, Madame Rimbaud became fiercely concerned with keeping her family together, much as did Ensor's mother. As a woman whose husband had cast her off, and she herself coming from a family of ne'er-do-wells and alcoholics, she was ill-regarded by the good bourgeoisie of Charleville, and, perhaps in consequence, she grew proud and authoritarian; she was to be described as "stubbornly Catholic" and "savagely rigid."

Some years later she wrote to Verlaine that what saved her from misery was the realization that "true happiness consists in the fulfilling of all one's duties, however painful it may be" (Starkie, p. 296). It was, among other things, against such a stiff-necked and self-righteous attitude that Arthur was to revolt. There is no evidence that he actually hated her; in fact, almost to the end of his life he yearned that she might mellow and that some sort of reconciliation between them could take place. However, she never did, and to his great sorrow such a reconciliation never took place; he died in a hospital in Marseille with only his sister present because Madame Rimbaud, after a brief visit, returned to Roche to take care of the farm, since it was harvest time. Her life-long concern about money was well known. She isolated herself and her children, as best she could, from other people, keeping her family under an "iron discipline." The children were obliged to dress "properly," to wear "sensible" shoes and clothes that had long been out of fashion. Every Sunday she marched her children off to church, two by two, with herself bringing up

the rear—under the ironic comments of the townspeople. When the boys began to attend the Charleville *Colle`ge* they appeared wearing derby hats, high white collars and slate blue broadcloth trousers that they would wear for several years, because Madame Rimbaud had at one time bought a large quantity of the material. At home the principal reading matter was the Bible. Visits of friends were forbidden, and the children played by themselves, although without toys. She accompanied them to school every day, supervised their homework, made them recite their lessons, and punished them for any errors by sending them early to bed without supper.

When he was about fifteen, he wrote *The Orphans' Gifts* (New Year's):

The room is full of darkness; indistinctly you hear
The soft whispering of two children . . .
....
Is there no mother for these small children,
No mother with a fresh smile and triumphant glances? So she forgot in the
evening, alone and leaning down, To kindle a flame saved from the ashes,
And to pile over them the wool and the quilt
Before leaving them, and calling out to them: forgive me!
....
Your heart had understood:—these children are motherless.
No mother in here! and the father far away! . . .
....
The parents' room is empty today:
No red reflection shone under the door;
There are no parents, no hearth, no stolen keys: And therefore no kisses, no
sweet surprises!
They murmur: "When will our mother return?"
....

On seeing them you would say they are crying in their sleep,
So swollen are their eyes and so painful their breathing! Small children
have such sensitive hearts!

"The Orphans' Gifts" (New Year's) 1869
(Fowlie, 1966)

A year later he wrote again of his childhood:

And the Mother, closing the exercise book,
Went off satisfied and very proud, without seeing
In the blue eyes and under his brow covered with bumps, The soul of her
child given over to repugnance.
All day he sweated obedience . . .

....

In the shadow of the corridor with their moldy hangings,
Passing through he stuck out his tongue, his two fists in his groin . . .

....

In summer
Especially, overcome, stupefied he was bent
On shutting himself in the coolness of the outhouse: There he meditated,
peacefully, opening his nostrils.

....

Seven-Year-Old Poets, 1871
(Fowlie, 1966)

Here, as throughout his poetry, as well as in hi letters, he cried out
for freedom, and decried being oppressed.

From his earliest years in school, Arthur showed himself to be a brilliant student, year after year winning prizes for his scholarly achievements, although he protested that he hated school. A new world of literature was opening up for the boy, along with a profound conviction that he would be a poet, despite his mother's arduous efforts to dissuade him. Arthur once wrote of her as ". . . a mother as inflexible as seventy-three bureaucrats in steel helmets" (Fowlie, p. 313).

On one occasion, outraged, she wrote to Arthur's mentor and teacher of rhetoric, Georges Izambard, protesting the assignment of *Les Misérables* "by V. Hugot" (sic). Pierquin, a childhood friend, later recalled that Madame Rimbaud "never had the slightest understanding, the least indulgence for the adolescent, who nevertheless in his work gave her every satisfaction" (Pierquin, 1924). In fact, his school work was stunning: for example, at nine he composed hundreds of remarkable lines of Latin verse.

Izambard, a teacher and confidant, remembered Rimbaud as a slightly built, shy, well-behaved, sweet young man, always immaculate, with scrupulously well-kept notebooks. In short, he was, to all appearances, the perfect type of the *"be^te à concours,"* the competitive "greasy grind."

And yet, behind this well-scrubbed face was an acidulous cynic, a shrewd ironist. He dismissed Napoleon III, the reigning monarch, suggesting to a friend that the Emperor should be sent off to the galleys; evoking the most ruthless revolutionaries of 1789, he called out: "Danton, Saint-Juste, Couthon, and Robespierre, [we] the youth await you." He railed against the "wheezy bourgeois," "men behind huge desks, bloated, (who) drag their fat wives . . .," "the grotesque priest whose feet stink as he mouths the divine babble," ". . . ladies from the correct neighborhoods . . . dip their long yellow fingers in the holy-water basins."

By the time he was fourteen, it was clear that the pressure of rebellion could scarcely be contained any longer; at first the explosion was contained through his poetry. However, he soon found himself no longer able, in and through poetry, to encapsulate, or to extinguish his feelings of rage, anguish and rebellion, and he fled to Paris. This was to be the first of several such elopements, and presaged a later obsession to move from one place to another.

Izambard tried, valiantly but in vain to placate Madame Rimbaud at the same time that he attempted to encourage Arthur to "settle down." When he asked the youth how much longer he intended to keep running away, Rimbaud replied, "As long as necessary." It was at this time that he threw away the derby hat and the slate blue trousers, allowed his hair to grow long and uncombed, and to walk around smoking a pipe upside down. He proudly proclaimed his vocation of poet. In a letter to his friend, Demeny, he wrote that the first task of one who would be a poet is to "totally understand himself." The poet, he announced, must make himself into a *Voyant* (a seer); he must experience "every form of love, of suffering, of madness," in this way only can he become the "great patient, the great criminal, the great accursed one" (Carre´ , p. 316).

He wrote Izambard that he was "rotting away [in Charleville] amidst the platitude the pettiness the grayness" (Carre´ , p. 41). In 1870, a year after he left school, his mother tried to impose a strict program on him; she followed him to Douai, where he had fled, and demanded that either he submit to "work" and "responsibilities" or he could stay away for good. He felt that a "rag of disgust" had been crammed in his mouth, and he refused her ultimatum, announcing that he'd probably end up in a reform school anyway.

The end of 1870 was a time of momentous change: France had suffered a massive, humiliating defeat by the German army; the Commune of Paris, with which Rimbaud sided, chiefly out of his own rebelliousness, was crushed in a bloody civil war, Napoleon the Third was deposed and the Third French Republic formed. Against this turbulent background the pubertal boy began to grow, physically, and become an adult. He adopted ragged clothes and behaved like a lout. He continued to run away from home, and did such things as to chalk, on a park bench in Charleville, "Merde a` Dieu" (shit on God). He bragged that he was so full of lice that he picked them off his clothes and threw them at priests. When he ate with family or friends, he delighted in being as slovenly as possible. With some people he managed to be infuriating by sitting with them for hours without uttering a word. Moreover, he frequently stole inexpensive things, such as books, from the people who were sheltering him. After visiting the Louvre, he walked away commenting that it was a pity that the Communards hadn't blown the place up.

Well-known is Rimbaud's dramatic liaison with Verlaine that ran its ragged course from 1871 to 1873. This tumultuous affair culminated with Verlaine shooting Rimbaud, wounding him in the wrist, an act for which he was sentenced to two years in prison. The implications of this homosexual relationship (presumably the only one he ever had) for his creativity and his ultimate renunciation of poetry are unclear. Verlaine, an older and already famous poet, who adored Arthur, praised his work and encouraged him. This obviously was of considerable importance for the youth, and indeed, the two years he spent with Verlaine were among the most fertile in his brief career as a poet. However, his genius had already been well on the ascendency before he met Verlaine (and he had had earlier mentors), and after the two lovers broke up he continued to write, completing *A Season In Hell,* and *Les Illuminations.*

After he left Verlaine he returned to the farm at Roche where he worked on *Une Saison en Enfer* (A Season in Hell). This lengthy suite of poems explores the hell which he constructed for himself, through which he lived, that he transcended and finally silenced through the creative world of his poetry—of all his poem s this astounding work may well be regarded as the centerpiece. In contrast to many of the earlier poems, where the focus was, more often than not, on people and events in his environment, *A Season in Hell* is profoundly introspective. This large and at times obscure work defies summary. The main issues revolve around his feelings of guilt, the reality of God and Satan, and the nature of sin. Having earlier flaunted his atheism, here he works through the problem once more, and plunges into his personal hell. Finally he rejects religion, seeing it as yet another form of restriction of his freedom. He will not be a "slave" to it, and so will forsake God. Except for a death-bed absolution, (for which we have only his sister's word) he never returned to religion or poetry. Indeed shortly before his death, spending a few months back at Roche, his physician tried to speak with him about poetry and literature, to which he made a gesture of disgust and answered coldly, "Shit for poetry" (Starkie, 1961). Towards the end of *Season,* he writes:

At least I will ask forgiveness for having fed on lies.
....
For I can say that victory is mine . . .
. . . All filthy memories fade out . . .
....
. . . and I shall be free to *possess truth in one body and soul.*

A Season in Hell, 1873
(Fowlie, 1961)

A Season in Hell was published, in 1873, by Poot et Cie, of Brussels. He later demonstrated his feelings about the meaninglessness of literature: The firm had sent him a half-dozen author's copies, and awaited payment for the remainder of the edition—some 500 copies. Rimbaud distributed those he had received, to people he knew in Paris, but never sent Poot et Cie the money for the balance, nor did he ever evince the slightest interest about the fate of *A Season in Hell.* When he sought the opinion of those who, presumably, had read the work, he met with deep disappointment. "It is very probable" Starkie observes, "that he was received with hostility and snubs, and that his book was not even read." Moreover, she continues, many had already regarded him ". . . as unworthy, as some sort of lunatic." Many sided with Verlaine and felt Rimbaud was a monster who was responsible for their imbroglio and Verlaine's imprisonment. Starkie believes that the reception he received in Paris left him with "a wound that he was never afterwards able to forget. He had come to them in all humility—even if pious humility—confessing his past errors and renouncing all that hitherto he had held dear, and they had repulsed him" (Starkie, p. 311).

(A curious footnote: the 500 copies remained, stored by Poot et Cie in their basement, until 1901, when they were discovered by a Belgian bibliophile, who did not reveal his purchase until 1914).

He was later (November, 1873) seen sitting by himself in a cafe, drinking, appearing gloomy. It was shortly after this that he returned to the farm and burned all his manuscripts and other papers. What continues to be a controversial matter is when he began and finished what may have been his final work, *Les Illuminations.* The consensus is that this long prose poem was begun in 1872 and extended over 1874. It is first mentioned by Verlaine in 1875, requesting it from a third person. But by 1874, at the age of twenty, Rimbaud had decisively slammed the door on poetry and begun a series of voyages, often travelling hundreds of miles on foot, criss-crossing Germany, Switzerland, Italy, North Africa, and Holland.

Serving briefly in the Dutch Army, he was sent to the Dutch East Indies, where he deserted. Later, there were trips to Cyprus and Egypt. After each excursion he returned to his mother's farm. The details of his extraordinary *epope´e* during the next seventeen years, that is until his death, are well beyond the scope or aim of this essay. Suffice it to say that from 1880 when he was 26 years old, he remained in the Middle East, working as a building foreman in Cyprus, running guns in Africa—and possibly involved in slave trade—and exploring in Somalia and Ethiopia (he was the first European to go to Bubassa and to cross the Ogaden; his report on these explorations was published by the French Socie´ te´ de Ge´ ographie in 1883. They enthusiastically wrote him requesting some biographical information, and a picture; he never responded). In 1891 he was found to have a malignant tumor of the right knee. Since there was no doctor in Harar, he was carried on a litter some 120 miles, a trip of two weeks, to Aden. In excruciating pain he was repatriated to France and died in November, 1801, in a hospital in Marseille.

Of consuming interest is that from 1874, when he abandoned poetry, he not only rigorously kept to that promise, but even refused to talk about or hear any one else discuss literature. When he was told, in 1886, that *Les Illuminations* had been published in Paris (with a preface by Verlaine), he didn't show the slightest interest. The following year, when his employer, Bardey, tried to draw him out on his thoughts about poetry, he responded, as usual, that it was all "absurd, ridiculous and disgusting" (Bardey, 1939). In 1891 he received a letter from the editor of *la France Moderne,* who had discovered his whereabouts, inviting him to be "one of us," the symbolist avant-garde; he never answered, but the letter was found in his effects after his death. Moreover, during the twenty years preceding his death, he showed no interest whatsoever in literature—whether it be novels, poetry or criticism. Instead, he frequently wrote his family for books on mathematics, surveying, agriculture, forestry, carpentry, metallurgy, and Eastern languages (he taught Arabic to natives in Harrar).

Like Ensor, he grew progressively bitter, misanthropic, and demeaning of other people, although he was described by many as extraordinarily kind and generous, and generally able to control his temper. He despised his primitive surroundings and scorned the natives; at the same time he claimed that returning to Europe was virtually impossible because he would never find work there, would be unable to tolerate the cold, and would find the mode of living insufferable. He wrote his family on many occasions that he was desparately bored. He yearned for peace and quiet described fantasies of some day making a killing and becoming financially independent, marrying, having children whom he would raise to be "new kinds of people," and a son who would become an engineer. Now all he wanted was to achieve something like bourgeois respectability, and feared that instead he was becoming an "abruti" (an idiot).

III.

If we consider the deterioration of Ensor's creativity, a link may be perceived between the waning of his artistic powers (from which he was never able to pull back, with the exception of occasional resurgences) and Rimbaud's deliberate abandonment of his vocation as a poet. For both men, what seems to have been critically implicated in the death of their creativity was the pervasive domination in their work of impulses, feelings and "needs," which neither arose primarily from aesthetic considerations nor were, for them, secondarily available or amenable to assimilation into an aesthetic imperative.

Of course, it could be that for Ensor or Rimbaud some intrinsic "reservoir" of talent may have been exhausted for reasons that are as mysterious as is the very concept of genius. Since such a possibility can no more be denied than affirmed, we can only set it aside, and assume that it neither enhances nor detracts from the following observations.

For Rimbaud, his poetical genius was placed powerfully in the service of a psychological *coup d'e'tat,* aimed at a world that he despised, rejected, that had rejected him, and from which he finally fled. His life was pervaded by fury and sadness, indeed, despair—in the first instance at not having a loving, caring home (no father, and a beloved grandfather who died when Arthur was four) but one under the iron rule of his authoritarian mother. She met his insurgency more than half way by her controlling measures, her response to his rebelliousness. Nor was her behavior modified in later years when Arthur attempted some sort of *rapprochment.* In 1885, when he was thirty-three, living in Aden, in her characteristic style, she wrote him complaining that she had received no news from him for eight months. "Happy are those who don't have children, or blissful are those who don't love them," she wrote, "they are indifferent to what may happen to them . . . It's useless to speak to you about us since what concerns us bothers you so little . . . Are you so sick that you can't pick up a pen? . . . Yours, V. Rimbaud" (Rimbaud, pp. 414–415).

Despite such guilt provoking letters, it is undoubtedly true that Madame Rimbaud did her best, according to her lights, to hold her family together, and if her standards of conduct and discipline affronted the sensitive temperament of Arthur, it was not only a matter of her actual behavior but of a tragic misfit, clearly beyond the control of either mother or son.

It was the fire in Rimbaud, his rebellion against his omnipresent mother, then against petty-bourgeois morality, culture, religion, the clergy, the monarchy of Louis Napoleon, and the military that fueled his revengeful impulses, his cynicism and profound despair. It was this adolescent's *cri du coeur* that propelled his poetic genius. When he had poured out, virtually as an abreaction, his bitter rage, sarcasm, pain, revolt—when, in short, he had given utterance to everything that seethed within him—the fire seems to have died, at least the desire to express it through poetry. Poetry, literature altogether, became an irritant, a reminder of everything in his youth that he now invested with loathing; perhaps, also, his liaison with Verlaine. It all seemed soft, weak, and unworthy. It was then that he threw himself into a life that was, at least unconsciously, the antithesis of everything from which he had sought to escape, and he set out on a life of exotic, rough, manly voyages and experiences. In this last chapter of his life he followed closely, in many ways, in the footsteps of his errant father, Captain Fre´ de´ ric Rimbaud, who had spent several years in North Africa. Thus, Rimbaud pawned his prodigious gifts for the imperative needs of his rebellion; when these needs were more or less sated, they became useless baggage, and he proceeded to live out his life in a vain, blind and selfdefeating exile from a world he both embraced and desecrated, much as he raged against his mother but was never able to detach himself from her. Indeed, his letters to her frequently express affection and devotion.

IV.

Although so different in many ways, Ensor and Rimbaud represent two among the many ways in which an artist's creativity may rapidly—or lingeringly—pass from view. For Ensor, the loss represented his inability to continue a devotion to art, as he had done for some fifteen years. For Rimbaud, the abandonment of a creative life seems nothing less than the loss of the very desire to continue any artistic activity, that is to say, to revolt through poetry. What characterizes these two lives, is the powerful intrusion of feelings and ideas that grew to choke off their aesthetic vision.

Ensor was unable to integrate his revengeful feelings into his work. In effect, his need for tendentious expression overrode artistic considerations. I have earlier discussed the place of revenge in art, using Edgar Allan Poe, in contrast to James Ensor, as an example of an artist who mostly succeeded in keeping his intense feelings of revenge subordinate to his art, if not absent (Werman, 1993).

Rimbaud's decision to abandon poetry, it seems, came as a consequence of the ultimate meaninglessness that such writing took on for him. This revolutionary youth had the magnificent gift to translate his bitterness and irony into poetry, but by the time he was in his early twenties he had poured it all out—most especially in *A Season in Hell*—once and for all. His catharsis was virtually complete. Nothing more needed to be said, and he was then able to chuck literature: the city to which he had laid siege had surrendered, and he could lay down his arms. He was then free to work out externally what other meaning life held for him, although even then we see he was still oppositional while attempting some sort of tenuous, uneasy reconciliation with his family. This was a conflict that was to be resolved only with his death.

In Thomas Mann's story, *Tonio Kröger* (Mann, 1903), Kröger, a writer, tells his friend, Lisabeta Ivanova, a painter: "If you care too much about what you have to say, if your heart is too much in it, you can be pretty sure of making a mess. You get pathetic, you wax sentimental; something dull and doddering, without roots or outlines, with no sense of humor— something tiresome and banal grows under your hand, and you get nothing out of it but apathy in your audience and disappointment and misery in yourself " (p. 103).

Such, for the most part, was Ensor's fate during the last fifty years of his life. Rimbaud, in contrast, avoided the possible path of slow deterioration by totally abdicating his vocation as a poet. Both men "cared too much" about what they felt compelled to say to permit that "regression in the service of their (aesthetic) ego" which seems critical to artistic creativity. Ensor was unable to escape from reiterating, in words and on canvas, his bitterness; Rimbaud, having uttered his thoughts in as powerful a way as was possible, seemingly felt that thereafter only silence sufficed. For both men art was so ardently enlisted to serve a non-artistic purpose that their creativity was ultimately extinguished. Fortunately, for posterity, before that occurred, both artists were able to achieve masterworks that stand as a mute rebuke to the later exhaustion of their creativity.

Works of art emerge from a network of tensions. From the outset, the artist must deal with his or her "inspiration"—or "primary process" material—and a simultaneous need to cast this in a form that possesses "aesthetic value." From the outset of the creative process, the artist inevitably must confront the work of masters who preceded him or her. This relation is marked by trends of emulation, identification, limitation, rebellion and travesty. Henry James described Maupassant as "a lion in the path" of those who would attempt to write stories. Moreover, it is virtually impossible for the artist not to struggle to express artistic "thoughts" in a form that will permit them to be more or less successfully realized"and communicated to the public. The "content" may enfold political ideas, emotional states, or philosophic concepts; the content may also mainly represent a means to "*e'pater la bourgeoisie*" or to take revenge on one's enemies, to serve as a catharsis, or to foster the artist's narcissism or rage. The possible paths in which a gifted artist may be blocked are numerous, and unfortunately many examples come to mind in which tendentious goals were not only not integrated or fused with aesthetic considerations, but actually suffocated them.

There are many artistic works with a "thesis;" one thinks, in painting, of Bosch, Goya, Picasso, and countless others—but in their work nonaesthetic values did not generally subdue their artistic imagination. Clendinnen (1999) spoke of an "inversion effect," where the actuality subdues the artistic imagination. For Ensor and Rimbaud, a time came when they no longer sufficiently revered the muse of their art but allowed themselves to be governed by interests that were not essentially aesthetic. For Ensor, art became the servant of his need to settle old scores; for

Rimbaud, once he had exorcized his rage, poetry ceased to have any meaning for him.

REFERENCES

BARDEY, A. (1939). Lettres d'Alfred Bardey à Paterne Berrichon, *Mercure de France,* 15 mai–15 juin.

DELAHAYE, E. (1925). *Souvenirs familiers à propos de Rimbaud, Verlaine, Germain Nouveau.* Messein.

ENSOR, J. *Mes Ecrits.* Lie` ge, Editions Nationales. 5ième edition.

IZAMBARD, G. (1946). *Rimbaud tel que je l'ai connu.* Paris, 1946.

MANN, T. (1903). "Tonio Kröger" in *Stories of Three Decades.* London, Martin Secker and Warburg, Ltd., 1946.

PIERQUIN, L. (1922). Les Souvenirs d'un ami de Rimbaud, publ. by Jean-Marie Carré, Mercure de France, I–IV.

RIMBAUD, A.(1954).Oeuvres Completes. Paris, Bibliothèque de la Pléiade.

WERMAN, D.S. (1989). James Ensor and the Attachment to Place. *International Review of Psycho-Analysis* 16:287–295.

——— (1993). Edgar Allan Poe, James Ensor, and the Psychology of Revenge. *Annals of Psychoanalysis* 301–314.

CHAPTER 5

Chance, Ambiguity, and Psychological Mindedness

[Werman, D.S. (1979). *Psychoanalytic Quarterly* 48:107–115.]

ABSTRACT:
The inability to believe in chance occurrences and an intolerance of ambiguity in the external world are often the outward manifestations of poor psychological mindedness. Such attitudes are frequently accompanied by beliefs in the occult and the mystical. It is suggested that these factors be considered when an individual is being evaluated for analytic treatment.

The crucial interest that psychoanalysts have in the psychological mindedness of their patients has led some analysts to a relative neglect of the patients' views of the external world, of which their attitudes toward chance and ambiguity are two significant aspects. Since the inward regard and the outward are opposite sides of the same coin, distortions in one are apt to be reflected in the other.

Freud wrote briefly about chance, distinguishing between "internal (psychical) accidental events" and "external (real) chance" (1901, p. 257). He observed that superstitious people deny the effect of mental processes on their actions and parapraxes but believe such processes exert an influence on external events. Subsequently he wrote, "A fair amount of intellectual education is a prerequisite for believing in chance; primitive people and uneducated ones, and no doubt children as well, are able to assign a ground for everything that happens. Perhaps originally it was a reason on animistic grounds" (Freud, 1932, p. 122). In a birthday congratulation to his son he once more mentioned chance, noting that " . . . not all things in life go according to merit, [hence] let me express the wish that luck will continue to remain faithful to you" (cf., E. Freud, 1960, p. 338).

A belief in external chance does not imply a negation of causality but rather relates to an awareness of the relative unpredictability of certain events, to one's ignorance of their precise causes, and to one's lack of control over them. Poincaré (1908) used the example of a roulette wheel to illustrate the nature of chance: whether the needle stops at red or black depends upon the initial impulse the wheel is given. Neither muscular sense nor even the most delicate instruments can distinguish the difference between neighboring impulses.

Ambiguity relates primarily to meaning and is defined in two different ways: the first relates to imprecision, uncertainty, or vagueness of meaning; the second concerns the presence of two or more meanings. In the latter sense it is analogous to the overdetermination of mental events and consequently characterizes many of the cultural derivatives of psyche. In contrast to the merely obscure, ambiguity in the second sense seems to be intrinsic to great works of art (Kris, 1952) which communicate and interact on several psychical levels. Arlow (1969a) has observed that "situations of perceptual ambiguity facilitate the foisting of elements of the life of fantasy upon data of perception" (p. 8). He further pointed out that the very "lack of specificity" in a work of art tends to "stimulate a wider range of unconscious fantasy activity" (p. 8). In an opposite manner, the trivial and the sentimental in art generally prove to be single-minded and unambiguous.

Chance and ambiguity (in both its meanings) may evoke anxiety by depriving the subject of a purposeful activity aimed at some control over an event which is perceived as dangerous. This situation is analogous to the anxiety evoked during therapy when resistance is diminished and hitherto repressed ideas move closer to consciousness. It should also be pointed out that in a quite contrary manner, ambiguity may support repression and limit anxiety: in dreams, for example, threatening material may be veiled from consciousness by condensation with other ideas or images forming an ambiguous and therefore tolerable composite.

The ability to believe in chance and to tolerate ambiguity are consequences of the development of secondary process thinking and may be regarded as specialized aspects of reality testing. Reality testing itself is a slow, developmental process. As Arlow (1969b) summarized it, "In addition to the maturation of the essential ego apparatuses, the vicissitudes of development are very important" (p. 28). We see ". . . the development of reality testing as a gradual evolution in the child from an attitude toward the world which is self-centered, pleasure seeking, animistic, and magical, to a later capacity to differentiate between inner fantasy and objective reality" (p. 29). Hartmann (1956), in particular, laid special stress on the life-long task of learning to differentiate subjective and objective elements in our perception of reality. In addition, Arlow (1969b) has shown how unconscious fantasies impinge upon and may critically distort one's images of the past and one's perceptions of the present.

The problem of causality, viewed primarily as a consequence of the human being's projection of internal perceptions, was conceptualized by Rado (1932). The thrust of his contribution was a critique of a mechanistic, pre-Heisenbergian determinism that was unable to integrate the newer contributions from natural science, in which fortuitous events loom so importantly. Determinism, he observed, has never freed itself from its earlier animistic impress: " . . . our whole scientific conception of the universe, based as it is on research, is a legitimate derivative of the animistic system of thought. Moreover, we should be ever mindful of the fact that the materialistic sovereignty of natural science obtains only for our consciousness; in the unconscious animistic thinking indeed holds unlimited sway" (p. 699).

Nunberg (1956) attributed man's "need for causality" to the synthetic function of the ego. Although not an instinctual drive, it had, he believed, the "compelling force of an instinct." "The seeking for connections in a chain of events in which the last link is determined by the first seems to be at the root of causal thinking" (p. 151). Rationalization is thus an illusory causality which, like the secondary elaboration of the dream, "reconciles contrasts which are too sharp, fills in gaps and gives the appearance of plausibility to illogical mental processes . . . " (p. 151). The ego's work of unifying, connecting, and breaking down contradictions may be further overextended, as in the psychotic patient, where delusions bridge the lacunae in consciousness. Nunberg added that "the younger, the less logical, the more primitive or the sicker a person is, the more easily will he find 'causes'" (p. 151).

It thus appears that problems in dealing with causality, and consequently with chance and ambiguity, arise from distortions in the development of reality testing, probably reflecting crucial animistic vestiges. A somewhat differing point of view has been suggested by Coltrera (1978), who noted that the tolerance of ambiguity and chance are "as much determined by nonconflictual autonomous ego gifts as they are by . . . conflictual determinants." This intriguing hypothesis seems, however, to present problems of verification.

As previously mentioned, the belief that one can control external events by one's thoughts is observable among many people. Indeed, magical thinking may occur in virtually all individuals when they find themselves in a perilous situation and realize they possess no effective means of dealing with it. If fight or flight is useless, an individual may enter a state of depressive withdrawal, experience feelings of derealization or depersonalization, or regressively attempt to control the situation magically. Freud (1901) described some of his "bungled acts" when, for example, his accidental destruction of a valuable object represented a sacrificial offering given to protect one of his children who was seriously ill.

Examples of difficulties with chance and ambiguity are commonly encountered in clinical practice. A female patient in analysis had an early spontaneous abortion. Her obstetrician outlined the usual causes of miscarriage, but was unable to establish the etiology of the one she had just undergone. She felt intensely guilty and was convinced that her miscarriage was caused by a weight she had lifted the week before the bleeding had begun. Her evident intolerance of the ambiguous situation was subsequently seen to be related to an induced abortion she had had performed several years before her marriage. Her inability to accept the unknowable thus served as a resistance against dealing with the earlier guilt-ridden event.

A student in psychotherapy, applying to a professional school, was told that despite his superior qualifications his chances of being accepted were only one out of four because of the large number of similarly qualified applicants. Not surprisingly, he became anxious during the weeks he waited for a decision. He soon began to have complicated fantasies, however, which "mathematically proved" that he would be selected. He also found himself making pacts with God that he would abandon his extramarital relationship if he would be accepted. As in the case of the former patient, his magical formulas not only served to deal with an uncontrollable, unpredictable situation, but also reflected a particular intrapsychic conflict.

During an extended evaluation to determine whether a young woman, who had applied for analytic treatment, was actually capable of introspection, she reported several dreams whose manifest content disturbed her and whose latent content, relating to incestuous wishes, was close to awareness. The patient was dissatisfied because the doctor did not explain (away) the dreams. It became apparent that her mounting anxiety impelled her to seek explanations of her dreams that would re-repress the emerging material. When no "explanations" were forthcoming, the patient supplied her own, characterizing her dreams as "precognitive." She related that she had had many such dreams in the past and described how they had foretold the future. In this way she effectively closed the door to the past. Although this patient demonstrated a number of characteristics that would make her an appropriate patient for analysis, her lack of introspectiveness, as shown above by her intolerance of uncertain material, was further evidenced by a generally alloplastic view of her psychological problems and an adamant refusal to talk about subjects which she decreed to be "off limits." Along with the other patients described she demonstrated a marked predilection to regress to the level of magical thinking when confronted with uncontrollable, potentially dangerous material.

In contrast to the preceding patient is the case of a thirty-five-year-old woman who was accepted for analysis. She had sought treatment because of a work inhibition, marital disturbances, and a poor self-concept. During the initial hours of evaluation, although she freely described her belief in astrology and an interest in various religious sects, for the most part she identified her difficulties as stemming from her own behavior, recognizing that she used these magical means in a defensive way. During the years of her analysis there were several occasions when she utilized magical behavior and thinking as a resistance; each time, however, the therapeutic alliance was sufficiently sturdy for her to work through these evasions from the analytic process. Most probably this woman will fall back on magical defenses at critical times when she feels out of control, but these will be infrequent and less urgent.

Perhaps the most dramatic preoccupation with chance is seen in gamblers. Although gambling has multiple determinants, in many gamblers one finds an isolation of ideas which permits them to reject the laws of probability despite their erudite understanding of those very laws. This allows the gambler not only to avoid a realistic appraisal of the chance event, but also to deny those unconscious and preconscious aspects of his behavior that impel him into believing that he can surmount odds that are often overwhelmingly against him. Luck, always maternally personified, will gratify all his wishes. In a case vignette, Fenichel (1945) observed, "A passionate gambler in the lotteries behaved as if it were assured and inevitable that one day he would win the Grand Prize" (p. 372).

The gambler, in his denial of the known probabilities of an event so that he can expect the odds to operate in his favor, is the mirror image of the individual who is completely unable to accept luck. In both situations there is a denial of the actual nature of chance in conjunction with the use of magical thoughts to control the event. It is therefore not surprising that gamblers are well known for their use of the paraphernalia of magic—rituals, signs, amulets, etc. Like the patients previously mentioned, compulsive gamblers use the denial of chance as a means of dealing with unconscious conflicts. Thus, through gambling, they simultaneously succeed in distorting both internal and external reality.

The matter of magical thinking and determinism (or, more properly, overdeterminism) not only has significant clinical implications but social overtones as well. Some observers have claimed that during the past twenty-five years there has been a significant increase in mysticism, irrationalism, and anti-intellectualism. In specific individuals this propensity for magical thinking and behavior can be seen to represent specifically an intolerance of ambiguity and chance and a concurrent rejection of psychic determinism. It has been suggested that the history of philosophy as well as popular attitudes demonstrate a cyclic pattern in which a society swings from a relatively Dionysian world view, characterized by experiential, body-directed, supernatural, and mystical concerns, to an Apollonian posture marked by naturalism, rationalism, and logic. Perhaps the contemporary rejection of rationalism represents yet another normal oscillation; it is, however, paradoxical that these attitudes thrive in an era of unprecedented scientific achievement. Freud's comment that "intellectual education is a prerequisite for believing in chance" implies only that such education is necessary but not in itself sufficient to develop a rationalistic outlook. It is not uncommon today to find individuals with higher education who reject rationalism, chance, and ambiguity in many areas of their lives and demand and discover the "answers" to all their questions in a wide variety of faiths ranging from astrology to oriental mysticism.

Perhaps the very successes of science and technology have thrown into relief not only our ignorance but our growing concern, often dread, over the destructive monsters that science is creating which appear to be progressively eluding human control. In this light, science itself is commonly regarded as synonymous with anti-humanism. Furthermore, scientific developments in many areas have led to heightened expectations, with the inevitable result that some people are embittered because their physical and emotional illnesses, as well as their problems of everyday life, are not quickly and painlessly eliminated. Such utopian expectations cannot fail to engender disappointment, frustration, and pessimism. Those individuals who are unable to accept the ambiguity of the unknown are led to denigrate science and the reality it studies. They repulse the mysterious and embrace the mystical.

Such regression may be partial and limited to times of stress or to particularly conflictual areas in the lives of individuals who at other times may be reasonably capable of introspection. In others, magical thinking widely pervades their mental functioning, and if they are in psychotherapy, this cognitive mode will constitute a powerful resistance. Although even prominent magical thinking may not in itself be a contraindication to psychoanalytic therapy, its presence represents an unfavorable factor unless there is reasonable evidence that the patient will be able to form a therapeutic alliance. Accordingly, the evaluation of patients for analysis or psychoanalytically-oriented psychotherapy may be enhanced by assessing not only their capacity for introspection, but also by determining their view of the external world. Assessment of patients' ability to believe in chance occurrences and their tolerance of ambiguity may be a useful adjunct in evaluating the extent to which they rely on magical thinking.

SUMMARY

The inability to believe in chance occurrences, along with an intolerance of ambiguity in the external world, are often the outward manifestations of difficulty with introspection. Case vignettes are presented to demonstrate how magical thinking and behavior, directed to the outside world, also serve to defend against intrapsychic conflict.

The contemporary vogue of anti-intellectualism and mysticism is seen as a sociocultural expression of individual magical thinking. Those who are strongly pervaded by these attitudes are apt to show poor psychological mindedness. It is suggested that information about a patient's ability to accept external chance and ambiguity may be important in the evaluation of the patient for analytic treatment.

REFERENCES

Arlow, J. A. (1969a). Unconscious Fantasy and Disturbances of Conscious Experience. *Psychoanalysis Quarterly* XXXVIII pp. 1–27.
——— (1969b). Fantasy, Memory, and Reality Testing *Psychoanalysis Quarterly* XXXVIII pp. 28–51.
Coltrera, J. (1978). Personal communication.
Fenichel, O. (1945). *The Psychoanalytic Theory of Neurosis* New York: W. W. Norton & Co., Inc.
Freud, E. L., Editor (1960). *Letters of Sigmund Freud* New York: Basic Books, Inc.
Freud, S. (1901). Psychopathology of Everyday Life *Standard Edition* 6.
——— (1932). New Introductory Lectures on Psycho-Analysis. Lecture 33: Femininity *Standard Edition* XXII pp. 112–135.
Hartmann, H. (1956). Notes on the Reality Principle In:*The Psychoanalysis*

Study Chi¹d Vol. 11. New York: International Universities Press, Inc.,
pp. 31–53.

Kris, E. and Kaplan, A. (1952). Aesthetic Ambiguity In: *Psychoanalytic
Explorations in Art.* New York: International Universities Press, Inc.,
pp. 243–254.

Nunberg, H. (1956). *Principles of Psychoanalysis. Their Application to the
Neuroses* New York: International Universities Press, Inc.

Poincar, H. (1908). *The Foundations of Science,* Translated by B. Halstead.
Lancaster, Pa.: The Science Press, 1946.

Rado, S. (1932). The Paths of Natural Science in the Light of Psychoanalysis
Psychoanalytic Quarterly I pp. 683–700.

CHAPTER 6

Normal and
Pathological Nostalgia

[Werman, D.S. (1977). *Journal of the American Psychoanalytic Association* 25:387–398.]

The experience of nostalgia is both ancient and widespread. It has been a major theme in myth and poetry; the Bible, Homer's Odyssey—the literature of all ages—give eloquent voice to this human phenomenon; indeed, there is scarcely a person who has never experienced it. The contemporary psychiatric literature that deals with nostalgia is limited, and the psychoanalytic studies can be numbered on one hand. Although these explorations sometimes converge, they tend to reduce nostalgia to a single particular view which necessarily excludes important normal and clinical findings. In this paper I shall attempt to clarify and integrate some of the conceptions about nostalgia that have previously been developed and present some new ideas.

The word nostalgia was introduced by J. Hofer (1678), in the late seventeenth century, as a literal translation into Greek of the German heimweh and, like the latter, means a painful yearning for home or country. Hofer regarded homesickness as a cerebral disease of essentially demoniccause. Since his time there has been an abundant literature dealing with homesickness and its physical and psychological aspects. Physicians of the eighteenth and nineteenth centuries devoted many studies to this problem, often based on observations of soldiers in the armies of the wars of the French Revolution, and later of those in Napoleon's Imperial Army. Pinel, Broussais, Esquirol, and Jean Colombier were among the many prominent physicians who contributed to this literature. Their work was critically reviewed by Bachet (1950) who himself examined some of the mentally disturbed deportees who were repatriated toFrance from Nazi prisoner-of-war camps during World War II. The most recent extensive review of homesickness was undertaken by McCann (1941) who studied a group of homesick students.

During the first half of the nineteenth century nostalgia began to taken on an additional, broader meaning, defined by Webster's (1966) as "a longing for something far away or long ago." Robert (1970) gives a quotation from Balzac employing this usage, thus dating this new meaning from the third or fourth decade of the nineteenth century. It is nostalgia in this sense that is the subject of this communication. However, while it may at times be difficult to differentiate nostalgia, in the broader sense, from homesickness, the latter generally follows upon the separation of a person from his home, homeland, or loved ones, and is resolved quickly by a return to that place; in fact, the mere promise of such reunion often alleviates the pain of homesickness. The homesick person is typically overwhelmed by sadness and suffers from a variety of more or less severe somatic symptoms. Nostalgia, on the other hand, is an experience with particular cognitive and affective components. The cognitive aspects consist of memories of a given place—rather than of objects—at a given time, and the affect associated with these memories is characteristically described as bittersweet.

Some authors equate homesickness and nostalgia; this reduces these phenomena to a single underlying dynamic configuration and thereby excludes much of their richness and variability. Fodor (1950), for example, regards nostalgia as a manifestation of an intense desire to return to the country, town, or home from which one came. He sees utopian fantasies as the same sort of experience, behind which is hidden the "yearning for childhood," which in turn derives from a longing for the prenatal home. He believes that whereas nostalgia is not a mental disturbance, it can develop into a "monomaniacal, obsessive mental state" under unspecified conditions. No mention is made of the affective nature of nostalgia, nor does Fodor deal with any psychodynamic features other than that just mentioned.

Martin (1954) is another who discusses homesickness and nostalgia as a single entity. The thrust of his view is that there exists a "true nostalgia," which is related to and involves a healthy surrender to a "biological and rhythmic homing tendency to return to the past," to childhood, to sleep, and to the unconscious. This conception is compatible with many observations both in and out of analysis, but exception must be taken to his s priori notion of a "biological and rhythmic" tendency. In contrast to this form of nostalgia, Martin describes the unbiological, unrhythmical, culturally induced phenomena of "nostomania" and "nostophobia," i.e., "compulsive movements toward and against the home and whatever home means, literally and figuratively" (p. 103). "True nostalgia" meets with many obstacles because our culture has taken flight from what it regards as emotional and old-fashioned and because the "compulsive-intellectual type" of personality has significant difficulties in permitting himself to experience such feelings. Martin seems to be referring here to an inhibition of "regression in the service of the ego."

Freedman (1956) reports on the analysis of a young composer who in the early months of his treatment nostalgically recalled locales where he had been taken as a child by his mother or father. At first, these recollections were used as a resistance to keep the analyst in ignorance of his current life situation.Analysis later revealed that they were related to an intense desire for the pregenital mother (corresponding to the joyful aspect of his nostalgia) and to his destructive wishes regarding the father (the "bitter" side of the memories) alongside of his wish to maintain the affectionate feelings he had for him. When analysis led to the lifting of repression,phobias for the previously desired locales developed, demonstrating the counter phobic nature of the patient's nostalgia. Freedman asserts that the depressive component of nostalgia is related to the turning back on the self of death wishes originally directed to the father.

Exploring the subjective nature of nostalgia from an existential point of view, Howland (1962) describes the mixture of joy and sadness for what had "formerly been part of our lives" and from which we are cut off by time and space; and, if we manage to "return home," we find it is not the way we remembered it. Although Howland suggests that the nostalgic memory may represent only a longing for something "dreamed about," like many of the writers dealing with nostalgia, he does not explore the dynamics of this idealization. Rather curiously, and without any supportive evidence, he notes that our nostalgic experiences are "unique" and cannot be shared; in fact,groups can and do share nostalgic memories, which is obviously not unrelated to their common ideals and therefore to the tensions in and between groups.

Nawas and Platt (1965), who also regard nostalgia as synonymous with homesickness, classify theories about it according to their relation to time: the "past-oriented view," which sees the nostalgic person as wishing to return to something in the past; the "present-oriented"conception, which regards nostalgia as a reaction to an unsuccessful adaption to the present environment; and their own view, which sees the nostalgic subject as suffering from a "concern over or dread of the future." Those then, who emphasize futurity are not likely to "fall victims to nostalgia." Middle-class people, the authors say, whose education emphasizes futurity, are less likely than "lower-class" or "tradition-bound" people to become nostalgic. They suggest that psychotherapy should help the patient to structure goals and plans rather than to "analyze the causes of his nostalgia." While Nawas and Platt reduce nostalgia to a dread of the future, which may indeed be a reality for some people, they do not elucidate the roots of that anxiety. Although writing about fantasy, Freud's words (1908) apply equally well here to nostalgia: "Thus past, present and future are strung together, as it were, on the thread of the wish that runs through them" (p. 148).

The relation between nostalgia and mourning is dealt with in a searching psychoanalytic contribution by Geahchan (1968), a French psychoanalyst. He regards the basic representations of nostalgia as a wish to go or return to a place, to a time past or a time to come, or to a beloved or awaited person. Nostalgia is essentially normal unless it dominates the psychic economy. He describes a "nostalgic relationship" to the lost object which avoids both internalizing the object and the work of mourning, and safeguards the subject from psychosis. While fantasy seeks to fulfill a desire, nostalgia repetitively tends toward a fantasy that never takes place. In this way the desire is "fulfilled" by not being realized, and so the subject is safe from the loss of the object, and the object is guarded by being kept in the nostalgic relationship. Outwardly the subject appears to mourn the lost object, but intrapsychically it is not actually given up; perhaps this is because the nostalgic relationship corresponds to the subject's own ego ideal. Hence, the nostalgic relationship is sought and maintained for itself.

The nostalgic relationship is characteristically indeterminate in its representations, and by its imaginary nature the subject is able to maintain separateness from the object. This leads to an indefinite and indefinable quest—and if an object should appear that seems to correspond to the nostalgic desire, it is promptly rejected, it becomes demythologized; it is not what it promised to be: the subject's projection of what it should be. The subject can thus only enjoy the search and never the possession. The nostalgic person may appear depressed because he cannot find an object to embody his ideal, but he does not have the sense of loss of the depressed patient, who, in losing his object, seems at the same time to lose his ego ideal.

Geahchan (1968) observes that patients with strong nostalgic tendencies regularly show a particular libidinal organization characterized by: intense narcissistic trends, pronounced analsadism, significant repression, marked homosexual trends in women, and a prominent feeling of repulsion for the female genitalia in men.

The multiple aspects of nostalgia are brought forth in a case presentation by Kleiner(1970) of an analytic patient who was constantly stimulated to experience nostalgic memories such as romping with playmates, a lazy summer afternoon, or cozy feelings of a winter evening. The patient felt these recollections as if they were foreign bodies, but she could not rid herself of them. Typically, they were idealizations of something lost in the past, never to be recaptured.

As a small girl this patient was traumatically affected by the death of her baby brother. She apparently attempted to deal with the loss and the guilt by denial, incorporation, and idealization, but her immature ego was unable to mourn his death adequately. Instead, she went back to an earlier time to seek a reunion with her preoedipal mother to whom she was orally fixated; this fixation followed an interruption of breast feeding due to a depression which the mother had suffered. Eventually, all phases of her libidinal development were influenced by the threat of objectloss, and so, for example, she was led to an idealization of her father—but at the expense of a depreciated husband. Later in life she was unable to mourn and found herself idealizing other lost objects in an attempt to defend them against her aggression. Ultimately she had to give up her search for the lost objects so that she could be free to accept new ones. As long as the past so massively intruded into the present, so long was the patient "governed as much by the pleasure principle as by reality" (p. 29).

Nostalgia, then, is an ambivalently felt, affective-cognitive experience. Its cognitive aspects typically consist of a memory of a particular place at a given time. The places usually have existed in reality, but they may also be derived from myths or literature or may be totally imaginary, such as the yearning for a Paradise Lost. Whatever their actuality, these scenes are uniformly idealized. The location in time is usually also in the past, but is equally flexible, and may be at any period in the subject's life, or even before, or indeed in the future—for subjects may yearn for a utopia or the millenium. The affects associated with these memories are characteristically described as bittersweet, indicating a wistful pleasure, a joy tinged with sadness. Whatever else the sadness indicates, it always acknowledges that the past is in fact irretrievable. It is the subtlety, irridescence, and ambivalence of these feelings that gives nostalgia its inimitable coloration. No better description of nostalgia can be given than the one found in the last lines of Eduard Mörike's poem Im Fruhling (1957, pp. 353–354): "I think about this and that, I wish longingly for something, I am not quite sure what; it is half pleasure, half mourning; oh, tell me, my heart, what memories are you weaving in the twilight of the golden green branches? Old times I dare not talk about."[1]

The ubiquity of nostalgia suggests that we are dealing with a human experience that for the most part is normal. Taking pleasure in the past recalls Freud's comment that "Actually, we can never give anything up; we can only exchange one thing for another. What appears to be a renunciation is really the formation of a substitute or a surrogate" (1908, p. 145).

Nostalgia resembles fantasy in certain limited respects. Like fantasy, it is stimulated by some current impression which leads the subject back to earlier experiences of gratification; nostalgia, however, seems more apt to be precipitated by sensory stimuli. Whereas fantasy is a substitute for the fulfillment, in the present, of a wish, usually, as Freud noted, for power or for erotic gratification, and diminishes or disappears when genuine gratification ensues, nostalgia is not a substitute for a wish but is an experience of the past that is recalled, normally or pathologically, for itself. The past is particularly tenacious when it was experienced as markedly pleasurable, painful, or ambivalent. All nostalgic thoughts do not necessarily indicate that the subject, in yearning for the past, wishes to return to it; one can briefly savour a time in the past without in the least wishing to exchange one's present situation in life for a former one.

The stimulus of unpleasant or painful current life situations in the evocation of nostalgia is well known, and Kleiner's patient clearly illustrates this. The aged, faced with limitations imposed upon them by their advanced years, and with some awareness of the end of life, often will delight in recalling their childhood. Soldiers will spend hours talking about earlier, idealized, days in civilian life, as an escape from the unfulfilling situation in which they find themselves; later, as veterans, they may look back on army days, now thoroughly mythologized, with shared pleasure.

The line between normal and pathological nostalgia, as with most mental phenomena, is not a sharp one. Proust, perhaps the most famous grand nostalgique, turned the tables on his neurotic symptoms and used these now classic episodes of nostalgia to create an imperishable masterpiece. It is through his literary "remembrance of things past" (more accurately, of time past) that he was able to hold on to the lost object, his mother, while avoiding that working through of mourning which might have enabled a reinvestment of a new love object—something neither

---

[1]Reprinted by permission of Penguin Books Ltd.

he nor his protagonist was able to do. His work became the aesthetic crystallization of his nostalgia. Miller, who has written the most thorough, large-scale psychoanalytic study of Proust(1956), suggests (in a personal communication) that Proust's problem of mourning is "solved by tapping the well-springs of the past, renewing joys stored in the unconscious"—thus art enables Proust "to live the true essences of life outside of time—death is overcome by escaping from time." No real object could be expected to embody the one which was lost, and so the past, like a fossil, lives on in the amber of his great novel; the quest for the object is continued by other means. All pervasive experiences of nostalgia are not, however, exploited so richly. In some individuals the very core of their psychopathology consists of nostalgic memories which dominate their mental life. A common neurotic use of memories is as a means of dealing with poorly resolved traumatic experiences of childhood. A patient who had suffered from early deprivation of both mother and father recalled coming home from school and being greeted by the redolent odors of cakes her mother was baking for church suppers. Another patient who, in fact, had been virtually ignored by her father, kept harkening back to her delight on a swing, which was probably being pushed by her father who, however, did not physically appear in the memory. In both these patients there is an attempt to master early feelings of rejection—and rage and guilt—by idealizing the past. A patient thus creates his private mythology and actually believes it. Another patient, after a period of analysis, wryly commented that he was no longer able to believe his "lies." This particular mechanism, consisting of denial and idealization associated with bittersweet feelings, is analogous to a screen affect.

The attempt and the failure to idealize and recapture the past is poignantly expressed by Hermann Hesse in Dies *Kindheit* (Childhood):[2]

> My farthest valley, you are
> Bewitched and vanished.
> Many times, in my grief and agony,
> You have beckoned upward to me from your country of
> shadows
> And opened your legendary eyes

---

[2]Reprinted with the permission of Farrar, Straus & Giroux, Inc. From *Poems by Hermann Hesse,* translated by James Wright, Copyright 1970 by James Wright.

Till I, lost in a quick illusion,
Lost myself back to you wholly.
O dark gate,
O dark hour of death,
Come forth,
So I can recover from this life's emptiness
And go home to my own dreams.

I described the role of nostalgia as a substitute for mourning in reviewing Geahchan's work. Briefly, the principle relates to the maintenance of the lost object in the nostalgic memory; this impedes an effective renunciation which would permit a new object to be libidinally invested. The failure of mourning leads to a continuing search for the idealized lost object, an inability to love new objects, a depreciation of objects in one's current life, and an endless pursuit of nostalgic memories for themselves at the expense of an inhibition in many areas of existence. Noteworthy is the disappointment of these patients in new objects which are regularly found to fall short of their idealized representation. There is, however, a normal aspect to this process. Inasmuch as mourning is probably never accomplished totally, it is natural that a part of the object is retained. This is borne out by the occasional recurrence of nostalgic memories of places associated with the loved one, in distinction to memories of the object itself.

In psychotherapy, nostalgia may prove to be a means of distorting the past; this can be very confusing to the analyst inasmuch as the patient himself intersely believes in the reality of this idealized, perhaps largely falsified, past, and because the memories are associated with poignant feelings. At the same time, nostalgia may operate as a powerful resistance against bringing current conflicts into the analytic situation.

The counter phobic mechanism of nostalgia, as Freedman described it, in which the originally yearned-for places represent, in part, destructive tendencies to objects, the ensuing guilt, and the turning of these feelings against the self, does not appear to be a common occurrence, but does occur. The possible defensive uses of nostalgia are surely not limited by the foregoing examples, but these seem to represent the most usual encountered. One fundamental trait of nostalgia, which must be explored, is the relative absence of a consciou srepresentation of objects in nostalgic memory. Their appearance tends to be rare and, when present, is shadowy, marginal, or exists as a mere feeling of its presence. This erasure of objects from the nostalgic memory is all the more curious since it is clear that these memories of places relate essentially to objects, and this situation prevails whether the remembrances are normal or pathological. The most plausible explanation of this phenomenon seems to involve an original displacement of the affective-cognitive memory from the object to an idealized place with which they become associated. Most probably this defensive process stems from the subject's need to repress direct memories of the object because they would evoke intolerably painful feelings of blissful gratifications from the object now lost, or frightening or depriving experiences related to the object, or intensely ambivalent feelings toward the object, especially when destructive, guilt-laden wishes conflict with loving feelings. As a result, nostalgia serves both as a screen memory and a screen affect, and, if it is associated with mild sadness, it also brings forth pleasurable, sweet feelings, ensuring the continuance of this particular kind of universally experienced memory.

SUMMARY

Nostalgia is distinguished from homesickness from which it was originally derived, and from fantasy to which it is related. It is described as an affective-cognitive experience, usually involving memories of places in one's past. These memories are associated with a characteristic affective coloration described as "bittersweet." It is concluded that the locales remembered are displacements from objects whose representation was repressed. Nostalgia is a ubiquitous human experience that is evoked by particular stimuli under special circumstances, and, while it is generally a normal occurrence, pathological forms occur. Among those discussed are: nostalgia as a substitute for mourning, as an attempted mastery through idealization and displacement of a painful past, as a resistance in analysis, and as a counterphobic mechanism. Nostalgia not only serves as a screen memory, but may also be said to operate as a screen affect.

REFERENCES

BACHET, M. (1950). Etude sur les tats de nostalgie. *Ann. Med. Psych.* 108:T.I. 559–587, T.II.:11–34.

FODOR, N. (1950). Varieties of nostalgia. *Psychoanal. Rev.* 37:25–38.

FREEDMAN, A. (1956). The feeling of nostalgia and its relationship to phobia *Bull. Phila. Assn. Psychoanal.* 6:84–92.

FREUD, S. (1908). Creative writers and day-dreaming. *Standard Edition*

9:42–53. London: Hogarth Press, 1955.

GEAHCHAN, D. (1968). Deuil et nostalgie. *Rev. fran. de Psychoanal.* 32:39–65.

HESSE, H. (1970). *Poems.* New York: Bantam Books, pp. 38–39.

HOFER, J. (1678). Medical dissertation on nostalgia. *Bull. Hist. Med.* 2:376–391 (1934).

HOWLAND, E.S. (1962). Nostalgia. *J. Exist. Psychiat.* 10:197–204.

KLEINER, J. (1970). On nostalgia. *Bull. Phila. Assn. Psychoanal.* 20:11–30.

MCCANN, W.H. (1941). Nostalgia: A review of the literature. *Psychol. Bull.* 38:165–182.

MARTIN, A.R. (1954). Nostalgia. *Amer. J. Psychoanal.* 14:93–104.

MILLER, M.L. (1956). *Nostalgia: A Psychoanalytic Study of Marcel Proust.* Boston: Houghton Mifflin.

MRIKE, E. (1957). *Im Fruhling* In: The Penguin Book of German Verse. L. Forster (Ed.). Harmondsworth, Middlesex: Penguin Books, p. 154.

NAWAS, M.M. & PLATT, J.J. (1965). A future-oriented theory of nostalgia *J. Indiv. Psychol.* 21:51–57.

ROBERT, P. (1970). *Dictionaire de la Langue Francaise.* Paris: Socit du Nouveau Littre.

Webster's New World Dictionary. (1966). Cleveland and New York: World Publishing Co.

CHAPTER 7

On the Nature of the Oceanic Experience

[Werman, D.S. (1986). *Journal of the American Psychoanalytic Association* 34:123–139.]

ABSTRACT:

It is postulated that consciousness is not simply an organ of perception, but that it possesses a structure, or organization, despite its enormous fluidity. In support of these views, the oceanic experience is explored. It demonstrates the impact, on this state of consciousness, of the subject's values and culture. Like the oceanic experience, every state of consciousness—what is in awareness at any given time—is a complex phenomenon that derives from all aspects of the psyche, including the subject's value system and the influences of his culture.

In the course of psychoanalysis, it is not unusual to observe that the patient's associations, that is, his verbalized conscious ideas and feelings, frequently reflect his value system and culture. In effect, these influences do not so much determine his associations, which are strongly derivative of psychodynamic factors, among others, as they frame and impart a particular coloration to the patient's associations. Indeed, as much might readily be said about the statements of people outside of analysis. The major and often qualitative difference is that these statements of thoughts and feelings are likely to be more conflict-free and goal-oriented than are those of a patient during an analytic hour. To explore this influence of values and culture on consciousness, and thereby to expand the concept of the nature of consciousness, is the purpose of this paper. I shall first focus on altered states of consciousness, in particular on the oceanic experience, which illustrates that consciousness is not a simple "organ of perception," but that it possesses an organization, albeit one of great flexibility. Finally, after reviewing some of the pertinent literature, I shall propose that consciousness, and its various altered states, can have various ego functions: goal-oriented, adaptive, defensive, creative, and so forth.

Presented in a slightly different version at the Fall Meeting of the American Psychoanalytic Association, New York, December 16, 1983. Accepted for publication September 12, 1984.

One altered state of consciousness that strikingly illustrates the influence of values and culture is the so-called oceanic experience. This condition, indeed the expression itself, entered the psychoanalytic literature almost by accident. After receiving a copy of The Future of an Illusion from Freud, Romain Rolland expressed his general agreement with Freud's views on religion, but criticized the monograph because it did not deal with a subjective experience which he characterized as oceanic (Werman, 1977). Freud later announced that he had been troubled by Rolland's communication, and after waiting a year and a half he finally considered it in some detail in the first section of Civilization and its Discontents, to which it is only tangentially related. Rolland had described the oceanic experience as a "subjective fact"—not concerned with any organized church or a personal hereafter—characterized by an unbounded sensation of eternity and of limitlessness. Freud (1930) believed the experience consisted of "a feeling of an indissoluble bond, of being one with the external world as a whole" (p. 65). He conceptualized this oceanic feeling in terms of ego boundaries: one aspect of the ego penetrating deeply into the unconscious, the other facing the exterior world and normally well demarcated from it, except "At the height of being in love [when] the boundary between ego and object threatens to melt away" (p. 66).

Freud noted that like the regressive loss of boundaries that presumably occurs during the oceanic experience, alterations also occur in several pathological conditions. In some states "parts of a person's own body, even portions of his own mental life—his perceptions, thoughts and feelings—appear alien to him and as not belonging to his ego; there are other cases in which he ascribes to the external world things that clearly originate in his own ego and that ought to be acknowledged by it. Thus even the feeling of our own ego is subject to disturbances and the boundaries of the ego are not constant" (p. 66). Freud argued that although the infant's boundaries and sense of its self develop under the impact of pleasurable and unpleasurable stimuli from the inner and external worlds, greater or smaller residues of the primitive state persist. "In that case, the ideational contents appropriate to [the oceanic feeling] would be precisely those of limitlessness and of a bond with the universe—the same ideas with which [Rolland] elucidated the 'oceanic' feeling" (p. 68).

In an extension of these remarks, Freud described "a friend" who practiced Yoga: "by withdrawing from the world, by fixing the attention on bodily functions and by peculiar methods of breathing," he is able "to evoke new sensations and coenaesthesias in [him]self, which he regards as regressions to primordial states of mind which have long ago been overlaid." The friend saw in them "a physiological basis, as it were, of much of the wisdom of mysticism." Freud did not give his opinion of these comments, except to observe that "It would not be hard to find connections here with a number of obscure modifications of mental life, such as trances and ecstasies" (pp. 72-73). This casual observation, which Freud did not pursue, suggests his awareness of a kinship between these various states of consciousness; regrettably, he did not choose to unravel the connections and divergences.

If we examine the oceanic experience we find that the subject's sense of merger with the universe is probably the specific, indeed the only characteristic that clearly differentiates it from other mystical or ecstatic states of consciousness. For an individual to undergo the oceanic experience, he must possess particular psychodynamic configurations which lead him to "reach out" to the ambient culture for gratifications; these are met by the presence, in that culture, of the elements that can imbue him with a pantheistic world view. There is, in effect, a confluence of the inner and outer world.

Although pantheism posits that "God is everything and everything is God" (Oxford English Dictionary, 1971), the concept depends on how the divine totality is defined. With numerous variations over the past 2500 years, pantheism is usually taken to mean that the universe is God, that God is the totality of all existence, and that God is in man as mankind is in God. Pantheism, as a philosophic concept, is not necessarily mystical; Russell (1959, p. 200) observed that Spinoza's pantheism had "not a trace of mysticism in it." The doctrine can, however, readily lend itself to mystical experiences. The oceanic experience characteristically affects people when they are in certain natural settings. We have all experienced an awesome sense of the vastness of space when we are in the middle of an ocean or gaze at the dome of the sky on a starlit night. We are aware of the apparent infinity of space and of our small finitude in that vastness. However, the oceanic experience goes beyond this commonsensical view of the physical enormousness of what surrounds us: the reality shades off and the subject's perceptions become distorted. Starbuck (1899, p. 325) described people who experience "awe, the sense of mystery, reverence, love, and aesthetic appreciation . . . " when contemplating God, nature, persons, and society. He quotes one person:

> I never felt emotion of the kind others have. Sometimes a contemplation of the world, of humanity, and of the universe, awakens a sense of sublimity and infinity. This arouses awe and wonder at the mystery of life and of its unity. Sometimes this grows into a sense of the great world spirit in and through all things.

James (1904, p. 398) cites a woman who professed not to have the usual religious feelings:

> I am satisfied that I feel more serene in church than most Christians. I feel most reverent in a Catholic church, whether it is empty or during service; and more reverent in an Episcopal than in any other Protestant church. There are some things that call forth my feelings—a burial service, an eclipse of the sun, the sight of Niagara, the power of the ocean—those have moved me most.

Consider the experience of Malvida von Meysenbug, a cosmopolitan German woman, who for years had been "unable to pray" owing to her "materialistic belief":

> I was alone upon the seashore as all these thoughts flowed over me, liberating and reconciling; and now again, as once before in distant days in the Alps of Dauphiné, I was impelled to kneel down, this time before the illimitable ocean, symbol of the Infinite. I felt that I prayed as I had never prayed before, and knew now what prayer really is: to return from the solitude of individuation into the consciousness of unity with all that is, to kneel down as one that passes away, and to rise up as one imperishable. Earth, heaven, and sea resounded as one vast world-encircling harmony. It was as if the chorus of all the great who had ever lived were about me. I felt myself one with them, and it appeared as if I heard their greeting: "Thou too belongest to the company of those who overcome" (James, 1904, p. 39).

This quintessential description of the oceanic experience richly conveys its pantheistic overtones. Her epiphanic experience is of particular interest because of the important, if not altogether clear, role she played in Romain Rolland's life.

In an autobiographical study, Rolland (1959) described three of his oceanic experiences. One of these occurred above Lake Geneva: before him lies a broad horizon backed by distant Alps; overhead is a vast field of sky, below, soft hills and meadows gently fall away to a wide expanse of lake. Whether at that time he recognized some extraordinary, uncanny quality in this and the other transcendental experiences of his youth, or whether he only did so retrospectively, perhaps by Malvida's suasion, is not known. But for him, as for her, these mystical experiences lent a shape and dimension to their tumultuous, troubled lives. For Rolland, life had been a painful journey: early sibling loss; a chronically grieving mother with whom he maintained an intense, life-long attachment; the disarray of the provincial adolescent thrust into mid-nineteenth-century Paris; despair, morbid self-absorption, and suicidal preoccupations during his years at the Lycée—this and more, provided the scaffolding for his search, and the discovery of a "special meaning" to his life which his devoutly Catholic education seemed unable to fulfill. Fortunately, this mystical side of Rolland did not intrude on the social man, the creative artist, the résistant. For him, as for Meysenbug, the oceanic experience became a refuge from their early religious training, which they had rejected, and a full-blown philosophic materialism which was not tolerable to either of them.

Undoubtedly, feelings of this union with the universe, as Freud postulated, are derivative of a re-merger with the mother in an archaic state of blissful narcissism. Dynamically, this beatific union can also represent an individual's defensive attempt to transcend the painful limitations of his oneness by totally merging with everything that exists. The experience may represent a restitutive act which undoes a previous unconscious withdrawal from ambivalently experienced love objects. Such a desire for fusion with the world may even function as a reaction formation to deal with a hatred of objects or self—of humanity altogether—which the individual negates by an acceptance, a veritable union, with everything and everybody in the universe. The universe and humanity may also symbolize the mother, whose infinite control can only be mastered by and through a fusion, now under the control of the subject.

A well-known source of the oceanic experience may be found among the Hindu mystics. Not surprisingly, in the same way that Rolland was deeply attached to Malvida von Meysenbug, so he developed an intense interest in Ramakrishna and Vivekananda, whose biographies he wrote. These he sent to Freud. The self-styled "Lantier" (terrestrial animal) promised his "Oceanic friend" that he would correct his ignorance of oriental philcsophy by penetrating "the Indian jungle," a step he had not taken earlier, he noted, inhibited by an "uncertain blending of Hellenic love of proportion, Jewish sobriety and Philistine timidity" (E. Freud, 1960, p. 392).

Rolland quoted Ramakrishna: the spirit is an ocean, " . . . boundless, dazzling with great luminous waves" by which he is swallowed up. "It is an ocean of ineffable joy" (Rolland, 1930).

In contrast to the foregoing where merger is with the universe, and thus is typically "oceanic," there are other typesa of fusion experiences in a wide var.ety of ecstatic, mystical states. St. Teresa of Avila, largely because of her detailed autobiography, letters, and other writings, is a particularly well documented mystic whose ecstatic states are typical of a fusion with God. She often wrote of the "orison of Union," when the soul enters God and when "God establishes himself in the interior of the soul" (James, 1904, p. 409). Although she described some feelings of "immensity," she principally felt herself engulfed in God.

The Saint wrote of her "spiritual marriage" with God. When St. John of the Cross wished to mortify her at the moment of communion by giving her only half of the host, she heard the Lord tell her not to be frightened: "No one will ever be able to separate you from Me . . . From today on you shall be my wife" (Renault, 1970). On another occasion she underwent a "profound ecstasy" while in prayer. "It seemed to me that our Lord bore me in spirit to his Father's side and said to him: 'She that thou gavest to me, I give to thee,' and it seemed to me that he drew me close to him. This is not an imaginary thing, but with so great a certitude, and so spiritual a delicacy, that I know not how to describe it; he said to me some words that I do not remember; some of them were about doing me favors. He had me close beside him for some time" (Graham, 1907, pp. 391–392). These citations are strongly suggestive of oedipal conflicts, and indicate that ecstatic experiences do not only represent regressions to infantile levels of preindividuation, but may implicate elements of fixation from any developmental level, and may deal with any psychological conflict or disturbance. The passages cited, and many others from Saint Teresa, suggest a lifelong struggle to resolve conflicts related to sexuality, in both its broadest and narrowest meanings.

Saint Teresa also strikingly demonstrates the profound impact of culture on the contents—affective, ideational, and imaginal—of states of consciousness. Graham (1907) observed that Teresa's visions were probably "moulded on the recollection of the vivid and realistic pictures of the early Spanish painters, full of force and emotion, which then abounded, as they did until very recently, in every old house in Spain— pictures which she had gazed at for hours, absorbed in devotion (note her expression, 'This most sacred Humanity was represented to me as he is painted after the Resurrection'), until they had so engraven themselves on her imagination that . . . the kneeling nun unconsciously reproduced them, flushing them with such life and vigor that she believed she was embracing the predisposing cause."

Throughout the history of psychoanalysis, the nature of consciousness has, understandably, received only modest attention. Freud's historic discovery of the dynamic unconscious focused attention on that system to the relative neglect of consciousness as a psychic structure. Before Freud, mind was virtually synonymous with consciousness—a point of view that is still prevalent. Freud regarded consciousness, systemically, "as a sense organ which perceives data that arise elsewhere" (Freud, 1900, p. 144). Consciousness is virtually equivalent to perception—a fluid system incapable of memory because its contents are transitory. Consciousness receives perceptions from the external world as well as from the interior of the mental apparatus. Perception itself, through the sense organs, comes about through "cathexes of attention" to the data registered in consciousness. Such cathectic processes are regulated by releases of pleasure and unpleasure. Furthermore, through the linkage of mnemonic residues with speech, consciousness also becomes "a sense organ for a portion of our thought-processes" (p. 574). This system of consciousness is ultimately able to correct its perceptions, that is, to test reality through action; consciousness possesses a motor innervation to carry out this function. Developmentally, consciousness becomes more important as the significance of external reality becomes prominent and consciousness learns "to comprehend sensory qualities in additon to the qualities of pleasure and unpleasure which hitherto had alone been of interest to it." In this regard, the function of attention is instituted, which serves to meet "the sense-impressions half way, instead of awaiting their appearance" (Freud, 1911, p. 220). Consciousness, Freud noted, is not an all-or-none function, but possesses "gradations of clarity" similiar to illumination (Freud, 1923, p. 16).

More recently a psychoanalytic model of attention and learning was elaborated by Schwartz and Schiller (1970). They described the apparatus of consciousness as an "agency" which receives excitations from three sources: perceptual systems, endogenous sources, and memory storage. In all situations the conscious experience is governed by a limited supply of attentional energy. The apparatus of consciousness possesses a threshold; accordingly, excitations become conscious when they receive an energic supplement from within the mental apparatus; this corresponds to Freud's attention cathexis. Inevitably, the concepts of attention and cathexis evoke the necessity of a selection among simultaneous stimuli. These authors suggest that selection is governed by variables such as intensity, duration, novelty, and familiarity. They are careful to note that although they base their model upon an economic foundation, they regard such energy as a theoretical construct. Underlying all psychoanalytic views of consciousness and attention to stimuli is an explicit or implicit acceptance of the role of affect and neurotic conflict on thought and the capacity to attend, as well as the influences of prior experience and motivation (Breuer and Freud, 1883–1895); (Freud, 1895), (1915). Clearly, consciousness is an ego function of which an aspect, such as perception, is a primary autonomous ego function.

In general terms, consciousness operationally denotes the mental contents that are in awareness at any given moment: thoughts, feelings, perceptions of sense data, fantasies, images, and impulses. Most authors agree that implicit in consciousness is the process or function of attention, which plays a pivotal role in perception. Attention may be directed to entities emanating from within oneself—such as one's fantasies, or to the external world—a bright light or a piece of music.

Furthermore, attention may be volitional, as in the attempt to recall a name, solve a problem, or assess the intensity of physical pain; or it may be in response to an external command. Attention may be highly focused or "relaxed"; it may be sufficiently intense to modulate or even extinguish a competing perception. Whether attention is directed or volitional, one is inescapably drawn to the idea that it embodies something we call, faute de mieux, "force" or "energy," in that it can contribute to the generation of motor behavior, thinking, feelings, and still other perceptions. Attentional "energy" also relates to memory, where selection plays a vital role; but as Freud (1895) pointed out, the selectiveness of consciousness relative to the function of attention depends on prior experience and motivation. Thus, a critical aspect of attention and consciousness inevitably relates to psychodynamic considerations or, more generally, is influenced by all elements of the psyche.

"States of consciousness" implies different "sets" of attentionality and awareness within the same individual, and relates to the "contents" present in the system "consciousness" at any given moment. One often becomes aware of a particular state of consciousness when it strikes a contrast with the state of consciousness that immediately preceded it—hence the designations of "altered" or "alternate" states of consciousness. Although all students of these phenomena agree that they exist, there are differences of opinion as to their nature. The range of these stages is extraordinary; Pribram (1977, p. 222) lists sixteen:

(1) ordinary perceptual awareness; (2) states of self-unconsciousness; (3) dream states; (4) hypnogogic states; (5) ecstatic states; (6) socially induced trancelike states; (7) drug-induced states; (8) social-role states; (9) linguistic states, as when a multilingual person thinks in one rather than another language; (10) translational states, as when one linguistic universe is being recorded (e.g., in stenotyping); (11) ordinary transcendental states, such as those experienced by an author in the throes of creative composition; (12) extraordinary transcendental states, which are achieved by special techniques; (13) other extraordinary states, such as those that allow "extrasensory" awareness; (14) meditational states; (15) dissociated states, as in cases of pathological multiple personality; and (16) psychomotor states manifest in temporal lobe epilepsies.

Pribram notes that most people have experienced close to a dozen of these "alternate" states.

To this list I shall add: the oceanic experience, as well as a great variety of mystical states, orgasmic experiences, Breuer's hypnoidal state—a special form of dissociation—and a gamut of more or less pathological conditions, many of which are also dissociative experiences. These include such phenomena as multiple personality, mentioned by Pribram; amnesia; fugue states; many culture-bound conditions such as Latah; depersonalization and derealization (or estrangement); and finally, aspects of schizophrenic and other psychotic reactions. Indeed, there is probably no mental disorder which is not accompanied by some alteration in consciousness.

In all states of consciousness, regardless of their differences, even if produced by drugs, there are cognitive and emotional contents which are dynamically determined. In all states there is an obligatory selection of perceptions through different patterns of attention, of which some are more vivid, or real, than others. Thus, at one extreme there may be a massive detachment of consciousness from both inner and outer perceptions. This occurs, for example, in some trance states, amnesias, and conditions such as hysterical blindness. At the other extreme there may be a tightly constricted, intense focus on a single perception, such as a hypnotist's ring, or a particular aspect of the self—as in multiple personality or physical pain. The affects that accompany these states include every known emotion. To some extent, adaptation, defense, and relatively conflict-free motivation are all present in every state of consciousness.

In the same manner that Teresa's visions were peopled with her memories of pictorial representations of Christianity, so too are the mystical, ecstatic, and hallucinatory experiences of all individuals stamped by the world around them, and their world view; we have but to think of the numerous ethnic psychoses. But it is evident that this is characteristic of all states of consciousness, for all people, whatever state they are in: "normal" waking, sleep, chemically induced "highs," religious experiences, transcendental states, or psychopathological conditions. In respect to the latter, perhaps the best-known patient who suffered from dramatic, pathological altered state symptoms was Breuer's patient Anna O. Her hallucinations and hysterical symptoms constituted a virtual encyclopedia of the conversion reactions apparently common among neurotic patients living in Vienna in the latter half of the nineteenth century. That she lost her ability to speak in German, and would, during her absences, speak only in English, is a bizarre symptom but surely suggests something about her previous conscious and/or unconscious attitudes toward these languages, the cultural "position" of English in Vienna at that time, and their symbolic meaning to her.

When the state of consciousness is powerfully driven by intrapsychic needs (defensive, adaptative, conflict-resolving, etc.), we find it to be chiefly characterized by those internal forces. In contrast, when the social imperatives are more dominant—as in such group phenomena as Cargo Cults—the external influences are more prominent. Between lies goal-oriented, conflict-free consciousness. In every situation, however, there is a fusion of the inner and the outer influences whose resultant is the contents of the state of consciousness.

Our understanding of altered states of consciousness is limited. We know that consciousness has a specific organic infrastructure in which the sensory apparatus subserves the perceptual system. We know that a large number of substances can affect the central nervous system and alter consciousness. The limbic system, especially the hippocampus, undergoes changes when exposed to idoleamines and catecholamines. But we do not know how the resulting neurophysiological and pharmacological effects pass from brain to mind, producing subjective and objective psychological phenomena which may be indistinguishable from states induced without exogenous chemicals.

When we return to the psychological basis of consciousness, we find that although metapsychological paradigms possess explanatory and organizing power, they ultimately stand or fall on the validity of the concept of psychic energy. One of the more useful of these models is Federn's (1952) extention of Freud's concept of ego boundaries. He conceived of the boundary as dynamic and flexible; like Freud, he described one face of the boundary turned toward and perceiving the external world; when it is "cathected" (or, let us say, invested with attention, interest, or emotionality) external objects are experienced as vivid and real. The face of the boundary that is turned toward the unconscious does not typically perceive, except, normally, in the process of falling asleep, when one passes through a hypnogogic state to finally enter sleep. To a large extent perceptions from the outer world are then shut off, and the boundary partially admits previously unconscious material which is cloaked in derivative forms. The inner boundary becomes critically "permeable" in psychotic conditions when the individual is overwhelmed by formerly repressed (id) contents, resulting, defensively, in a massive distortion and misperception of external reality, taking the forms of delusions and hallucinations.

Federn postulated that the breakdown of the outer boundary gives rise to specific feelings, chiefly derealization (estrangement) and depersonalization. He characterized the various states of consciousness as dynamic changes in the "permeability" of ego boundaries which are selectively and dynamically overly rigid or overly flexible. The feeling tones experienced by a subject at any given time reflect the contents of the boundary at that time; furthermore, such feelings derive from bodily sources, themselves "a compound feeling including all motor and sensory memories concerning one's own person" (Federn, 1952, p. 27) and from "mental sources," relating to the ideational content of consciousness. Either body or mental "ego" may predominate at a given moment.

Ultimately, Federn's ego-boundary model, though a valuable means of conceptualizing perceptual processes, remains a metaphor for a group of phenomena which are still elusive. One negative conclusion from these considerations can, however, be drawn: although the relative absence of boundaries in the infant may be the prototype for the oceanic experience and for states of consciousness where self-boundaries are blurred or disappear altogether, it is clear that these experiences are not simple regressions to an infantile level.

The oceanic experience, for example, is an adult phenomenon which in no significant manner can be duplicated by the infant; indeed, what an infant actually experiences in its relative union with the world is only dimly understood. In contrast to the infant, the adult lives in a world of culture; psychologically, he carries an ego that is staggeringly complex compared to the rudimentary islets of ego formation present in the infant. The adult's ego is thoroughly imbued with culture and his world view. Moreover, the adult is often aware of his states of consciousness. It also seems likely that the oceanic experience, as well as some of the other states of consciousness, may influence creativity in that, to use Kris's (1952) formula, such experiences constitute a "regression in the service of the ego." Klein (1959) observed that by departing from ordinary awareness, with its necessary "blinding function," the artist transcends the laws of constancy and is able to discern new or latent forms in objects; he seeks out hidden qualities that are not apparent in the more accessible schemata of things. It is not difficult to see how the oceanic experience can play an incisive role in creative activity, particularly where feelings of awe, vastness, solemnity, high-purpose, or intense love pervade the artistic product; writers such as Milton and Blake come to mind in this respect.

Nor is the impact of such experiences limited to formal artistic behavior. Bertrand Russell (1967) described a "semimystical" experience, lasting but five minutes, that occurred when he was twenty-seven. From a self-styled "imperialist" he became a pacifist. His highly analytic and materialist stance quickly reasserted itself and those attitudes remained intact until the end of his long life. The psychogenetic foundations and psychodynamic forces that precipitated this "mystic illumination" were carefully explored and persuasively argued by Simon and Simon (1972). Noteworthy in their contribution is the emphasis on the defensive role of Russell's "turn to pacifism," which dealt with aggressive feelings related to the early loss of both his parents. But the specific elements of his "illumination" clearly partake of his intellectual makeup and the sociocultural climate around him.

Similarly, Rolland's oceanic experiences, in and of themselves, do not permit us to characterize him as a mystic: for half a century he was a tireless creator of realistic novels, plays, and biographies; he was an eminent musicologist and art historian; he was a leading figure in the doomed struggle to contain fascism during the nineteen-thirties. We may even hypothesize that these reality-focused achievements were actually enhanced by his oceanic experiences, which by their very nature brought Rolland into greater connection with humanity. As Hartmann (1939) described, defenses against unacceptable impulses sometimes lose their raison d'être and radically change their function. Although Rolland's oceanic experiences may have been mere epiphenomena, standing outside of and unrelated to the reality of his daily life, it is more credible on both theoretical and empirical grounds to assume an intimate relation between these experiences and the totality of his mental, and hence social, existence.

In exploring the oceanic experience, it seems clear that Freud's observation that this particular state of consciousness represents a regression to the level of the preindividuated infant is correct only in part. The transitory loss of ego boundaries that accompanies this state is undeniable. However, the regression model omits several crucial elements: the impact of the totality of the patient's conscious and unconscious mental life, comprised of instinctual drive impulses and their derivatives; the organization of the defensive processes that deal with these impulses; and the relatively enduring characterological patterns of attitude, affectivity, fantasy, cognition, and goal-oriented and conflict-free behavior. Furthermore, there is the subject's Weltanschauung which condenses the foregoing psychogenetic and psychodynamic processes with the influences of the subject's culture. The evidence suggests that to some extent the oceanic experience carries out defensive and adaptive functions—especially in relation to aggressive strivings.In a final extension of this point of view, it is apposite to apply the same criteria to all states of consciousness—indeed to ordinary consciousness itself. I would argue that consciousness (and its various states) may be conceptualized as a flexible organization—or process—of perception that possesses a structure which, ever-changing as it is, generally adheres to specific intrapsychic and cultural markers. Such a focus on the nature of consciousness stresses once again that biological man's mind is ever the resultant of the confluence of his inner psychological and external social world.

REFERENCES

BREUER, J. & FREUD, S. (1893–1895). Studies on hysteria. *Standard Edition* 2.

FEDERN, P. (1952). *Ego Psychology and the Psychoses*. New York: Basic Books.

FREUD, E.L. (1960). *The Letters of Sigmund Freud*. New York: Basic Books.

FREUD, S. (1895). Project for a scientific psychology. *Standard Edition* 1.

———— (1900). The interpretation of dreams. *Standard Edition* 4 & 5.

———— (1910). The psychoanalytic view of psychogenic disturbance of vision *Standard Edition* 11.

———— (1911). Formulations on the two principles of mental functioning. *Standard Edition* 12.

———— (1915). The unconscious. *Standard Edition*.14.

———— (1923). The ego and the id. *Standard Edition* 19.

———— (1927). The future of an illusion. *Standard Edition* 21.

———— (1930). Civilization and its discontents. Standard Edition 21.

GRAHAM, C. (1907). *Santa Teresa*. London: Eveleigh Nash.

HARTMANN, H. (1939). *Ego Psychology and the Problem of Adaptation*. New York: Int. Univ. Press, 1958.

JAMES, W. (1904). *The Varieties of Religious Experience*. London: Longmans, Green, 1935.

KLEIN, G. (1959). Consciousness in psychoanalytic theory: some implications for current research in perception. *J. Am. Psychoanal. Assoc.* 7:5–34.

KRISIS, E. (1952). *Psychoanalytic Explorations in Art*. New York: Int. Univ. Press.

Oxford English Dictionary (1971). Compact ed. Oxford: Oxford Univ. Press.

PRIBRAM, K.H. (1977). Some observations on the organization of studies of mind. In *Alternate States of Consciousness*. N. E. Zinberg (Ed.). New York: Free Press, pp. 220–230.

RENAULT, I. (1970). *Ste. Thrse d'Avila et l'Exprience Mystique*. Paris: Ed. du Seuil.

ROLLAND, R. (1930). *Prophets of the New India*. New York: Boni.

———— (1948). *Choix de Lettres Malvida von Meysenbug*. Paris: Albin Michel.

———— (1959). *Le Voyage Interieur* Paris: Ed. Albin Michel.

RUSSELL, B. (1959). *Wisdom of the West*. New York: Crescent Books.

———— (1967). *The Autobiography of Bertrand Russell Vol. I: 1871–1914*. Boston: Atlantic, Little Brown.

SCHWARTZ, F. & SCHILLER, F.H. (1970). A Psychoanalytic model of attention and learning. *Psychol. Issues Monogr* 23. New York: Int. Univ. Press.

SIMON, B. & SIMON, N. (1972). The pacifist turn: an episode of mystic illumination in the autobiography of Bertrand Russell *J. Am. Psychoanal.*

Assoc. 20:109–121.

STARBUCK, E.D. (1899). *The Psychology of Religion.* New York: Scribners, 1908.

WERMAN, D.S. (1977). Sigmund Freud and Romain Rolland. *Int. J. Psychoanal.* 4:225–242.

CHAPTER 8

Sigmund Freud and Romain Rolland

[Werman, D.S. (1977). *International Review of Psycho-Analysis,* 4:225–242.]

I

In his last personal letter to Romain Rolland, in May 1930, Sigmund Freud remarked: 'I may confess to you that I have rarely experienced that mysterious attraction of one human being for another as vividly as I have with you; it is somehow bound up, perhaps, with the awareness of our being so different' (E. Freud, 1960, p. 406).

Their differences were indeed many and profound. Freud: the Central European, a nonbeliever, a Jew; a scientist, the 'archaeologist' of the mind. Rolland: from the heartland of France, a former Catholic and lifelong mystic; a musician and creative writer; an exponent of Hindu religion; a moralist, pacifist and social revolutionary.

The following communication explores that remarkable relationship, with particular attention to the two areas which linked Freud and Rolland: their mutual concern with the problems of war and peace, and their respective views of Rolland's concept of the 'oceanic experience'.

In order to clarify the Freud–Rolland relationship, certain events and trends in Rolland's productive and tumultuous life must be described, although such a summary must, regretfully, be brief.

Rolland was born in 1866 in the Burgundian town of Clamecy, to an old bourgeois family. His mother, whom he worshipped throughout his life, was highly religious, Jansenistic, a sensitive amateur musician, who had a profound influence on her son. Quite the contrary, Rolland's father, a notary, was a disbeliever, a robust man with a taste for hearty living. At less than one year of age, Rolland developed a severe bronchial infection which left him frail throughout his life and he probably and several episodes of pulmonary tuberculosis. He later observed that 'respiratory expressions' and derivatives of them abound in his writing. When he was five, his three-year-old sister died suddenly, leaving him with perhaps a partially resolved grief, and a debilitating fear for his own life, which

The author is responsible for the translation of all quotations from sources originally in French. The author wishes to express his deep gratitude to Miss Anna Freud, Mme. Marie Romain Rolland, and Mme. Solange Weiss, for their gracious assistance.

lasted until 10 or 12 years of age. Scarcely a night thereafter would pass that he did not think of her before falling asleep. Nor could his mother accept the death of the child. Though devout, she railed against God for taking her daughter and hovered over her sickly son, fearful of his health. Exactly one year after Madeleine's death, another daughter was born and given the same name. Throughout her life she was always close to her brother and allied with him in all his activities.

In 1882 the mother decided that her son's evident intellectual gifts required better schools than Clamecy could offer. Instead of sending Romain to Paris alone to study, as his father and grandfather had done before him, she organized a move of the entire family, which proved to have distressing repercussions. For one, the father had to take a subordinate position in a bank; and for Romain, Paris turned out to be a frightening 'jungle' after the secure prison of his provincial nest. The shock of puberty reinforced the transplantation to Paris to disturb his total emotional equilibrium; he entered a phase of intense religious doubt, engulfed by the desires and anxieties of adolescence, and found himself without a mooring. From the age of 15 to 17 he 'breathed the vapors of the abyss' and was plagued with suicidal thoughts. He ultimately broke with Catholicism, but the strong relationship with his mother survived.

After attendance at two distinguished lycées in Paris he was accepted to the École Normale Supérieur, the most prestigious school of higher education in France, where he studied history and geography. His major intellectual influences then were Empedocles, Spinoza, Shakespeare, Beethoven and Tolstoy. Following a letter he wrote to the Russian master, he received a 38-page response which, by elevating service versus art, was crucial, he felt, in his lifelong aim of serving man, if not in his creative writing.

He was awarded a scholarship to study art history in Rome where he spent two years. It was there that he became close friends with a German woman, Malwida von Meysenbug. She was then 73 years old and had been a close friend of Wagner, Nietzsche, Mazzini, Kossuth, Herzen and many other leading intellectual and political personalities. A free spirit, dedicated to the arts, especially music, she had a strong liberating influence on Rolland: by the time of her death in 1903, 15 years later, the Rolland-von Meysenbug correspondence comprised over 1200 letters.

In Rome, he wrote a History of the Opera in Europe before Lully and Scarlatti, a study of 16th-century Italian painting, and the first of some 20 plays. For the next several years he taught art history in lycées and at the Sorbonne. The Dreyfus Affair became the arena of his first public involvement; he tried to avoid the political and partisan aspects of the case and defined the intellectual's role as the search for truth and insistence on ethical issues. Stefan Zweig notes that at this time Rolland already seems to have found his glorious place, of being a 'solitary combatant' (Zweig, 1921).

In 1900 he and Charles Péguy launched the literary journal Cahiers de la Quinzaine, through which they called for an 'uncorrupted literature'. It published Rolland's (1905–12) multi-volumed novel, Jean Christophe, as well as some of his biographical studies and other articles. At the same time he served as a music critic and became the first professor of musicology at the Sorbonne, a chair which he held until he retired from it in 1912. He produced studies of Handel and Michelangelo and began his monumental series of volumes on Beethoven. During this time he was emotionally overwhelmed by the breakup of his marriage with Clotilde Bréal, the daughter of a leading academician and Jewish intellectual. Badly injured by an automobile accident in 1910, he was bedridden for many months and suffered thereafter from the sequelae.

While his name was becoming well-known through his books, plays and literary prizes, in 1914 it suddenly became universally recognized, but only to be dishonoured and disgraced. For, at the outset of the Great War, he declared the conflict to be a monstrous and brutal deception of all the nations involved. His opposition was moral, and as Jouve wrote: 'he refused to be carried away in the hour of panic. . . . One of those extraordinary moments when one man, without even being clearly conscious of it, incarnates part of humanity, expresses it, animates it, and causes it to be born' (Jouve, 1920, pp. 43–44).

His first salvo was a letter to Gerhardt Hauptmann, the erstwhile liberal German playwright, calling on him to denounce 'with every bit of energy' the destruction of Louvain. The author of The Weavers never replied. Later Rolland attacked the German government for the bombardment of Rheims. But with his criticism of the French he was immediately accused of treason in the French press. In September 1914 he published his historic article 'Above the Mêlée' (cf. Rolland, 1953), an appeal to governments, intellectual leaders, churchmen and laymen, socialists and people of all persuasions to oppose the war. A nightmare of hatred and calumny descended on him and he was obliged to move to Switzerland, but even there his life was endangered. 'The French superpatriots cried out as if they had picked up a red hot iron by mistake. In a trice [he] was boycotted by his oldest friends, the book-sellers no longer dared to display Jean Christophe, the military authorities were already considering measures against him' (Zweig, 1943). One pamphlet after another denounced him. As late as 1926 he was still a pariah to the French: Hesse had dedicated the first part of his novel Siddhartha to Rolland, but the French editor deleted it. Despite being rejected from military duty because of his poor health, he ceaselessly combated the war and was in turn pilloried and hounded for his efforts. He spent the war years in Switzerland, at first working for the International Red Cross and corresponding with thousands of families whose sons and fathers were in the armies. He took as his motto that of William of Orange, 'Je n'ai pas besoin d'espérer pour entreprendre' ('I do not need to hope in order to undertake'). A small number of friends and supporters rallied around him: among others, Einstein, Stefan Zweig, Jules Romains, Hermann Hesse; and from England, Bertrand Russell and Norman Angell. Repeatedly, during and later after the war, he preached a gospel of love, action, commitment, responsibility of the thinker, and of truth to oneself. As Doisy (1945) notes, like his friend Gandhi, he could never separate his political from his moral thinking. In 1916 he was awarded the Nobel Prize for literature and despite his penury he contributed it entirely to charitable causes.

His activities after the First World War were not less significant than those during it and before, but are less pertinent to this communication. He continued to be in the forefront of European pacifism and, later, of the collective opposition to the rise of Fascism in Italy and Nazism in Germany. From the mid 20s onward, he was perhaps Gandhi's leading spokesman in Western Europe; he adopted a strongly supportive posture towards the new Soviet state but retained his independent and critical views, and with Maxim Gorki decried the repressive forces in Soviet life. Increasingly, he called for some form of socialist revolution, but never threw in his lot formally with the Communists.

As Nazi totalitarianism grew more threatening, he devoted himself to increased efforts to denounce it, isolate it and impede its inexorable takeover of Europe. In 1933, with Hitler in power, Marshal von Hindenburg awarded him the Goethe Medal for Art and Science, which he refused, citing the crushing of freedom in Germany and the brutal proscription of Jews. Gradually he moved from pacifism to civil disobedience, and finally, in the late 1930s, he supported armed resistance to the Nazi terror.

During the Second World War, once more living near his birthplace, he lived to see Nazi officers billeted in his home. German publishers sought his approval for a new edition of Jean Christophe, 'revised and edited' by them; he showed them out. Although close to 80 years of age he produced four or five important works including the final volume on Beethoven, and a two-volume, definitive study of Péguy. He barely survived the liberation of France and died on 30 December 1944.

On 9 February 1923, Freud wrote to Edouard Monod-Herzen, the grandson of Alexandre Herzen, and son of the eminent historian, Gabriel Monod (one of Rolland's professors at the École Normale Superiéur, and the person who had introduced him to Malwida von Meysenbug). He asked Monod-Herzen as 'a friend of Romain Rolland . . . to pass on to him a word of respect from an unknown admirer' (E. Freud, 1960, p. 341). Jones suggests that Freud was thinking of 'Au-dessus de la Mêlée'. Two weeks later Rolland responded, saying that he was 'very touched' by Freud's letter. He observed that if Freud's name has now become illustrious in France, he, Rolland, was one of the first Frenchmen to know and read Freud's works. Amazingly, he says that some 20 years earlier he found the 'Dream' book (Freud, 1900) and some other books, in Zurich, and was fascinated by Freud's views which corresponded to some of his own intuitive thoughts. He characterized Freud as the 'Christopher Columbus of a new continent of the mind' which he has opened up to other explorers. Not only medicine, but psychology in all its forms has benefited from this work, and now literature also benefits from these conquests without always even being aware of it. He mentioned that he often discussed Freud with his friend Stefan Zweig, who affectionately worships him.

Freud's letter made him aware of the sadness and misery of living in a country defeated in war, but he believes that it is not less depressing to live in the victorious country, and to be únable to identify oneself with its victory—for he has always preferred to be among those who suffer rather than with those who cause suffering.

Western Europe is in political ruins, he thinks, but he is confident that man will endure; the price will be high, but 'as you know, nature is profligate and without pity' (Rolland, 1977).

Freud responds on 4 March 1923 and writes that Rolland's name has been associated with the most precious of beautiful illusions, that of love extended to all mankind. Referring to his Jewish origins, he writes that he belongs to 'a race which in the Middle Ages was held responsible for all epidemics and which today is blamed for the disintegration of the Austrian Empire and the German defeat'. Most of his life's work has been spent trying to 'destroy illusions of my own and those of mankind'. He writes of the need to 'divert our instincts from destroying our own kind', warning that if we do not do so, but 'continue to hate one another for minor differences and kill each other for petty gain, if we go on exploiting the great progress made in the control of natural resources for our mutual destruction, what kind of future lies in store for us?' The very survival of the species is in question. 'My writings cannot be what yours are: comfort and refreshment for the reader. But if I may believe that they have aroused your interest, I shall permit myself to send you a small book which is sure to be unknown to you: Group Psychology and the Analysis of the Ego, published in 1921.' He does not consider the work especially successful, but believes that 'it shows a way from the analysis of the individual to understanding of a society' (E. Freud, 1960, p. 342).

Rolland quotes part of the letter in his diary and adds that it seems that the plight of the Jewish people—proscribed and humiliated in the Middle Ages, now held responsible for the Central Powers' defeat—must weigh heavily on Freud (Rolland, 1977).

Freud's pleasure at receiving Rolland's letter was reflected in a letter to Abraham, in March 1923, where he speaks of it as a 'breath of Spring' and relates Rolland's 20-year interest in analysis (Abraham & E. Freud, 1965).

During the second and third weeks of May 1924, Rolland was visiting in Vienna. After many years he had renewed contact with Richard Strauss, attended several performances of his operas and visited, with Stefan Zweig, Schnitzler and other Viennese writers and musicians.

On reading in the paper that Rolland was in Vienna, Freud wrote to Zweig that he 'immediately felt the desire to make the personal acquaintance of the man I have revered from afar'. He had been concerned as to how to approach him and was pleased to learn from Zweig that Rolland, too, wanted to meet Freud. The latter proposed a visit, either in the afternoon 14 March or preferably 'the pleasure of taking a cup of tea (with you both) at nine (after supper) with my family'. He regretted that Rolland had to be so careful of his health and counted on Zweig's presence since 'during the past six months my speech has been seriously affected; above all my French would hardly be adequate for conversation'. He closes with with cordial greetings to Zweig and his 'great friend' (E. Freud, 1960, p. 348–349).

Freud's keeness to meet Rolland is underscored by the difficulties he was experiencing from the surgery he had undergone six months earlier. Just the day before Rolland's visit he wrote Lou Andreas Salomé about his feelings in the face of the 'awful realities' of his disease, the 'possibilities' stemming from it and the limitations of his prosthesis.

On 13 May Zweig gave a lunch for Rolland at the Hotel Meissl und Schadn, in the Neuer Markt, with Richard Strauss, Schnitzler and others (Rolland, 1951) and the following evening they visited Freud at his home in Bergasse.

Little is known of the exchange that took place that evening. Rolland (1951) subsequently mentioned in his diary a letter from Freud (6 Dec. 1924) that spoke of their meeting in his study, and that he 'often thinks of the hour that you gave to me and my daughter, and I recall your face as you sat in the red chair, pulled forward. Things are not going well for me; I am taking leave of life, but I must await the end [Abwicklung]' Rolland notes: 'I can see there his stoical persuasion.'

The meeting apparently occupied a special place in Rolland's memories for in 1936, when he responded to Freud's (1936) contribution to his 70th birthday celebration, he evoked his gratitude to Stefan Zweig for bringing Freud and himself together, because their 'friendship was born out of that encounter', and he speaks of the deep respect and admiration he has for Freud who 'was able to penetrate to the depths of the internal abyss' (Rolland, 1977).

Zweig's presence at this meeting was more than as a simple intermediary; for almost three decades his closest links were to Rolland, Freud, and the Belgian poet Emile Verhaeren (who had died in 1916). He was the 'cross-pollinator' between Freud and Rolland, had written biographies about them, and considered his 'friendship [with Rolland] together with that of Freud and Verhaeren, . . . the most fruitful and, at certain times, the most decisive for the future course of my life' (Zweig, 1943, p. 202). 'On

no writer did Rolland have a greater moral influence, nor as abundant a correspondence and as vast and regular an exchange of thoughts for 30 years; nor was anyone as loyal to Rolland as Zweig' (Nedeljkovic, 1970, p. 7. Perhaps more than any contemporary Frenchman, Rolland had always been powerfully attracted to German culture, 'I am the son of Beethoven, Leibnitz and Goethe' (Rolland, 1953 b, p. 91). The two men were intensely concerned with the failure of faith in reason, with the deception of the war, the socialist revolution, and the rise of fascism and its growing power. Zweig repeatedly avowed his dependency on Rolland, regarding him as the greatest moral event of their epoch. From 1900 until Zweig's death in 1942, the two men remained in close contact, discussing in great detail their respective work, plans, thoughts and preoccupations. As the Nazis progressively enslaved one European nation after another, Zweig became demoralized and deeply pessimistic. While he had been able to draw strength from Rolland during the Great War to sustain his opposition to it, he now became uprooted, a displaced person, criss-crossing from Paris to London, to New York, to Rio de Janiero. He cried out against the use of violence and recalled that the 'good great Freud was right to distrust our "progress" and to fear the implacable force of our instincts' (Nedeljkovic, 1970, p. 212).

Settled in Brazil, he was cut off from everything and everyone who had sustained him. Freud, who had 'helped him combat pusillanimity' had died, and as Allday (1972) notes, 'On Freud's death in September, 1939, he mentally turned the page in his own earthly saga' (p. 227). Living in Nazi occupied France, Rolland vainly tried once more to strengthen Zweig's will. But Zweig had long been convinced of Hitler's invincibility and could not conceive of his defeat. On 22 February 1942, he and his wife carried through a carefully planned suicide. For Rolland, Zweig was more than a 'man with great human qualities, he also loved him as the born artist who touched all the strings as a master . . . He was the poet armed with the powerful keys of Freud' (Nedeljkovic, 1970, p. 356).

Zweig's relationship with Freud went back to 1908, when Freud had praised his verse drama, Tersites. Despite some sympathy for oriental thought, he welded his romantic vision of emotion to Freud's scientific approach and followed Freud's development of psychoanalysis with passionate interest often discussing it with Rolland. Both Dumont (1967) and Prater (1972) suggest that Zweig had also had some therapeutic sessions with Freud; the latter quotes Arnold Bauer that 'their talks may in fact have taken on the character of a Lehranalyse'. Zweig's important biography of Stendhal may have been written in large part to explore Stendhal's position as a precursor of Freud in attributing a dominant role in life to the instinctual drives.

Their relationship was not without its vicissitudes: although Freud admired Zweig's work, he was not entirely pleased with his amateur approach to psychology, nor did he conceal his criticism when he felt the occasion demanded it. In a letter to Arnold Zweig, with whom he was very close, Freud apologized for mistaking the two, attributing his error to irritation over Stefan Zweig's biography of him in Healers of the Mind, where he is one of three subjects, the other two being Mesmer and Mary Baker Eddy, the founder of Christian Science.

What familiarity did Rolland have with the psychoanalytic literature, and what was his understanding of it? Freud had sent him 'The Future of an Illusion' (1927), 'Group Psychology and the Analysis of the Ego' (1921) and 'Civilization and its Discontents' (1930). And, as previously mentioned, many years before, he had read his book on dreams and 'some others'.

Most evident throughout Rolland's comments on psychoanalysis is his ambivalence, and his rejection of infant sexuality and the Oedipus complex. However, despite his most strenuous objections, he never stints in his high regard for Freud

For several decades, he was a close friend of the Swiss psychoanalyst and man of letters Charles Baudouin, within whom he discussed many of Freud's discoveries. In January 1922 he recieved a book from Baudouin on psychoanalysis, which he found 'lucid, of good sense and well balanced'. However, he protests against the explanations of child psychology with which his own experiences and observations do not concur. Psychoanalytic interpretations are 'forced'; psychoanalysts have erected a symbolism which has crystallized and become monotonous; they insist on categorizing people rather than individualizing them.

'I'm speaking to you, my dear friend, in all affectionate candour: nothing seems more false and revolting to me than this obsession—not in the child but imputed to him—with sexual things.' He mocks the sexual interpretations of children's drawings, behaviour and dreams. Much of a child's behaviour he believes is due to simply doing what he is able, at a given age or through observation of the parents. 'Whatever he says, writes or draws, you are ready to reduce it to three or four motifs: Oedipus or Electra complex, sexual themes, etc. . . . But it is you, the psychoanalysts, who are obsessed with all this' (Rolland, 1977).

He recalls his own childhood feelings, having 'analysed' himself, and has the clearest memories of sexual matters: during his childhood, along with his chums, the only sexual thing they evoked was the chamber pot. Sexuality as such was absent. 'We never suspected any connexion between the organ that excreted beverages and . . . and what? We didn't even know there was a possibility of another 'what', and it didn't interest us' (Rolland, 1977). He doubts that 'subconscious' eroticism is normal in the child; and when it does appear, later on, it is due to outside influences, and it causes 'stupor, disarray and a crumbling of their earlier framework' (Rolland, 1977).

As for the Oedipus complex, he at first denied its reality, but later admitted that it did exist, but only as an exception. 'For myself, although I have always loved my mother, as I have never nor ever shall love anyone else in the world, I recall the insignificant place she occupied in my childhood thoughts. I was much too taken up with other children and especially myself' (Rolland, 1977). Never, in his extensive day-dreaming, he recalls, did either his mother or his father ever figure prominently.

He predicts that Baudouin will undoubtedly assume that all of this is due to repression. 'You psychoanalytic devils! whether one thinks black or white or neither, you'll prove that one is killing Laios and sleeping with Jocasta. And when I read that to dream of a damp cellar means to return to the "maternal breast"!!!' He is sure that if Baudouin had ever seen the inside of the frightening cellar he had known as a child, he would understand why a child would be frightened and dream of it.

He explains psychoanalytic interpretations by pointing out that analysts are, for the most part, very intelligent but 'not very normal' people, and thus are inevitably, almost unconsciously, drawn towards the exceptional. This is true not only of Freud (who 'at least has a powerful vitality') but of the Geneva psychologists, 'repressed types', whose instincts are constricted by their 'race'. He warns Baudouin about the formulation that psychopathology is an exaggeration of the normal, and offers numerous analogical arguments to refute this view (Rolland, 1977).

In his memoirs, Le Voyage Intérieur (Rolland, 1959) the chapter entitled 'Le Sagittaire' ('The Archer') is a free attempt at self-analysis. While he credits Freud with having discovered the importance of dreams, his own treatment of dreams indicates a blurring of the distinction between dreams and fantasies; nor does he appear to have differentiated manifest from latent content. Although he alludes to childhood as well as adult sexuality, it is difficult to ascertain if the ambiguity is due to discretion or resistance. He assumes that he can and does 'analyse' himself, and while there are many insightful aperçus, these merely hint at the psychogenetics and psychodynamics of his personality development.

He also questions the applicability of the Oedipus complex to himself:

I have the greatest respect for Freud, the man, whom I have known, and I honour the courage of the pilot, who like his great Phoenician ancestors, was the first to brave the circumnavigation of the black Continent of the Soul. He has related what his eyes have seen. And he has also sorted out and grouped the masses of half-true, half-fictional tales that disorganized people brought to their great confessor. For the middle ages of human intelligence— that are yet to come — his Summation of the subconscious [sic] describing unknown lands, will surely supplant Pliny the Elder. But with a calm certainty I aver that the dark Continent which he describes is not mine. I come from a different race. In the conche of its memory, my race carries down through the ages the howling of other monsters and the chants of other gods . . . Let them leave me in peace, with their myths of Oedipus and Electra! If ever a son felt as much as I the soulful intimacy of filial affection, never had a child felt more than I the barrier of age that separated me from my elders.

He had already begun to analyse his dreams at the age of six or seven and by ten or twelve was 'a master ofhtr the art of sticking together the fragments of my desires and my visions of life' and they contained no incestuous ideas. While he acknowledges the prominent role of Eros, of sexuality, he hastens to point out that while it is the first of desire's channels, it is not the only one (Rolland, 1959, pp. 112–114). The language of this chapter is so allusive that it lends itself to a variety of interpretations. In his books on Ramakrishna and Vivekananda there is further mention of psychoanalysis. Although these books will be dealt with later when the issue of the 'oceanic experience' is discussed, at this point, certain aspects of them are worth noting. He groups together Freud, Jung, Janet and Bleuler and he believes that almost all psychologists 'are possessed by the theory of Regression' (Rolland, 1930, pp. 633–634). It is obvious that he possesses some knowledge of psychoanalysis, but it is imprecise and unsystematic. Freud, to whom Rolland sent these books, immediately pointed out to him that the concepts 'introvert' and 'extrovert' came from Jung, whom he qualifies as

a bit of a mystic himself [who] hasn't belonged to us for years. We don't attach any great importance to this distinction and are well aware that people can be both at the same time and usually are. Furthermore, our terms such as regression, narcissism, pleasure principle are of a purely descriptive nature and don't carry within themselves any valuation. The mental processes may change direction or combine forces with each other; for instance, even reflecting is a regressive process without losing any of its dignity or importance in being so.

He states that analysis has its scale of values, but its sole aim is the enhanced harmony of the ego, which is expected to successfully mediate between the claims of the instinctual life (the 'id' and those of the external world; thus between inner and outer reality. (E. Freud, 1960, pp. 392–393).

Some years later, in an introduction to a presentation to J. J. Rousseau's writings (Rolland et al., 1953) Rolland endeavours to present a psychological interpretation of his subject. Although the approach is not, properly speaking, psychoanalytic, the 'flavour' is occasionally there in the use of words such as 'subconscious', 'repression' and 'libido'. However, his understanding of these words remains unclear.

The same anti-psychoanalytic themes recur as late as 1940 when he again expressed his repulsion against the 'morbid, maniacal use' of Freudian explanations by psychologists, hisorians and scientists. He had received from E. Monod-Herzen a study on Napoleon's handwriting, which approached its subject uniquely from an oedipal point of view. (It is unclear whether the article in question was actually written by Monod-Herzen or simply transmitted by him.) Rolland's diary quotes part of his letter to Monod-Herzen begging to be excused from believing in the 'famous complex and Freudian symbols'. As far as he can see, these complexes attack only those whose personality is already out of balance: 'I never had any difficulty in harmonizing mother and father.' Life is richer and more complex than a 'simple reservoir of psychoanalytic pictures'. And yet, he concludes that the living must tear themselves away from the past (Rolland, 1977). Indeed, throughout his life he exhorted his readers to reject a 'neurasthenic' way of life, and to commit themselves to deeds, service and to strength.

As to what Freud had read of Rolland we know little. He read 'Above the Mêlée', the play Liluli (to be discussed later), Gandhi, and the three volumes on Ramakrishna and Vivekananda which Rolland sent him. There is also the strong likelihood that he had read other works of Rolland since some of these had been either translated by and/or introduced into Germany by Stefan Zweig, and it is improbable that Zweig had not at least spoken to Freud about them, particularly the Jean Christophe series.

Anna Freud recalls (personal communication) her 'father's very high regard for Romain Rolland and his vivid pleasure in reading his books and in telling or thinking about him. Romain Rolland was one of the figures my father admired, not only [for] his literary achievement but his courage, his penetrating intellect and his superior view of the world'. The courage alluded to by Miss Freud relates to many aspects of Rolland's multifaceted career, but must in the first place refer to Rolland's position during the First World War, when he denounced the belligerent nations on both sides of the conflicts. It is my contention that Sigmund Freud later developed a powerful identification with Rolland's active pacifism. The roots of this lie not only in his profound aversion to war in general, and to his penetrating regard of man's potential for destructiveness, but to his own position, at the beginning of the Great War which was far from pacifistic and from which later he decisively turned.

Just before the outbreak of hostilities he doubted that war would occur, and maintained that view even after the assassination of the Archduke Franz Ferdinand. He largely took the official position of the Austrian Government, particularly regarding the 'impudent' Serbs, a view that Jones, who had been studying the history of Croatia, felt was rather one-sided:

> Freud's immediate response to the declaration of war was an unexpected one. One would have supposed that a pacific savant of fifty-eight would have greeted it with simple horror, as so many did. On the contrary, his first response was rather one of youthful enthusiasm, apparently a reawakening of the military ardors of his boyhood . . . for the first time in thirty years he felt himself to be an Austrian. . . . He was quite carried away, could not think of any work, and spent his time discussing the events of the day with his brother Alexander. As he put it: 'All my libido is given to Austria-Hungary' (Jones, 1955, p. 171).

Despite his long-standing feelings about German arrogance, he rejoiced in their victories and was shaken by their defeats. When Jones predicted the ultimate defeat of the Germans, Freud wrote to Ferenczi that Jones talked about the war 'with the narrow-minded outlook of the English'. But shortly thereafter he wisely warned Jones: 'Don't forget that now there is much lying (on both sides).' These dual attitudes of enthusiasm and repulsion, acceptance and scepticism, seem to have been characteristic of his position, especially during the earlier phase of the war. He grew gloomy about the future and about his own life; his superstitions about his own death were revived and enhanced by the death of his half-brother Emmanuel, at the age of 81, the same age at which their father had died. Despite everything, however, he maintained contact with Jones, and until the United States entered the war, Putnam regularly served as an intermediary for letters between the two.

With his three sons involved in the war, two in actual combat, his position is only too understandable.

He even turned against his beloved England, who now had become 'hypocritical'. He evidently accepted the German version that Germany was being 'encircled' by envious neighbours who had been plotting to destroy her. It was only late in the war that the Allies' 'propaganda' aroused his suspicions about the moral issues involved, so that he then became doubtful about both versions and could stay au dessus de la mélée (Jones, 1955, p. 170).

Jones's use of the French idiom, in this context, strikes the eye because it is also the title of Rolland's powerful denunciation of the war in 1914.

Freud's metapsychological understanding of war was epitomized in a letter written on 12 December 1914 to Frederik von Eeden, a Dutch psychopathologist and social reformer:

> Psycho-analysis has inferred from the dreams and parapraxes of healthy people, as well as from the symptoms of neurotics, that the primitive, savage, and evil impulses of mankind have not vanished in any of its individual members, but persist, although in a repressed state, in the unconscious (to use our technical terms), and lie in wait for opportunities of becoming active once more. It has further taught us that our intellect is a feeble and dependent thing, a plaything and tool of our instinct and affects, and that we are all compelled to behave cleverly or stupidly according to the commands of our (emotional) attitudes and internal resistances.
>
> If you will now observe what is happening in this war—the cruelties and injustices for which the most civilized nations are responsible, the different way in which they judge their own lies and wrong-doings and those of their enemies, and the general lack of insight which prevails—you will have to admit that psycho-analysis has been right in both its theses (Freud, 1914, pp. 301–302).

Writing to Lou Andreas-Salomé, he observed that he and his contemporaries will never again see a joyous world, 'it has all come out just as our psychoanalytic expectations' predicted. 'Since we can only regard the highest civilization of the present as disfigured by a gigantic hypocrisy it follows that we are organically unfitted for it. We have to abdicate, and the Great Unknown, He or It, lurking behind Fate, will sometime repeat such an experiment with another race' (Jones, 1955, p. 177).

Behind these pessimistic thoughts one can discern Freud's frustration with the course of history and his powerlessness to deal with it. On 7 June 1915, he wrote to Putnam:

> My chief impression is that I am far more primitive, more humble and less sublimated than my dear friend in Boston...... The unworthiness of human beings, even of analysts, has always made a deep impression on me, but why should analyzed people be altogether better than others? Analysis makes for unity, but not necessarily for goodness (Jones, 1955, p. 182).

In the spring of 1915 he wrote two essays under the general title: 'Thought for the Times on War and Death' (Freud, 1915). The first article, 'The Disillusionment of the War' evokes the barbarous manner in which the war was being conducted and the flaunting of treaties and other international obligations. Freud consoles himself that disillusionment is not altogether justified since it was based on an illusion in the first place, which the war is destroying.

In peace time, moral behaviour is based either on the dominance by the love instinct of the underlying hostile ones that are always present, or 'hypocritically', on a fear of punishment. It is the latter form which more readily collapses when external controls are lacking.

In the second essay, 'On Attitudes to Death', Freud deals with many aspects of the subject of which most are not pertinent here. Regarding war, he states (Freud, 1915):

> It strips us of the later accretions of civilization, and lays bare the primal man in each of us. It compels us once more to be heroes who cannot believe in their own death; it stamps strangers as enemies, whose death is to be brought about or desired; it tells us to disregard the death of those we love. But war cannot be abolished; so long as the conditions of existence among nations are so different and their mutual repulsion so violent, there are bound to be wars. The question then arises: Is it not we who should give in, who should adapt ourselves to war? Should we not confess that in our civilized attitude towards death we are once again living psychologically beyond our means, and should we not rather turn back and recognize the truth? Would it not be better to give death the place in reality and in our thoughts which is its due . . . ? (p. 299).

The essay concludes with the observation that it would be in keeping with the times to change the old saying, si vis pacem, para bellum (if you want to preserve peace, arm for war) to si vis vitam, para mortem (if you want to endure life, prepare yourself for death).

Here, as in other writings, Freud seems to intertwine two attitudes about war: one, a theoretical, pessimistic view that man is instinctually destructive; the other gives voice to his pacifistic loathing of war, his desire for peace, but also his painful scepticism about the possibilities of securing it. Rolland's apparently unquestioning assumption of such possibilities and his courageous personal commitment to that end, despite its perhaps unrealistic character probably attracted Freud's admiration, and was an alluring, although Utopian goal; for despite his perspective of man's instinctual destructiveness, Freud never suggested that men abdicate their responsibility to contain evil whether it be war or any other product of civilization.

As the war progressed, Freud not only grew increasingly doubtful of a German victory, but he could write Abraham at the end of 1917, that he had 'definitely' reached the position of rejecting both sides. However, his feelings about man's destructive impulses remained mixed. While he could question if a 'handful of ambitious and deluding men without conscience could have succeeded in unleashing all these evil spirits if their millions of followers did not share their guilt?' (Freud, 1916a, p. 146), he could also write: 'the war neuroses which ravaged the German army have been recognized as being a protest of the individual against the part he was expected to play in the army . . . ' (Freud, 1921, p. 95), and to Theodore Reik: 'Although I agree with your judgement about the world and the present race of human beings I cannot, as you know, regard your pessimistic rejection of a better future as justifiable' (Jones, 1955, p. 414).

One of his more powerful indictments of war, as well as an expression of his personal desolation in the face of it, occurs in 'On Transience' (Freud, 1916b):

> [War] destroyed not only the beauty of the countrysides through which it passed and the works of art which it met with in its path but it also shattered our pride in the achievements of our civilization, our admiration for many philosophers and artists and our hopes for a final triumph over the differences between nations and races. It tarnished the lofty impartiality of our science, it revealed our instincts in all their nakedness and let loose the evil spirits within us which we thought had been tamed forever by centuries of continuous education by the noblest minds (p. 307).

It is difficult to assume that the pronouns in this paragraph are merely rhetorical and do not embody to some extent a self-criticism directed against his early enthusiasm for the war.

But by 1930 his position seems to have crystallized and he wrote:

As a result [of man's powerful share of aggressiveness] . . . their neighbour is for them not only a potential helper or sexual object, but also someone who tempts them to satisfy their aggressiveness on him, to exploit his capacity for work without compensation, to use him sexually without his consent, to seize his possessions, to humiliate him, to cause him pain, to torture and to kill him. *Homo homini lupus*(Freud, 1930, p. 111).

The well-known exchange of letters with Einstein in 1933 carried these thoughts still further. Einstein's letter asks 'Is there any way of delivering mankind from the menace of war?' and he speaks of the 'lust for hatred and destruction' in man. Freud (1933) agrees with Einstein's thoughts and amplifies them at some length; but he is able to project that 'wars will only be prevented with certainty if mankind unites in setting up a central authority' with the power to deal with international conflicts. He delineates the dual instinct theory, Eros versus the destructive or death instinct, and while he characterized this hyopthesis as 'our mythological theory of instincts', he based his programme on it: 'to bring Eros . . . into play against it [the aggressive instinct]. Anything that encourages the growth of emotional ties between men must operate against war.' Men can love each other as they do sexual objects but without the erotic component, and they can be emotionally tied to each other through processes of identification. Despite these theoretical possibilities of avoidance of war, he fears that the 'mills . . . grind so slowly that people may starve before they get their flour'. At several points in this communication, Freud describes himself as a pacifist. The inherent contradiction between his (and others') pacifism and the universal wish for death (whether directed inward or outward) is dealt with in the concluding part of the essay where he suggests that we rebel against war for 'organic reasons': that throughout the ages there has been a 'progressive displacement of instinctual aims and a restriction of instinctual impulses'. Consequently, the intellect has been strengthened, and aggressive impulses have become internalized. Thus, 'we pacifists [now] have a *constitutional* intolerance of war . . .'; 'we simply cannot any longer put up with it'. The last paragraphs of the letter richly reveal, on the one hand, Freud's pervasive, grim appreciation of the future of man, and on the other, his highly qualified view that war may be preventable. Despite his harshest statements about man's ruthless destruction of others, he never lapses into a state of hopeless resignation in the face of the threat of future wars which he predicts as probable (Freud, 1933).

It is as simplistic to characterize Rolland as a 'pure idealist' as it is to regard Freud as a dyed-in-the-wool pessimist. At many points throughout his works one can see Rolland's exasperation and anger with mankind's destructiveness, folly and cowardice. Freud (1930, p. 65) observed that Rolland had 'himself once praised the magic of illusion in a poem ..'. *Liluli* (Rolland, 1920) the verse play in question, is a satirical allegory about man's gullibility and servitude to illusion. On the evidence of the play itself, there is no question of its pessimism: The State, the Church, public opinion, intellectuals—all are pilloried, and the masses of the people depicted as willing sheep led to destruction. Rolland later wrote that *Liluli* was but part of a trilogy whose ultimate meaning, the consolation of faith, had been ignored by the public. But, as one writer observed, 'The critics can scarcely be blamed . . . [Rolland was] judged by his public performance, not on his private intentions '(March, 1971, p. 94). Nor was he a muddle-headed 'do-gooder', oblivious to the harsh realities of the world. He regarded Einstein's call for individuals to become war resisters as childish optimism and illusionary, for it was personal and involved no risk.

Despite the vast and varied differences between Rolland and Freud, there are important affinities. In the first place, both men had suffered physical and emotional pain. They had endured isolation from their fellow men: one had been cast out from his professional world and virtually declared to be a charlatan; the other had been ostracized by his countrymen and branded a traitor. But both men were, each in his own way, combatants, rarely ceding an inch in their struggles. They profoundly revered the fruits of human intellect (for both, Shakespeare, Goethe and the ancient Greek writers were lifelong companions). They were torn by their observations of man's destructiveness, in contract with his creative potentialities.

Rolland and Freud were the favoured sons of their mothers, and as Freud (1900, p. 398n) wrote, 'I have found that people who know that they are preferred or favoured by their mother give evidence in their lives of a peculiar self-reliance and an unshakeable optimism which often seem like heroic attributes and bring actual success to their possessors'.

Similarly, both had suffered the early loss of a sibling. Did this enhance the survivors with a sense of 'specialness', or feelings of 'survivor guilt' with a need to atone through humanitarian contributions (as Pollock, 1972, has described) ?

The relationships with siblings bring to the fore a curious and still poorly explained event. In January 1936, Freud wrote Arnold Zweig that he had been

> much besought to write something for Romain Rolland's 70th birthday and have finally agreed. I managed to write a short analysis of a 'feeling of alienation' which overcame me on the Acropolis in Athens in 1904, something very intimate with scarcely any connection with RR [sic] (apart from the fact that he is exactly the same age as my brother [Alexander] with whom I was in Athens at the time). But combine the two proverbs about the rogue who gives more and the beautiful girl who will not give more than they have and you will see my situation (E. Freud, 1970, p. 119).

Schur (1972) described the last sentence as 'tantalizingly unclear'.

> The 'rascal' is obviously engaged in some kind of deception. The 'beautiful girl' leaves one in doubt. Did she really give everything she had? What did Freud want to convey to Zweig? Did he mean to say only that this paper was all he could produce at that moment, or were the play on words and the few hints he gave in the letter a conscious or unconscious indication that he was not divulging all he knew about the incident on the Acropolis and was thus apparently giving away more in the paper than he actually was (p. 460).

Schur connects the letter to Freud's preoccupation during the trip '"later described in a letter to Jung in 1909. The letter to Zweig 'begins to resemble free associations' Schur notes. 'Freud started a word, crossed it out, and continued with the remark that this analysis was "something quite intimate".' That Rolland was the same age as Alexander 'meant that both were "younger brothers", as were Jung (born in 1875), Fliess (who died at 70), and of course Freud's younger brother Julius. Moreover, Freud was getting closer to his 80th birthday, and his apprehension about this very "critical term" was to show up soon' (Schur, 1972, p. 460).

The paper itself (Freud, 1936) is subtitled: 'An Open Letter to Romain Rolland on the Occasion of His Seventieth Birthday.' It opens with Freud stating that he had been urged to make some contribution to Rolland's 70th birthday, and has made

> long efforts to find something that might in any way be worthy of you and might give expression to my admiration for your love of the truth, for your courage in your beliefs and for your affection and good will towards humanity; or, again, something that might bear witness to my gratitude to you as a writer who has afforded me so many moments of exaltation and pleasure. But it was in vain. I am ten years older than you and my powers of production are at an end. All that I can find to offer you is the gift of an im ed creature, who has 'seen better days' (p. 239).

In itself the article adds no information to our knowledge of the Freud-Rolland relationship. However, in its analysis of the strange feeling of unreality which Freud experienced when he and Alexander stood on the Acropolis, the essay is a scientific attempt to plumb an experience which some individuals might describe as mystical. Certainly, Freud was well aware of this aspect of Rolland's *Weltanschauung*.

The paper also brings to mind through the frequent use of French expressions (and an anecdote taken from French history) Freud's lifelong pleasure and interest in France and French culture. It is well known that he possessed a wide-ranging knowledge of French history and his taste for its culture ranged from its novelists and poets to his admiration of Yvette Guilbert, the cabaret singer. The last book he read was Balzac's *La Peau de Chagrin* (The Fatal Skin), which he felt appropriate to his terminal condition. The mirror image of this special interest and knowledge of France was Rolland's adoption of German culture as his second patrimony. His lifelong reverence for Goethe, his studies of Beethoven (begun in 1903 and finally completed in his last years), his friendships with S. Zweig and Hesse, and finally, his magnum opus, *Jean Christophe,* which among other things is a paean of praise for the brotherhood of the German Jean Christophe and his French friend Olivier, all attest to Rolland's attachment to the people across the Rhine. Some of this mutual esteem of the two men is handsomely embodied in Freud's greetings to Rolland on his 60th birthday, 29 January 1926:

> Unforgettable man, to have soared to such heights of humanity through so much hardship and suffering!
> I revered you as an artist and apostle of love for mankind many years before I saw you. I myself have always advocated the love for mankind not out of sentimentality or idealism but for sober, economic

reasons: because in the face of our instinctual drives and the world as it is I was compelled to consider this love as indispensable for the preservation of the human species, as say, technology. When I finally came to know you personally I was surprised to find that you hold strength and energy in such high esteem, and that you yourself embody so much will power.

May the next decade bring you nothing but fulfillment (E. Freud, 1960, p. 364).

This message was included in the volume of greetings to Rolland edited by Gorki, Duhamel & Stefan Zweig (1926). Among the 131 contributors, intellectuals and artists whom Rolland counted among his friends, were Einstein, August Forel, Gandhi, Hermann Hesse, T. G. Masaryk, Nansen, Schnitzler, Schweitzer, Tagore, Unamuno, H. G. Wells, Zangwell and others.

II

Among the profound differences between Freud and Rolland, their respective understanding of the 'oceanic experience' is outstanding.

Soon after its publication, Freud sent a copy of 'The Future of an Illusion' (Freud, 1927) to Rolland. In December 1927 Rolland wrote back, thanking him for his 'lucid and courageous little book'. He lauded Freud's calm good sense and moderation and acknowledged his agreement with his analysis of religions, but observed that he would have liked to have seen an analysis of spontaneous religious feelings, or 'more precisely of the religious sensation, which is quite different from religion, properly speaking and much more lasting'. The letter enters with some detail into Rolland's concept and personal experience of the 'oceanic feeling', and mentions that he is writing a book on two Eastern thinkers for whom this oceanic feeling was a powerful force. The letter closes with regrets about the 'everlasting confusion of words' (Rolland, 1967).

Freud did not answer Rolland until almost a year and a half later (14 July 1929) when he wrote that the description of the oceanic experience 'has left me no peace'. In a new work ('Civilization and its Discontents'; Freud, 1930) which he is completing, he is using Rolland's concept as a starting point, and is trying to interpret it from a psychoanalytic point of view. The essay will also deal with happiness, civilization, and the sense of guilt. He adds that while he does not mention Rolland by name, he nevertheless drops a hint that points towards him, and is beset with doubt whether he is justified in using Rolland's private remark for publication. Perhaps it might even be contrary to Rollands' wishes. Would Rolland permit him to use his idea of the oceanic feeling; if he has slightest objections, he could easily use a different introduction (E. Freud, 1960, p. 388).

Only three days later Rolland replied that Freud should feel free to bring his ideas before the public. However, after a year and a half, he is no longer very sure of just what he had written to Freud in 1927. He recalls that he had already undertaken the three books on the Hindu prophets and since then has found hundreds of examples of the oceanic feeling, not only among contemporary Asians, but in the codification of the emotions in treatises on Yoga. He has also found that East and West are not so far apart for he has discovered similar experiences among European mystics, especially during the Alexandrian epoch, the fourteenth century, and the sixteenth and seventeenth centuries in France (Rolland, 1977).

Six days later, writing from Berchtesgaden, Freud writes thanking Rolland for his permission but he adds that he cannot accept it until Rolland rereads his own letter of 1927, which he is returning to him, but remarks: 'I possess so few letters from you that I do not like the idea of renouncing the return of this, your first one. I am not normally a hunter of relics, so please forgive this weakness.' He is pleased to learn that Rolland's book on the Indian philosophers will appear before his 'small effort', 'Civilization and its Discontents', which he doubts will be in print before February or March.

> But please don't expect any evaluation of the 'oceanic' feeling; I am experimenting only with an analytical version of it; I am clearing it out of the way, so to speak.
> How remote from the other worlds in which you move! To me mysticism in just as closed a book as music. I cannot imagine reading all the literature which, according to your letter, you have studied. And yet, it is easier for you than for us to read the human soul! (E. Freud, 1960, p. 389).

On the 24th of July, 1929, Rolland returned the earlier letter to Freud, noting that it accurately conveys his current views. He finds it difficult to believe that the mystical and music are alien to Freud for 'nothing human is foreign to you'. Rather, he believes that Freud mistrusts these areas in order to maintain the integrity of his 'critical reason'. He himself has no difficulty because 'since birth' he has been capable of both critical and intuitive approaches—he can 'see, believe and doubt' (Rolland, 1977).

Freud received the three books (I. *La Vie de Ramakrishna* and II and III, *La Vie de Vivekananda et l'évangile universal* ; published in English in one volume: (Rolland, 1930) and wrote Rolland in January 1930, thanking him for them. Contrary to his calculation, his '"discontented" little book' came out several weeks earlier than Rolland's. With Rolland's guidance, he intends to try to 'penetrate into the Indian jungle in which until now an uncertain blending of Hellenic love of proportion, Jewish sobriety and Philistine timidity have kept me away'. He feels he should have gone into all this earlier, 'but it isn't easy to pass beyond the limits of one's nature.' (Actually, Freud's avowed ignorance of Oriental philosophy is belied by his evident knowledge of the Upanishads in his discussion of the relationship of this philosophy and that of Plato.) The beginning of one of the volumes was especially interesting to Freud, for it is there that Rolland deals with extreme rationalists—such as Freud (E. Freud, 1960, pp. 342–393).

As with many of Rolland's philosophic ideas, his conception of the oceanic feeling is difficult to delineate with precision; indeed, his ideas about religion are elusive and often contradictory (Werman, 1971). His writings teem with both assertive statements and fleeting allusions. It is clear that in his adolescence he already rejected all forms of organized religion. His criticism of the formally religious 'who shut themselves in their chapel and not only refuse to come out (as they have a right to do) but would deny to all those outside . . . the right to live, if they could . . . is balanced by his negative views of the 'super-rational' who combat religion. He distinguishes 'religious consciousness' from the 'profession of religion':

> It is the quality of thought and not its object which determines its source and allows us to decide whether or not it emanates from religion. . . . If it turns fearlessly towards the search for truth at all costs with singleminded sincerity prepared for any sacrifice, I should call it (the quality of thought) religious; for it presupposes faith in an end to human effort higher than the life of the individual, at times higher than the life of existing society, and even higher than the life of humanity as a whole. Scepticism itself when it proceeds from vigorous natures true to the core, when it is an expression of strength and not of weakness, joins in the march of the Grand Army of the religious soul. Religion is never accomplished. It is a ceaseless action and the will to strive—the ourpouring of a spring, never a stagnant pond' (Rolland, 1930, pp. xviii-xix).

It is in this sense, in the *quality of feeling*, that Rolland sees himself as religious. Elsewhere he has described mystical revelations he had, as well as 'oceanic feelings'. These experiences entailed sensations of ecstasy and fusion with the world or the universe. Rolland offers as examples the ecstasy of St Theresa of Avila, and the reports of such experiences which E. D. Starbuck (1905) collected; these were later cited by William James (1904). Like Freud, James avowed that his 'own constitution shut (him) out from their enjoyment almost entirely', so he could speak of them only at second hand (p. 370). Starbuck's subjects generally described feelings of infinity and sublimity; sometimes the feelings are evoked by some actual experience: a burial service, a solar eclipse, the power of the ocean, etc. One person declared, 'I lost myself in the recognition of freedom, power and love'. Another noted that she felt herself to be 'part of something bigger than I that is controlling' (Starbuck, 1905, pp. 325–6).

Of special interest is an example of mysticism which James extracted from a book of memories of Rolland's friend, Malwida von Meysenbug, published in 1900. She describes being alone at the seashore where she felt impelled to kneel down 'before the illimitable ocean, symbol of the infinite'. She had been unable to pray, owing to her 'materialistic belief', and now discovered that she could; she went from feelings of solitariness to a 'consciousness of unity with all that is. . . . I felt myself at one with all the great who had ever lived . . . (James, 1904, p. 386).

It is of great interest that this woman who played such an influential role in Rolland's early adult life, should also have experienced the same oceanic feelings which many years later Rolland was to describe to Freud. An examination of his published letters to von Meysenbug, covering the period 1890 to 1903, unfortunately reveals no discussion of the issue. At various times he engages in explanations of his religious position, which include both his belief in God and 'free-thinking'. In December 1895 he writes that 'Art is hateful to me when it is not the instrument of thought; thought is odious to me when it does not work for God. Thus I am entirely at the service of God' (Rolland, 1948, p. 157). Yet only one month later he is proclaiming that 'For me the essence of art is Passion and Action'. Far from there being evidence of her influence on Rolland, the letters show him constantly lecturing her, expatiating on his artistic, musical, religious and political opinions. He does mention reading her memoirs, and so he must have at least been aware of her experiences at the seashore.

In *Prophets of the New India,* Rolland (1930) quotes Ramakrishna who likens the spirit to an ocean, 'boundless, dazzling with great luminous waves' by which he is 'engulfed—swallowed up'. It is an ocean of 'ineffable joy', it is 'the divine Mother' [of the Hindu religion]. Emerging from a trance, Ramakrishna was heard to say 'Mother! . . . Mother!'. The symbolism of water, linking fecundity, mother, sister, the breast, etc. has been studied by Niederland (1956–19577) and further discussion of it would lead us away from the subject. What is significant is that Rolland defends the oceanic experience against 'almost all psychologists [who] are possessed with the theory of Regression'. His understanding of regression is taken from R.A. Ribot the French psychologist (1839–1916) whom he quotes: 'The psychological functions most rapidly attacked by disease were the most recently constituted ones, the last in point of time in the development of the individual (ontogenesis), and then reproduced on a general scale in the evolution of the species (phylogenesis).' (Rolland, 1930, pp. 634–635). Ribot was well-versed in neuroanatomy and his conception of regression was essentially as a somatic process, rather than a psychological one. An exception among psychologists, according to Rolland, is Baudouin, who protested the indiscriminate application of regression to all phenomena of psychological recoil. Rolland can only agree with the concept 'within the bounds of . . . functional disorganization . . . but [it] has been erroneously extended to the whole realm of the mind, whether abnormal or normal'. Janet, Freud and their followers are among those who applied the concept of regression 'to all the nervous affections and from them to all the activities of the mind . . . Freud with his customary energy, asserts that reverie and all that emerges from it, is nothing but the debris of the first stage of evolution.' Rolland cannot accept this, and announces that withdrawal into oneself to dream, to imagine, to reason—describing in short, 'regression in the service of the ego'—is indispensable and not pathological: Some day, he believes, psychologists will carry forward James's attempts to clarify mysticism and metaphysics.

In Freud's letter to Rolland of 18 January 1930, previously quoted in part, he observed that he and Rolland

> seem to diverge rather far in the role we assign to intuition. Your mystics (Ramakrishna and Vivekananda) rely on it to teach them how to solve the riddle of the universe; we believe that it cannot reveal to us anything but primitive, instinctual impulses and attitudes—highly

valuable for an embryology of the soul when correctly interpreted, but worthless for orientation in the alien, external world.

Poignantly, he closes by saying:

Should our paths cross once more in life, it would be pleasant to discuss all this. From a distance a cordial salutation is better than polemics. Just one more thing: I am not an out-and-out skeptic. Of one thing I am absolutely positive: there are certain things we cannot know now (E. Freud, 1960, pp. 392–393).

'Civilization and its Discontents' appeared a few weeks before Rolland's books on the Indian prophets and he wished Freud had been able to read them first, for he might have found in them some 'useful indications'. In his work Freud deals directly with Rolland's idea of oceanic feelings in the first pages. He describes Rolland as one of the 'few men from whom their contemporaries do not withhold their admiration' although their attributes and accomplishments may not be generally appreciated. He relates that Rolland responded to 'The Future of an Illusion' by agreeing with his view of religion, but went on to describe a 'peculiar feeling' which is always with him, and which he would like to call a 'sensation of "eternity", a feeling as of something limitless, unbounded—as it were, "oceanic"'. For Rolland, it is a subjective fact, not an article of faith, and while he differentiated it from the religion of the Church, he believed it to be the source of the religious energy which is seized upon by the Church.

Freud expresses some difficulty with the views expressed by the friend he honoured so much, for he has never discovered this oceanic feeling in himself. Attempting to analyse the feeling, he identifies it with an indissoluble bond—with the external world as a whole, it is an intellectual perception with an accompanying feeling tone, but from his own experience he cannot convince himself of its primary nature. He does not challenge its occurrence in others but seeks only to interpret it, and to question 'whether it ought to be regarded as the fons et origo of the whole need for religion'.

In love and in various pathological states, he continues, the ego's boundaries with the external world may be lost. In the course of the development of the body ego and its individuation from the mother's breast, the infant tends to locate all unpleasurable experiences in the external world, as against a 'pure pleasure-ego' that resides within.

Consequently, the adult's ego-feeling is merely a residue of an earlier 'all-embracing feeling which corresponded to a more intimate bond between the ego and the world about it'. In certain individuals, more than in others, this 'primary ego-feeling' would have persisted, to a larger extent, alongside of more mature ego feelings. 'In that case, the ideational contents appropriate to it would be precisely those of limitlessness and of a bond with the universe—the same ideas with which my friend elucidated the "oceanic" feeling.' The oceanic feeling is probably not the source of religious needs, which Freud believes arise from the child's helpless dependence on the father's protection. This feeling can later on, he assumes, become connected with religion, perhaps as a consolatory effort. He acknowledges the difficulty in dealing with these almost intangible quantities, and mentions another friend, who practises Yoga, body control, peculiar methods of breathing, etc., and who sees these techniques as providing a physiological basis for mysticism. Though Freud himself believes these occurences are connected with obscure modifications of mental life, such as trances and ecstasies, he concludes with a quotation from Schiller: 'Let him rejoice who breathes up here in the roseate light.'

On the 3rd of May 1931, on the occasion of Freud's 75th birthday, Rolland (1977) wrote

him an extremely warm letter of good wishes, hoping he will long be able to continue his research for the truth 'without desire and without fear!' And he takes note of Freud's affectionate and ironic dedication to him in the copy of 'Civilization and its Discontents' which he received: 'From the Terrestrial Animal [Landthier] to his Oceanic friend'. Since this opposition occurs within individuals as well as between them, Rolland considers himself also a 'Landthier', from the centre of Old France—the part best defended from the 'murmurs of the sea!'. He characterizes himself as an 'Old Frenchman', without illusions and none the worse for it, and begs Freud's indulgence to differentiate certain aspects of himself: 'First—what I feel ; second, what I am ; and third, what I desire'. What he feels is the 'oceanic'. The knowing is the 'que saisje?' ('what do I know?') of Montaigne; and his desires are, for himself, nothing, only for others—for himself he wishes merely rest and total effacement, for he has had enough pain in his life. Therefore his oceanic feelings are completely disinterested. Curiously, the oceanic feelings are a 'psychological trait' that is stamped on the forehead of many European 'land-animals' who mostly know nothing of the East; he has received whole files of letters from people describing such feelings in themselves; this could be significant, he thinks, in terms of its possible effects on history.

Binswanger (1957) recalls a conversation in 1927, when he asked Freud why certain obsessional patients fail 'to take the last decisive step of psychoanalytic insight, which the physician expects of them, and instead, persist in their misery in defiance of all efforts and technical progress made so far'. He suggests to Freud that the phenomenon might be due to a 'deficiency of spirit . . . an inability on the part of the patient to raise himself to the level of "spiritual communication" with the analyst. Only on the basis of such communication', continued Binswanger, 'could they gain insight into the "unconscious instinctual drive" in question and be enabled to take the last decisive step toward self-mastery.'

> I could hardly believe my ears when I heard him [Freud] say, 'Yes, spirit is everything.' I presumed that by spirit Freud meant something like intelligence. But then he continued: 'Mankind has always known that it possesses spirit; I had to show that there are also instincts. But men are always unsatisfied, they cannot wait, they always want something whole and ready-made; *but one has to begin somewhere and only very slowly move forward.*'

Encouraged by this 'admission', Binswanger went on to suggest that perhaps 'something like a basic religious category' exists that is not derived from something else; by 'religious' he meant the 'I–thou' relationship. At that point Freud responded sharply, stating that 'religion orginates in the helplessness and anxiety of childhood and early manhood; it cannot be otherwise', and showed Binswanger the manuscript of 'The Future of an Illusion' which he had recently completed.

Binswanger poses what for him is the 'most authentic problem' in interpreting Freud's work: 'Does his work signify only a "slowly progressing" beginning, that is, a torso that may legitimately be thought of as part of the "whole"? Or is his "great idea" about the instinctual nature of mankind of sufficient compass to stand in no need of any "enlarging"?'.

Believing in the former, Binswanger wonders if the 'enlarging' is to be undertaken with Freud himself, partly with him, or attempted entirely without him. On the strength of the conversation just quoted, he felt that perhaps Freud does not totally identify his instinctual theories with the whole of mankind's spiritual or intellectual existence; and yet he was unable to find anywhere in Freud's writings any mention of 'mind' or 'spirit' described as arising independently of the instinctual drives; and this is most markedly absent where Freud derives the ethical from narcissism.

Thus Freud's remark that man has always known that he possessed spirit, remained for Binswanger a 'singular admission'. But he then quotes Freud's letter to Rolland (on the occasion of the latter's 60th birthday): 'Unforgettable man, to have soared to such heights of humanity through so much hardship and suffering'. For Binswanger, this one sentence expresses 'a deep awareness of man's spirit . . . For, if soaring to such "heights of humanity" through hardship and suffering does not refer to spirit, to man's basic, autonomous spirit then I should like to know what else spirit may mean.' But in a footnote Binwanger appears less certain, and recognizes the role of repression and sublimation of the instinctual drives. However, he sees in Freud's 'admiration' of the spiritual, a spiritual act. *The problem of spirit is, in general, not a problem of origin or genesis, but of content.* It is the "content" that the repressed assumes in its return that decides a man's worth and the degree to which we admire him'.

It is precisely this admiration that Freud had for Rolland's 'spirit' that appears to have formed the basis of his feelings for him. Although Freud never conceded one iota of his belief in psychic determinism, or of his belief in a material world, he was nevertheless able to see beyond an individuals' philosophy to his role as a person in the real world; thus, he was fully able to appreciate courage, integrity, intellectual rigorousness, creativity and struggle against the vicissitudes of self and society.

In his 'Thoughts on War and Death' Freud (1915) described two types of social behaviour: 'cultural hypocrisy', or conformism, and an 'organized cultural adaptation', that is, a firmly grounded ego organization that does not shatter under stress. In discussing these forms of adaptation, Mitscherlich (1963) cites Rolland as one who possessed this aequanimitas to a high degree, the 'imperturbability of a highly sensitive mind, and that is why his 1914–1919 diaries (Au-dessus de la Mêlée) are a document of such great importance. Perhaps no one else saw with such inexorable clarity the extent of the 1914 collapse of the sense of reality that extended into the highest ranks of the intellectual aristocracy of the belligerent nations on both sides' (p. 20).

It was, clearly, Rolland's character to which Freud had so warmly responded. Freud had more than once pondered this question of character.

In a frank letter to Putnam, he wrote, in 1915:

> When I ask myself why I have always aspired to behave honourably, to spare others and to be kind wherever possible, and why I didn't cease doing so when I realized that in this way one comes to harm and becomes an anvil because other people are brutal and unreliable, then indeed I have no answer. . . . So one could cite just my case as a proof of your assertion that such an urge to the ideal forms a considerable part of our inheritance.

He suspects that if one could study the sublimation of instincts as thoroughly as repression, it might render Putnam's humanitarian assumption' unnecessary. But he knows nothing about this and finds it quite incomprehensible that he, as well as his six adult children are 'thoroughly decent human beings' (E. Freud, 1960, pp. 308–309).

I believe it is a similar respect for Freud that animated Rolland's intense admiration for him. Writing to Marie Bonaparte in 1936, he speaks of the pleasure and the honour it would give him to nominate Freud for the Nobel Prize, but he realizes that, unlike Bergson, Freud does not reassure people, and so his chances of being awarded the prize are negligible. There can be no doubt that despite his deep criticisms of psychoanalytic theory, he perceived his 'great friend' as a towering intellectual figure and as a man of courage and honour. His feelings were perhaps most concisely stated in his birthday greetings to Freud in 1926: 'May the light of your mind for many long years pierce the night of life!' (Rolland, 1977).

REFERENCES

ABRAHAM, H.C. & FREUD, E.L. (Eds.) (1965). *A Psychoanalytic Dialogue: The Letters of Sigmund Freud and Karl Abraham, 1907–1926.* New York: Basic Books.

ALLDAY, E. (1972). *Stefan Zweig, A Critical Biography.* Chicago: O'Hara.

BINSWANGER, L. (1957). Freud and the Magna Charta of clinical psychiatry. In *Being in the World: Selected Papers.* New York: Harper Torchbooks, 1963.

DOISY, M. (1945). *Romain Rolland, 1866–1944.* Brussels: Ed. Botie.

DUMONT, R. (1967). *Stefan Zweig et la France.* Paris: Didier.

FREUD, E.L. (Ed.) (1960). *Letters of Sigmund Freud.* New York: Basic Books.

———— (Ed.) (1970). *The Letters of Sigmund Freud and Arnold Zweig.* New York Harcourt, Brace, World.

FREUD, S. (1900). The interpretation of dreams. *Standard Edition 5.*

———— (1914). Letter to Frederik von Eeden. *Standard Edition* 14.

———— (1915). Thoughts for the times on war and death. *Standard Edition* 14.

———— (1916a). Introductory lectures on psychoanalysis: Part II. *Standard Edition* 15.

———— (1916b). On transience *Standard Edition* 14.

———— (1920). Beyond the pleasure principle *Standard Edition* 18.

———— (1921). Group psychology and the analysis of the ego. *Standard Edition* 18.

———— (1927). The future of an illusion. *Standard Edition* 21.

———— (1930). Civilization and its discontents. *Standard Edition* 21

———— (1933). Why war. *Standard Edition* 22.

————(1936). A disturbance of memory on the Acropolis. *Standard Edition* 22.

GORKI, M., DUHAMEL, G. & ZWIEG, S. (Eds.) (1926). Liber Amicorum. R.R. Zurich: Roniger.

JAMES, W. (1904). *The Varieties of Religious Experience.* London: Longmans, Green, 1952.

JONES, E. (1955). *The Life and Work of Sigmund Freud Vol. 2.* New York: Basic Books.

JOUVE, P.J. (1920). *Romain Rolland Vivant 1914–1919.* Paris: Libr. Ollendorf.

MARCH, H. (1971). *Romain Rolland.* New York: Twayne.

MITSCHERLICH, A. (1963). *Society Without the Father.* New York: Harcourt, Brace, World, 1969.

NEDELJKOVIC, D.D. *1970 Romain Rolland et Stefan Zweig.* Paris: Klincksieck.

NIEDERLAND, W. (1956-1957). River symbolism. *Psychoanal. Q.* 25:469–504; 26:50–75.

POLLOCK, G. (1972). Betha Pappenheim's pathological mourning: possible effects of childhood sibling loss. *J. Am. Psychoanal. Assoc.* 20:476–493.

PRATER, D.A. (1972). *European of Yesterday: A Biography of Stefan Zweig.* London: Oxford Univ. Press.

ROLLAND, R. (1905–1912). *Jean Christophe.* Paris: Ed. Albin Michel, 1950.

———— (1920). *Liluli.* New York: Boni & Liveright.

———— (1930). *Prophets of the New India.* New York: Boni.

———— (1948). *Choix de Lettres Malwida von Meysenbug.* Paris: Ed. Albin Michel.

———— (1951). *Richard Strauss et Romain Rolland, Correspondance et Fragments de Journal.* Paris: Ed. Albin Michel.

———— (1953). *L'Esprit Libre. [including Les Precurseurs and Au-dessus de la Mle].* Paris: Ed. Albin Michel.

———— (1959) *Le Voyage Interieur.* Paris: Ed. Albin Michel.

———— (1967). *Un Beau Visage tous Sens: Choix de Lettres de Romain Rolland 1886-1944.* Paris: Ed. Albin Michel.

———— (1977). Unpublished letters to and from Rolland, and excerpts from his personal diary; courtesy of Mme Marie Romain Rolland, Paris.

ROLLAND, R., MAUROIS, A. & HERRIOT, E. (Eds.) (1953). *French Thought in the Eighteenth Century.* London: Cassel.

SCHUR, M. (1972). *Freud: Living and Dying.* New York: Int. Univ. Press.

STARBUCK, E.D. (1905). *The Psychology of Religion.* New York: Scribner's.

WERMAN, D. (1971). Letter: Rolland et Freud French Rev. (Chapel Hill) 45:416–417.

ZWEIG, S. (1921). *Romain Rolland: The Man and His Work.* New York: Seltzer.

———— (1943). *The World of Yesterday: An Autobiography.*

CHAPTER 9

Freud, Yvette Guilbert, and the Psychology of Performance: A Biographical Note

[Werman, D.S. (1998). *Psychoanalytic Review,* 85:399–412.]

The friendship of Freud and Yvette Guilbert, the famous French "diseuse," well-known today by Toulouse-Lautrec's pictures of her, was based manifestly on mutual admiration, affection, and respect, if not on reciprocal understanding. Guilbert had little or no knowledge of Freud's research into unconscious processes, and Freud seemed not to have understood or empathized with Yvette.

Their superficial albeit congenial friendship was challenged when Yvette asked Freud to explain how she was able to enter into the characters she portrayed on the stage. Freud provided an answer based on the influence of early unconscious memories. Yvette roundly rejected this view, and defended the intense effort of the performer.

It is the opinion of the author that Freud and Yvette had each seized one end of the performer's activity: the regressive, on one hand, and the conscious, creative ego work on the other. While advancing the concept of "regression in the service of the ego," psychoanalysts have paid little attention to the actual work of the ego.

On a wall in Freud's study, at Bergasse 19, were the photographs of three women: The first two were of Lou Andréas-Salomé and Marie Bonaparte, well-known to psychoanalysts as among Freud's cherished friends and colleagues. The third photograph was inscribed "Au savant Sigmund Freud le salut d'une artiste," and was signed Yvette Guilbert, the French *diseuse* (Engelman, 1976).[1]

Freud was given this photograph in 1926 by the world-famous entertainer whose name was known throughout Europe and in major cities on

---

This paper was presented at the Mid-Winter Meeting of the American Psychoanalytic Association, in New York, December 17, 1995 in a slightly shorter version.

[1]A diseuse is, literally, a speaker. Actually, a diseuse is a women who usually sings and recites, generally popular songs of the past and present, usually in a cabaret or music hall. Guilbert principally appeared in the café-concert (or caf'-conc'). Such a singer was often called a divette.

the east coast of the United States. Today, although her name is less familiar, she is immediately recognized in the scores of pictures of her painted and drawn by prominent artists—principally Toulouse-Lautrec, but also Forain, Degas, Steinlen, and many others. Typically, she is portrayed as a tall, gawky woman, with henna-red hair, a turned-up nose, and a large mouth. She usually wears a green gown with a deep decolleté, and black gloves that reach above her elbows.

Beyond being simply a biographical footnote, Freud's relationship with Yvette (as she was called) presents two aspects that are of interest. The first is that it casts some light on a facet of Freud's personality that is frequently lost in the welter of idolatrous or demonizing stereotypes. The second aspect relates to the psychodynamics of the performer, and, more broadly, may have some implications for the mysterious process of creativity.

It has been said that Freud first heard Yvette sing in 1889, when he spent a few days in Paris, attending, and growing bored, at a Congress on hypnotism.[2] He had spent several weeks in Nancy and Strasbourg observing Hippolyte Bernheim and A. A. Liébault practice hypnotism. Freud had arranged for one of his patients to undergo hypnosis by Bernheim. Like Freud, Bernheim was also unsuccessful in hypnotizing this patient. Later, along with Bernheim and Liébault, Freud went on to Paris to attend the Congress. Jones notes that Madame Charcot, whose acquaintance Freud had made during his stay in Paris in 1885, had advised him to "attend one of Yvette's little concerts." In any event, after a few days Freud returned to Vienna.

The first authenticated, personal encounter of Freud and Yvette took place in Vienna, in 1926, as a consequence of a series of somewhat convoluted coincidences. In 1892, in New York City, two brothers, Carl and Theodor Rosenfeld, formerly of Berlin, theatrical producers and managers of performers, were attempting to organize an American tour for the great Italian actress Eleanora Duse. Their efforts seemed to take them from one difficulty to another, both with theater managers on one hand,

---

[2]How and where Freud could have heard Yvette sing at that time is unclear. Until the summer of 1889 she had been playing small parts in the Variétés theatre. She toured with this group until the end of August and didn't begin to sing publicly until November 1889, at the Eldorado café-concert—except for a few disastrous days in the Casino de Lyon, in Lyon. What is certain is that in later years when she toured in Vienna, Freud regularly attended her concerts, sometimes with Ernest Jones, with whom he shared his admiration for Yvette.

and with the very shy and sensitive Duse on the other. In desperation they called upon Theodor's brother-in-law, Max Shiller, a biochemist, who was working in Berlin. Biochemistry was a career which he had pursued chiefly in response to his father's urging. After receiving his doctorate he began to work in Berlin, where the Shiller family had moved from Romania as a result of revocation of citizenship to Jews.

Arriving in New York, Max was able to successfully organize Duse's tour, and soon began to have a love affair with her. Yvette herself had earlier come to New York in December 1895, when she performed at Oscar Hammerstein's Olympia Theatre. She returned to New York the following year, and in the winter of 1896 she met Max and they soon became lovers. He ultimately became her husband, manager, nurse, adviser, and buffer against all difficulties, and he remained with her until she died in Aixen-Provence, in 1944, during the Nazi occupation of France. At the war's end Max had her remains exhumed and brought to Paris, where she was buried in the Père Lachaise cemetery. He joined her there one year later.

Early in the century, Theodor Rosenfeld and his wife, Rose, (Max's sister), with their child Eva, left New York and moved back to Berlin where he continued to work in the theater. Eva, born in 1892, had many occasions over the ensuing years to see her uncle Max and his famous wife, Yvette Guilbert. Since Max was very attached to his family, the Shillers frequently visited Berlin, where Yvette often performed to enthusiastic audiences. When Eva Rosenfeld grew up she became a psychologist and eventually moved to Vienna to become a psychoanalyst and underwent analysis with Freud. It was in the course of one of Yvette's visits to Vienna that Dr. Rosenfeld introduced Sigmund and Martha Freud to the Shillers. As mentioned earlier, following this encounter, Freud attended Yvette's concerts in Vienna whenever possible. She sent him copies of books she had written, the photograph I described earlier, and another, dated May 6, 1939, inscribed: "De tout mon coeur au grand Freud" ("with all my heart, to the great Freud"). (E. Freud et al., p. 315). Jones noted that Yvette was one of the five people who regularly addressed Freud by his surname, without any title.

On several occasions Freud mentioned Yvette in letters or conversation, always with warmth and acknowledgment as a "friend." From the "rain" of congratulations he received from allover the world on his seventieth birthday, he said that there were five that most pleased him: from

Georg Brandes, Einstein, Romain Rolland, the Hebrew University of Jerusalem, and Yvette Guilbert.

Verbal communication between Freud and the Shillers grew more difficult as his cancer progressed. At one meeting he commented to Max: "Meine Prothese spricht nicht französisch" (Jones, vol. III, p. 103) ("My prosthesis doesn't speak French"); indeed, he was already encountering difficulties in making himself clearly understood even in German.

Freud has variously been described as the one person who more than any other, opened the floodgates to the looser sexual behavior that is presumed to have developed, chiefly, as a result of the *Three Essays on Sexuality,* and his concept of the sexual drive. In apparent contradiction to this portrayal is that of Freud the rigid, stern, patriarch who ruled his family and colleagues with an iron hand. Both views are, at the least, simple caricatures. In fact, from his letters and the reports of those who knew him well (and the list is long) he was a man of warmth, who loved jokes, the theater, and enjoyed the risque songs that Yvette sang. He was also much more enthusiastic about music and the theater than he himself—or others—credited him with being. During his first visit to Paris, in 1885, his letters to Martha Bernays, then his fiancée, recounted his pleasure at the remarkable high comedy of the two Coquelin brothers—great actors of the time. He gives Martha a description of Sarah Bernhardt who was "alive and bewitching": "As for her caressing and pleading (in *Theodora,* a play by Victorien Sardou) and embracing, the postures she assumes, the way she wraps herself around a man, the way she acts with every limb, every joint—it's incredible" (Jones, pp. 179–1980). After his initial bemusement, if not alienation, from Paris, he finally concluded that it was a "magic city."

In his personal life, Freud was probably a devoted and faithful husband and father, but his view of humankind recognized, in theory and in earthy reality, the power and the pleasure of sexual behavior, whether it be in the infant's sucking or the adult's sexual life. Nowhere is there any evidence of smirking or winking about sex, nor is there any castigation of what has been described by some as "immoral behavior." He did not scold his colleagues or his patients for even serious lapses in their conduct, but always sought to help them understand it and its possible consequences. If psychoanalysis has one goal above all others, he never tired of pointing out, it is surely that of self-understanding, not moralizing. Freud scarcely deviated from that position.

The second matter, which I mentioned earlier, deals with the process of how an actor successfully takes on the personality of a character he or she is portraying on the stage. In 1931, in the process of writing a new book of her memoirs, Yvette wrote Freud, asking for an explanation of why and how she was able to so richly and authentically dramatize the songs and recitations she offered the public.

February 28
My dear Professor

I am going to prepare a new book to follow "my memoirs," which will be titled *Mes lettres d'amour*—what I myself call my letters of love, and which come from those who help in my concert work. I shall put together these numerous letters from the public telling me "their impressions." I would combine my correspondence with some very important *poets interpreted* by me—some Parisian celebrities of my youth. In the preface that I am preparing for my book, I am trying to "explain myself to myself" I am attempting to reveal my system: *effacement of my own personality* in order to take on all those others whom I personify among the characters of my songs—now I ask you, my dear professor, to *tell me,* whether what I say of myself has been experienced by you? What impression have you experienced in listening to me? In the prologue I am sending you do you find that I am *fair with myself?* Or am I *fooled by myself?*

Four lines in German (my husband will translate them) will make me wild with joy.
My hands in yours, faithfully
Yvette Guilbert (E. Freud et al., p. 405)

Freud responded a week later:

Vienna IX, Berggasse 19 8.3.1931
Dear Friend

I wish I might be near when your dear husband translates this letter for you, for because of my bad health I was able to profit so little from your last visit to Vienna.

It is very fine to learn that you want to write once more something about yourself, and if I understand correctly, to revealthe secret of your work and your success and you imagine that your technique consists of setting aside your own personality in order to replace it by the character you wish to present, and you ask that I give my opinion as to whether this process is improbable and whether it is the case with you.

I wish I knew more about the process and I would certainly then tell you all I know, but not knowing much about all that, I beg you to be content with the following observations: I believe that what seems to you to be the psychological mechanism of your art has been often, even generally accepted. But this theory of the displacement of the proper personality and its replacement by the personality to be presented has never entirely satisfied me. It says so little, it does not teach how one can do it, and above all it does not explain why this [end] to which all artists apparently aspire is more successfully reached by one performer than another.

I theorize rather the additional influence of a mechanism quite opposite, which the proper personality has in no way dismissed but which springs from it; for example, from faculties undeveloped, suppressed desires are made use of for the presentation of the imagined character. It is thus that they manifest themselves and give to the character the appearance of real life.

This is less simple than the transparency of your own ego which you put forth.

I would be very curious to know whether you experience anything of this other situation.

In any case it is only one contribution to the solution of the great secret as to why we shiver before *La Soûlarde* and answer "yes" with all our hearts to the question "Dites-moi si je suis belle?'—But one knows so little!

In affectionate remembrance . . .

Freud (Knapp & Chapman, 1964, pp 333–334).

Freud's explanation was not the one Yvette had either wanted or expected.

Almost by return mail she responded with the following protestation; rambling and fuzzy, it was probably written with much emotion.

March 14
My dear great friend

Thanks for your letter! *No,* I do not believe that what *comes out of me* on stage is "the surplus" suppressed and made use of, for if life has made me understand many things I am still ignorantof so much! However, I would know how to imagine without having *"experienced."* I could be the Tsarina, the Tsar, Saint Francis of Assisi if *a text were given me* in order to express them,—I would feel the *physical* side because of my habit of carrying over from my *brain* to my *flesh* everything that I want my public to see.

It is by my eyes that I learn most about the lives of others—to me my eye is the great revealer—I see—I think—I decide—all this *very quickly*—My personal knowledge includes all human beings who have known poverty, love, illness, and all the struggles to overcome these three dangers—I do not possess all the virtues, but neither do I have all the human vices, but my sensitiveness, my painter's eye, help me to divine everything about what I do not know and to reveal everything I do know. I believe, myself, on the contrary, that it is what we have not yet been that makes it possible in art for us to become *that for the public.* Artists are full of electricity . . . For example, the atmosphere indicates to me physically the coming of snow, or rain. A face tells me sympathy for me, or the opposite—I sense very readily at the *approach* of a person (whether he is sincerely my *friend* or simply amiable). My soul (what I believe to be my soul) prompts me always to want *to be beautiful,* it is a form of pride? perhaps! But *I have cultivated it in myself* and I try *always* to tear out the human and habitual nastinesses from *that soul*—I have never had vices—I have had some meannesses and weaknesses from which I have suffered which when I have to interpret them in others, the heroes of my songs, I have felt a sense of pity mixed with a little scorn and *it is of myself that I am thinking* when I express a sadness, for both cause and effect—I am often quite bare on stage, and I offer myself unclothed of all lies—my heart is bare—my soul—my spirit—my temperament—my character—stamped with the sins of the universe, I add those of others to my own, *I adapt myself to them.* But they are not "suppressed"? No! No! they were never mine? I become on stage what I want to become *by a force of the artist's cerebral will,* and if I succeed in

being *Beautiful* (as you say) when I sing: *Dites-moi si je suis belle*—it is because my *brain* knows what I lack
  to be that
  and I create "the illusion."
   Ah, well . . . all this at bottom is such a mystery, is it not, my dear and wise friend . . . ? We are animals, very complicated and at the same time very simple. . . .*The great battle* is the search for *Happiness* in *Truth,* and our follies are only our rages over finding only *Lies!!* For myself it was the torment of *my life*—Truth, Truth, and again Truth, I wanted only Truth and I have found only Truth— and which lasts so short a time.—I was born for the *"Eternities"*— the absolutes—*exaggerations* in everything!
   And human beings are so poorly endowed. . . . I have known how to make my happiness with what they have given me however— To you my friend Freud, all my friendship, loyal and firm.

There is nothing surprising in this reply. In virtually all of her interviews and in her writings, she expresses a grandiosity and a self-centeredness that is often embarrassing to read. Moreover, her superstitions, although only suggested in this letter, colored much of her thinking, except when it concerned contracts, salaries, and the like. What is perhaps not so surprising is her ignorance of Freud's theories, and even of his nonmystical view of human behavior.

We may wonder at what in Freud appealed to Yvette. Perhaps the answer lies in a comment she made just before her return to New York in 1895. "I like brainy men, literary men—men with ideas . . . The cerebral quality is what enchants me . . . I hate fools. I hate Johnnies. Ah! *Quelles bêtes.* They talk and talk, and give birth to no single idea. They disgust me" (Knapp & Chapman, p. 158).

To round out the qualifications in a potential husband, she declared, she wanted a man who "would love me as a child, whose every caprice is catered to—like a sweetheart, like a sister." And, he must be "a person who will be competent and place a profound value on a dollar." Max Shiller filled this description to a T. Freud was important to her, I suggest, not because of what he discovered, but because by 1926 he was important throughout the world.

But the exchange of letters did not end with Yvette's riposte, for Freud seemed to want the last word, and presumably had it. On March 26, 1931, he wrote, this time, addressing his letter to Max.

Dr. Shiller,

It is a very interesting experience for me to be called upon to defend my theories to Madame Yvette and Uncle Max. Despite my impeded speech and hardness of hearing I wish I didn't have to do it in writing.

Actually, I don't intend to yield much beyond the confession that we know so little. Just recently, for instance, Charlie Chaplin was in Vienna; I almost caught sight of him, it was too cold for him and he left in a hurry. He is undoubtedly a great artist— although he always plays one and the same part, the weak, poor, helpless clumsy boy for whom life turns out all right in the end. Now do you think he has to forget his own self in order to play this part? On the contrary, he invariably plays only himself as he was in his grim youth. He cannot get away from these impressions and even today he tries to compensate himself for the humiliation and deprivation of that time. He is of course an especially simple, transparent case.

The theory that the achievements of artists are conditioned internally by their childhood impressions, vicissitudes, repressions and disappointments, has already clarified many things for us, and we therefore think highly of it. I once dared to tackle one of the very greatest of all, Leonardo da Vinci, of whom unfortunately too little is known. I was able at least to point out that *The Virgin and Saint Anne,* which you can see any day in the Louvre, couldn't be understood without some knowledge of Leonardo's peculiar childhood.

Now you may point out that Madame Yvette doesn't play just one part, that she plays with equal mastery all kinds of characters: saints, sinners, prostitutes, the righteous, criminals and ingénues. This is true and testifies to an unusually rich and adaptable psychic life. But I wouldn't hesitate to trace back this whole repertoire to experiences and conflicts of her early youth. It is tempting to continue on this subject, but something holds me back. I know that unwarranted analyses call forth antagonism, and I don't want to do anything that could disturb the warm sympathy that dominates our relationship.

With friendly greetings to you and Madame Yvette.
Your Freud (E. Freud et al., p. 406).

As Knapp and Chapman observed, although Yvette never subscribed to Freud's explanation of her talent, she continued to puzzle over it, and once said that "When I sing the vices of my life, I have the feeling that I am whipping them, that I am freeing the national reputation of the transgressions of a minority" (Knapp & Chapman, pp. 336–37). This statement is sufficiently ambiguous, or confusing, as to lend itself to several interpretations; I suggest that Yvette herself was not altogether clear about what she wanted to say.

What was the nature of the mutual attraction of Freud and Yvette Guilbert? For Yvette, it was always very important to be able to boast about the famous people whom she knew, even if her contact with them had been only fleeting. Her praise of these people was more or less proportional to their esteem of her. She gushes over Edward VII, who found her highly amusing, but she had only disdain for Queen Alexandria, who didn't ever reward her singing with a gift or souvenir.

There were many prominent people whom Yvette pursued or cultivated. The second volume of her *Memoires* (1927) consists, literally, of laudatory statements from a number of mostly literary admirers, and comments solicited from them by Yvette herself (much as she requested the ribbon of the Legion of Honor from Aristide Briand, then Minister of Foreign Affairs, at a formal dinner; the general embarrassment was profound).

She was once asked what she would like to accomplish if she could start her life over again. "If I came back to the world," she answered, "I would like to found a circle of philosophers and inspire them with modesty and wisdom. I would like to found schools of generosity, of goodness, of pity." She desperately wanted to be accepted as a serious, scholarly person, a researcher into old French songs, etc. She tried to start schools of singing and acting, but none of them succeeded.

But what did this relationship with Yvette hold for Freud? At the most immediate level it was clearly his facination with this world famous "star". She was alluring but not threatening, and so pleasurable and appropriate. When he first met Yvette, in 1926, she was 61 and he 70, nevertheless, she still carried the aura of the *caf'-conc'*, and the witty bawdy songs she sang and the poems she recited; these, by the way, were then written by many contemporary poets. Freud, like Jones and many others, relished the "double entendres" and other rules the diseurs and diseuses used to evade the censors.

It is possible that Freud experienced some *frisson* in the relationship, but it seems doubtful; there were several beautiful and brillant women in his life—Lous Andreas-Salomé and Hilda Doolittle, for example. Probably, meetings with Yvette brought back memories of his first visit to Paris in 1885, of Sarah Bernhardt, of the urbane soirees at the Charcot's home, when he revelled in the "magic city."

The exchange of letters between Yvette and Freud encapsulates a long-standing controversy that may be stated briefly: To what extent is the performer (perhaps the creative artist as well) under the dominion of his/her dynamic unconscious, and to what extent is the product of performance essentially the result of a conscious process? This often rehashed argument is especially strident when the artist is still alive and can jeer at the spectacle of the analyst who interprets his work for him, telling him what it "really means"; Nabokov, for example, was particularly sarcastic on this matter.

The controversy is but another version of the old "free will" versus "determinism" conflict. The matter was brought to the fore in the psychoanalytic literature in 1911, when James Jackson Putnam once more set forth his views on the necessity to fuse a particular philosophical outlook with psychoanalysis for the purpose of "ennobling" the patient's mind. Although his address was received politely, at the International Psychoanalytic Congress in 1911, in Weimar, out of respect for Putnam's courageous championing of analysis in the United States, his proposition was rejected (Putnam, 1921; Werman 1977).

A brief résumé of Putnam's talk and a commentary on it by Theodor Reik, appeared in the Zentralblatt in 1912 (Reik, 1912). A lengthier rebuttal to Putnam was contributed by Ferenczi. Of relevance here is his concern with what he characterized as Putnam's "attack on psychic determinism," which Ferenczi declared was the most "decisive advance of psychoanalysis." Our acts are not the "simple expression of a laissez-faire principle," he stated, "because by actively taking into our own hands the steering of our fate we observe not an act of free will, but the result of phylogenetic and autogenetic determinants that protect us from falling into an inactivity to self and species destruction" (Ferenczi, 1912). However, dynamic determinism, Ferenczi was careful to point out, should not be confused with "fatalism." In his ensuing discussion he makes it clear that our acts are not, nor can they be, without determinants from which "we cannot emancipate ourselves." In short, in what appears to be an apparent contradiction,

Ferenczi is stating that there is a conscious will, but it is a consequence of specific determinants.

To resolve the problem of free will and determinism is beyond the scope of this paper, as it has been for philosophers for well over 2,000 years. Perhaps a more fruitful path may be in the direction being traced by chaos theory, being articulated by mathematicians, where a subtle dialectic pulls together determinism

in natural phenomena with a series of seemingly chaotic everchanging "random" phenomena.

At this point, the most parsimonious construction one can make of the Freud-Guilbert exchange is that each was correct from his and her respective point of view. There is much more to the performer's work than powerful but limited concepts such as "regression in the service of the ego.'

To turn from these theoretical issues to how it was actually possible for Yvette Guilbert to successfully embody the characters she dramatized, is a huge leap from theory to reality. One after another she could be a Paris cabdriver, a poor student, a tipsy young woman, an Apache murderer about to be guillotined, a woman giving birth in the street, and many others. Although she believed she created her songs and the characters who inhabited them out of a deliberate willed process of "pure creativity," from her personal history it is likely that there were, often strikingly, identifiable sources for them in her own actual, fantasied, and vicarious experiences.

Are there some intrapsychic configurations that may be characteristic of the performer? It is most unlikely that any relevant character traits are universal; our clinical experience with performers militates against any generalizations. We may however, point to the role of narcissism, of a talent for mimicry and imitation which may emanate from an "as if" personality We may conjecture that some performers may possess a flexibility of character makeup that permits them to slip out of their own selves and into that of another. Undoubtedly, empathy plays a role in the activity of the performer. Clearly, there are many questions here to be explored.

But to explore the unconscious aspects of the performer in no way diminishes the struggle and sweat of the creative act. I believe Yvette was offended by Freud's remarks because she experienced them as devaluing her labor of creation and performance, something that was probably not Freud's intention. He did, however, demonstrate a lapse of empathy toward this woman who was always hungry for acclaim, and the final lines of his last letter to her, suggest that he was aware of a "something" that "held [him] back from continuing the subject."

Fortunately, this deep misunderstanding did not, apparently, affect Freud's relationship with Yvette. On their way to London, after leaving Vienna, the Freud family spent 12 hours in Paris, where Marie Bonaparte gave a reception for them. Among those present at this extraordinary moment both in world history and in the history of the Freud family, were Ernest Jones, who had come over from England to escort the Freuds to London; their son, Ernest; and Yvette Guilbert. "In an unexpurgated mood Yvette kept the dinner guests in gales of laughter by ribald stories, one after another. When later in the evening Dr. Jones asked her to sing *Il était seul* (He was alone), a particularly 'ambiguous' song, as he terms it, she readily obliged, following it with the equally 'ambiguous' *Elle avait le nombril en forme de cinq.* (She had a bellybutton shaped like a 5)" (Knapp & Chapman, p 349). Later, Freud wrote that that day ". . . surrounded by love for 12 hours, we left proud and rich under the protection of Athene" (Jones, vol. Ill, p. 228).

On the face of it, the relationship between Yvette Guilbert and Freud seems to have been idiosyncratic for both. But without further speculation, it seems that these two extraordinarily creative people recognized the genius of the other. Separated by light years of difference, they were able to value something in each other, and in their limited relationship, to experience a warmth, recognition, and affection.

REFERENCES

ENGELMAN, E. (1976). *Bergasse 19: Sigmund Freud's Home and Offices, Vienna, 1938.* New York: Basic Books.

FERENCZI, S. (1912). Philosophy and psycho-analysis. In *Final Contributions to the Problems and Methods of Psycho-analysis.* London: Hogarth Press (1955).

FREUD, E., FREUD, L., & GRUBRICH-SIMITIS, I. (1976). *Sigmund Freud: His Life in Pictures and Words.* New York: Harcourt Brace Jovanovich.

GUILBERT, Y. (1927). *La Chanson de ma Vie (Mes Memoires).* Paris: Bernard Grasset.

JONES, E. (1957). *The Life and Work of Sigmund Freud.* New York: Basic Books.

KNAPP, B. & CHAPMAN, M. (1969). *That Was Yvette.* New York: Holt, Rinehart and Winston.

PUTNAM, J.J. (1911). A plea for the study of philosophic methods in preparation for psychoanalytic work. In Addresses on psycho-analysis. Vienna: *The International Psycho-Analytical Press* (1921).

REIK, T. (1912). James J. Putnam, etc. *Z. f. Psychan.* 3:43–44.

WERMAN, D.S. (1977). James Jackson Putnam: Philosophy and psychoanalysis. *American Imago*, 34:72–85.

CHAPTER 10

Freud's *Civilization and Its Discontents*—A Reappraisal

[Werman, D.S. (1985). *Psychoanalytic Review* 72:239–254.]

A half-century has passed since Freud wrote *Civilization and Its Discontents*. This questing, speculative essay is Freud's most extensive application of psychoanalysis to society, and it endures as one of the revolutionary documents of our time. Although deeply flawed in certain areas, and now suffering from relative neglect, *Civilization and Its Discontents* demands attention because its implacable analysis of the nature of man and of his relations with civilization is even more pertinent today than it was in 1930. It is, therefore, fitting and perhaps urgent that we reexamine this work, taking advantage of the enriched perspective offered by the past 50 years of history.

At the time Freud wrote this manuscript, scarcely a decade had passed since the Great War had ended. The 10 to 12 million dead and 20 million wounded, the untold carnage, poorly evoke the barbarity of that war; perhaps the thought of the 600,000 men who perished at the single Battle of Verdun does so more strikingly. The madness of war-fever was not unknown to Freud, who had enthusiastically supported the Central Powers during the early months of the conflict. With three sons in the armed services, he could ill afford the emotional luxury of neutrality or indifference. But later he recoiled from such jingoism and unequivocally identified himself as a pacifist.

During the catastrophic social and economic conditions that followed the armistice, the Freud family barely eked out a living; their savings eroded and even Freud's modest life insurance became a worthless scrap of paper with the debacle of inflation. The situation improved somewhat during the '20s but by 1929 when the Great Depression unfurled over Europe, the Freud family once again suffered economic hardship. In Germany the Nazis began to bludgeon their way toward power. Communism appeared as an alternative and many people looked

This paper was presented at the Annual Meeting of the American Psychoanalytic Association, San Francisco, California, May 1980.

toward Soviet Russia for the answer to the crisis of the Western world. Freud had at first given the Russian Revolution the "benefit of the doubt," but by the end of the 1920s he saw that communism was no panacea for man's ills. Art and science reflected this instability and the brooding sense of worse things to come was frighteningly and prophetically evoked in several films produced during this time.

Freud's existence was not only affected by these social storms but suffered its own upheavals, for in 1923 he underwent the first of 33 operations for cancer of the palatinal arch. Only a few months prior to writing *Civilization and Its Discontents* he was fitted with a new prosthesis—the "monster" in his mouth that he could neither live with nor live without. On the heels of the diagnosis of cancer came a blow that, he avowed, caused him more suffering than the disease: the death of a grandson. He later wrote to Binswanger, whose eldest son had recently died, "it is the secret of my indifference—people call it courage—toward the danger to my own life" (Jones, 1957). Heinerle's death, he said, led to his first real depression. Two years later, when Karl Abraham died at the age of 48, Freud observed that no one could replace this personal loss.Despite these blows, the overall tone of *The Future of an Illusion* (1927), written two years earlier, is guardedly optimistic; in some "distant, distant future," Freud believed, man may finally put away his superstitions, religion, and illusions and confront reality with his intellect, that "soft voice [that] does not rest until it has gained a hearing" (p. 3). But this relatively hopeful attitude is largely dissipated when, a few years later, he writes *Civilization and Its Discontents.* The most plausible, immediate cause of this change was the growing menace of the Nazi movement, which was daily tightening its grip over Germany. The final words of *Civilization audits Discontents* give credence to this view.

Any attempt to summarize *Civilization and Its Discontents* must slight the richness of the work, for beyond the principal hypotheses there are several suggestive detours that Freud chose not to develop. As a prelude to *Civilization and Its Discontents* Freud briefly speaks about the relations of man to the universe as a whole. Evoking the concept of the oceanic experience—that "sensation of 'eternity'," that "feeling as of something limitless, unbounded"—he raises the question of religious faith. He posits that this feeling of oneness with the world is not a primary experience but a residue of the infant's absence of ego boundaries, of the archaic union with the world. Early experiences tend to be preserved, relatively intact, and may be summoned forth in later life; the feelings of helplessness that we may experience as adults resonate with the sense of protection felt at the parent's knee. Thus the "fear of the superior power of fate" becomes the psychogenic basis for religion to which the oceanic feelings later become attached.

The body of *Civilization and Its Discontents* rests chiefly on some half dozen organizing propositions that Freud advances to support his sociologic superstructure. The overarching theme is the unresolvable conflict between the individual and civilization. Here, as everywhere in psychoanalytic theory, conflict is the *primum mobile.*

Freud asks if there is a purpose to human life. He can find no answer to a question that "seems to derive from human presumptuousness." Only religion, he notes, can supply an answer; indeed, "the idea of life having a purpose stands and falls with the religious system" (p. 76). The religion he refers to here is that of the common man for whom it explains "the riddles of his world... and assures him that a careful providence will watch over his life and will compensate him in a future existence for any frustrations he suffers here" (p. 74). It is to this popular view of religion, not the "deepest sources of religious feeling," that Freud speaks.

If one observes human activity, it is evident that men and women strive to achieve happiness and to avoid unhappiness. But this pleasure principle is constantly being undermined from various sources. Man's earliest civilizing behavior probably entailed the control of fire, cooperative work, and the use of tools—making man a "prosthetic god." Species survival led to the formation of the family and the beginnings of social organization in which a group banded together to protect themselves against the individual who threatened their happiness. In this obligatory organization, man abandoned some individual freedom, placing himself under the dominion of the reality principle, gaining some security at the cost of bridling his sexual and aggressive appetites. He also began to develop some concept of justice, that is, that the law, once made, would not be broken for any one individual. However, despite the ineluctable necessity of civilization, Freud believed that the demands and frustrations it imposed on man are the root causes of neurosis.

How does man deal with this suffering? He attempts to escape from it through a variety of mechanisms: intoxicants, quietism; the displacement of libido onto joyful work (a path whose gratification is mild compared to the prototype of sexual pleasure, and moreover, is accessible only to a few); escape through illusion, imagination, delusions, the world of madness; or an existence devoted to aesthetic pursuits. There are also individual paths stemming from constitution and character, such as with those who devote themselves to eroticism, narcissism, or action.

Civilization restricts man's instinctual life so it may harness his aim-inhibited libido, bringing him into ever larger societal groups which can then fulfill social tasks. While man only seeks a partner for love, and experiences others as intrusive, civilization regards the dyad as subversive to its grander schemes. Thus men are required to restrict their sexual life, and women are limited to child rearing. Ideally, for civilization, sexual activity would be restricted to monogamic, heterosexual relations whose unique role would be procreation. This explains society's intolerance of promiscuity, incest, homosexuality, and perversion. But what if, *mirabile diclu,* we did away with this limitation on sexual behavior, even did away with the family itself—that "germ cell of civilization?" Such a Utopian prospect would not resolve our problems, Freud says, because man would still be under the dominion of that other indestructible feature of human nature—aggression.

The evolution of Freud's thinking on aggression need not be reviewed here. At the time of writing *Civilization and Its Discontents,* and for the remainder of his life, he conceptualized aggression as the outward expression of the death instinct; protected by his libidinal investment in himself, man's self-destructive drive is directed toward his fellow man. The individual is thus spared at the cost of a disintegrative effect on the connective tissue of society. Although Freud claims that this aggressive propensity in man is a derivative of the death instinct, in *Civilization and Its Discontents* he focuses on the external thrust of these impulses. He asserts that men are not intrinsically gentle creatures who only defend themselves when attacked, but are instinc-tually aggressive. While his destructiveness often waits for a provocation, man responds savagely when milder means might serve as well. When the mental constraints against aggression are inadequate, man is revealed as a "savage beast." Freud reiterates: *homo homini lupus;* man is a wolf to man.

Society is protected against this danger through the development of the superego—a psychological entity within the individual that watches over him, to use Freud's simile, like a garrison in an occupied city.

The tension that develops between the superego and the ego, which carries out aggressive acts, is experienced as a sense of guilt and expressed as a need for punishment. Whereas initially the child fears the external authority, parents, who can withhold their love, the authority is later transferred to society. However, this contingent control is relatively weak and may crumble when the individual believes his bad deeds will not be discovered. In contrast, when the authority is internalized, a more powerful modality of inhibiting aggression comes into being because the superego can then arrest destructive behavior even before it occurs since it is aware of the individual's intentions. Thus the severity of the superego is a continuation of the severity of the perceived external authority, which is then in part replaced. The sense of guilt engendered by inevitable temptations becomes the *sine qua non* of the intactness of society; without it civilization would be fragmented. But the individual often finds it intolerable, even if such intolerance may remain unconscious or may often appear as a malaise or feeling of discontent. Historically, society has fostered a superego of a severity that simply does not take into account either the desire for happiness or strength of the instinctual drives; nor does society consider the differences between individuals and different environments. Psychoanalysis often deals with just such situations by helping the patient modulate the demands of a cruel and implacable superego.

The community too, in effect, evolves its own superego embodied in its ideals and demands, advanced as ethical standards that in the main concern the relations of human beings with each other. A central ethical demand is that "thou shalt love thy neighbor as thyself." Freud regards this as psychologically untenable because it devalues one's love and so is unjust to those whom one does love. Love should go only to those who deserve it. Furthermore, Freud observed that, only too often, he saw that a neighbor had more claim to one's hostility than one's love because he injures one even without advantage to himself. Indeed, the more helpless you are, the worse he often is. And Freud said he would treat him with consideration if he were treated in the same way, without the need of ethical precepts. Thus, ethics also ignores the differences between individuals, and as long as those differences exist, obedience to high ethical demands will entail "damage to the aims of civilization, for it puts a positive premium on being bad" (p. 111). Ethical behavior is often tied to a religious concept of an afterlife that would richly compensate the individual for the sacrifice of some happiness in this life. Freud suspected that ethical precepts might be followed more effectively if the desired behavior were rewarded in this life.

His skepticism about the efficacy of religion in dealing with the conflict between the individual's happiness and the demands of civilization was matched by his doubts about the program of communism to resolve this conflict. Whereas religion is derivative of man's abiding sense of helplessness and dependency and the need to have a universal father, communists err by assuming that men are fundamentally good: If we could only abolish private property no one would regard the other as the enemy. Freud acknowledged that although the abolition of private property might deprive aggression of one of its strongest incentives, it would not change man's inherent destructiveness. However, he affirmed that a "real change in the relation of human beings to possessions will be of more help... than any ethical commands" (p. 143). Unfortunately socialists have obscured this by their "idealistic misconception of human nature."

Freud asks if civilization has any value in and of itself; for himself he cannot say. However, since most of man's judgments are influenced by wishes for happiness, his illusions are supported with arguments. In any event, the question is probably rhetorical, since the development of civilization seems inevitable and we can only submit to it. But then, Freud observes, the history of mankind has demonstrated many other so-called "inevitable" trends that were later thrown aside or replaced. *Civilization and its Discontents* concludes with Freud posing the "fateful question": whether and to what extent our cultural development will succeed in mastering the assault on our communal life by the human instinct of aggression and self-destruction.

> It may be that in this respect precisely, the present time deserves such a special interest. Men have gained control over the forces of nature to such an extent that with their help they would have no difficulty in exterminating one another to the last man. They know this, and hence comes a large part of their current unrest, their unhappiness and their mood of anxiety. And now it is to be expected that the other of the two "Heavenly Powers," eternal Eros, will make an effort to assert himself in the struggle with his equally immortal adversary, (p. 145)

One year later, in 1931, with the crescendo of the Nazi movement in his ears and the brushfire spread of anti-Semitism and barbarity sweeping across Europe, Freud added a grim and prophetic sentence: "But who can foresee with what success and with what result?" (p. 145).

The infrastructure of *Civilization and Its Discontents* is defined by a series of basic propositions; the most central of these is that man is fated to unhappiness primarily because of the restrictions society places on instinctual pleasure, of which the ideal is the sudden discharge of instinctual drive that has been "dammed-up to a high degree" (p. 176). Thus, "constitutional" factors limit our pleasure from the outset since they stand in direct conflict with the demands of society. Freud also identified three other major sources of unhappiness: our vulnerable bodies, which ultimately must deteriorate; the destructive forces of nature; and "most painful of all," the suffering we experience from our relations to other people. These sources of human misery are not directly drive-related—in the sense that they involve restrictions on our instincts. Moreover, though they have a powerful impact on the psyche, they are initially extrapsychological in terms of their place of origin; they are, in fact, aspects of the unhappiness of everyday life.

Contemporary psychoanalytic views of the instinctual drives (and their energic qualities) are markedly heterogeneous. In regard to libido, where there is more agreement than in regard to the aggressive instinct, the opinions include considering libido as a purely neurophys-iological phenomenon; accepting the drive but rejecting its energic qualities; conceptualizing libido as a wish, with or without a physical substrate; and rejecting libido, psychic energy, and all other related concepts as irrelevant, unverifiable, and of no explanatory value. There are few ardent advocates of psychic economics today. The hypothesis of a closed energic system, however, is central to *Civilization and Its Discontents,* because if such a system does not exist it is pointless to hypothesize a struggle for libido between society and the individual. In an open system man can cathect society, work, and sexual objects equally well, analogous to the parent who can love many children.

Freud's argument that society must place a rein on man's libidinal drives lest they run away with him fails to account for the physiological limitation of man's—specifically *men's*—potential for genital sexual pleasure. Moreover, in *Civilization and Its Discontents*, Freud views the sexual impulse as largely a male phenomenon, in contrast to the mothering, child-bonding wishes of women. Although the latter are still generally regarded as powerful cultural and/or biological trends in women, it is now recognized that women seek sexual gratification no less than men.

The idea of a "sexual revolution" has become an abused cliche; it is imprecise and poorly documented at best. Nevertheless, there is considerable evidence to support the view that there have been vast changes in sexual behavior. It would be a simplistic error to assume that such outward manifestations necessarily represent or are derivative of intrapsychic changes across a population. Yet, it is likely that the code of sexual morality that held sway 50 years ago, in the Western world, has much less effect on the way individuals behave today. While the combined institutional forces of society still maintain that earlier code, important chinks in its armor are appearing. Indeed, at times it appears as if society covertly grants a license for sexual behavior. These developments cast doubt on the inhibiting, restrictive role of civilization on sexual behavior that Freud described. Perhaps a less restrictive code is indicative of a more affluent society that can permit greater sexual freedom since the technological level of that civilization does not require maximum efforts for survival from its population. Such a society can afford to be less concerned with what its people do outside the time they devote to socially necessary tasks; in fact, fewer and fewer people are directly occupied in the production of the necessities of life. In the same vein the marked change in the public attitude toward homosexuality may be regarded as a harbinger of a still greater relaxation of restraints on sexual behavior.

But what has happened to the sense of guilt that Freud proposed as society's way of controlling man's drive impulses? On a social level the response is unclear. Psychoanalytic data alone seem to be able to provide a useful basis for forming an opinion since an individual's overt behavior is imperfectly relevant to this matter. Information from psychoanalysis demonstrates that human beings have not ceased experiencing a sense of guilt when they act, or have fantasies of acting, in ways that are forbidden by their superego; thus we see many patients whose behavior is, to a large extent, motivated by an unconscious need for punishment. However, whether people experience more or less guilt over sexual impulses today, as compared with 50 years ago, is an open question. It is also unclear whether, and to what extent, society actually has a manifest interest in developing a sense of guilt over sexual behavior. Although it is understandable that an individual who develops a sense of guilt because of unconscious, incestuous impulses, may be responding to the demands and needs of society, it is difficult to relate the contemporary changes in sexual behavior to society's needs. It might be supposed, however, that even though the demands of society are, historically, refracted through the family into superego development, when society's demands are modified, they live on unchanged within the family in a pseudohereditary manner, neither particularly in congruence with society's canons nor in sharp conflict with them.

When we turn to current psychoanalytic theory pertaining to the aggressive drives we find an even greater diversity of opinions than those relating to libido. In the first place there are few psychoanalysts today who support the concept of the death instinct, although the split-off, exteriorized aggressive-destructive drive, seems to enjoy a wide acceptance as part of the "dual drive theory."

A theoretical complication appears in Freud's view of civilization's attitude vis-a-vis the death instinct, in that it is apparent that such a self-destructive drive would spell the very end of the species; to inhibit such an event, civilization must in fact support the *outward* thrust of aggression. But such a phenomenon, while preserving the individual, and therefore the species, is inimical to the group-binding of civilization. This contradiction may be partially resolved by assuming that society can tolerate and even foster some degree of outward aggression, but only by diverting that destructive force to other societies or cultures that have been designated as enemies. This is indeed so, in the particular form described by Freud, where antagonisms seem to be especially fierce between contiguous peoples and nations. In a bitter piece of irony, Freud evokes the "most useful services" to those civilizations that have been the hosts of the Jewish people, scattered everywhere. The persecution of Jews has been a "convenient and relatively harmless satisfaction of the inclination to aggression, by means of which cohesion between the members of the community is made easier" (p. 114).

The many arguments against an innate destructive drive were marshalled by Stone (1971) who regards aggression as an ego function that is integrated with basic instincts such as hunger and sexuality in order to carry them to gratification. Such a nondestructive drive can become destructive in those situations of frustration that precipitate feelings of traumatic helplessness. This theory is in contrast to Freud and those who support his view that the external, frustrating event merely unleashes a destructive impulse already *in situ*.

When we examine aggression as a clinical phenomenon we find that the communications of psychoanalytic patients, their dreams, fantasies, and associations, leave no doubt that aggressive impulses are a prominent part of the human psyche. But here, too, there are no indisputable data to support whether these impulses arise from man's genetic endowment, some sort of learned response to frustration, or an amalgam of both. In either of these situations it is clear that there is a range of possibilities related to the means used to express these impulses, and for civilization as a whole, everything inheres in those differences. To stress the obvious, the difference between a fantasy and the execution of that fantasy might translate into a matter of life and death.

In terms of their impact on society, I doubt whether there is any significance if destructive impulses are innate or learned. In the latter instance, when individuals become destructive only when severely frustrated, such hostility might be tamed either by reducing the frustration or by enhancing the individual's potential for modifying the aggressive response. However, if the impulse for aggression is an inborn instinct there is still a need to limit provocative frustrations and/or to shore-up intrapsychic defenses.

In the last several decades the claims of ethologists that they could explain human behavior were accepted by many analysts because they seemed to validate the dual drive theory. Thus, Lorenz extrapolated a hypothesized destructive-aggressive instinct in animals to man. There is, however, no unanimity even among ethologists on this matter, and such reasoning by analogy is at best suggestive. More recently the biologic position has been advanced once more by the socio-biologists, with E. O. Wilson in the vanguard. Their claims have not been generally accepted by biologists, to say nothing of psychoanalysts.

The grim prophecy contained in the coda Freud added to *Civilization and Its Discontents* was realized on a scale far vaster than he had probably imagined in his most pessimistic conjecture. By the end of World War II, some 45 million people had perished, among them the six million Jews destroyed in a planned program of genocide unprecedented in human history. The horrors, systematically and institutionally associated with this enterprise, were at first disbelieved by the public as being beyond human behavior. Unfortunately, the subsequent filling in of the hitherto blank spaces of those years only magnifies previous information. How comforting it would be if we could only ascribe this nightmare to a given nation or a particular people; and that indeed has been attempted. But the daily newspaper ceaselessly demonstrates that no given society has a monopoly on aggression, and I speak not only of individual acts of violence but especially of national policies.

On the other hand, there is evidence that certain societies have evolved where the aggression of their people is intrapsychically and socially dealt with in ways that are neither destructive to the individual nor to others. The ethnopsychoanalysts, Parin and Morgenthaler (Parin, 1972)—in a work that has received insufficient attention-have described such circumstances in the Dogin and Agni tribes in West Africa. Their argument is that man's ego, molded under the influence of specific cultural influences, ultimately determines the way in which destructive aggression is managed. Moreover, they assert that the form of the social environment itself is a function of aggression. Thus, if "it is a characteristic of our Western ego, that, above all, repression and internalization of aggressive strivings are necessary to social functioning... this is neither the only nor even necessary normal destiny of aggression" (p. 256). The Dogin also demonstrate not only little harmful discharge of aggression toward each other but toward outside enemies as well. These authors recognize that the ego qualities demanded by the postindustrial society of the West—a sense of order, organizational talent, technical and economic expertise—probably preclude the possibility of developing the modalities of psychosocial management of aggression that emerged from and served the needs of a primitive, less destructive society. But even in the Western world, there are qualitative differences between countries regarding national and individual violence. Firm explanations of these phenomena are lacking.

And what of the various ways Freud described that men use to lighten their suffering from civilization's constriction of instinctual pleasure? If we consider religion we are struck by the apparent correctness of Freud's conjecture, enunciated more specifically in *The Future of an Illusion,* of the waning of organized religion. What is curious, however, which he did not foresee, is the large number of people who, while leaving a traditional sect, adhere to a new one. What is even more arresting is that while there is a steady erosion of orthodoxy in Judaism and the traditional Christian sects, the newer cults are often more ascetic and inflexible than the earlier ones. Whatever the nature of religious practice today, to all intents and purposes religion does not play a significant role in taming man's destructive impulses, if it can be said to have ever done so. Whatever influence religion may have on individual aggression appears to be overshadowed by its inability to affect "ignorant armies that clash by night."

Freud briefly addressed a related matter, the liberation of the self from the imperious demands of the instinct by, in effect, smothering them, "as is prescribed in the worldy wisdom of the East, and practiced by Yoga" (p. 79). This defense against suffering bypasses the sensory apparatus and goes directly to the internal sources of our needs by sharply limiting or even negating the instincts. Freud's objection to this quietist solution is simply that "the feelings of happiness derived from the satisfaction of a wild instinctual impulse untamed by the ego is incomparably more intense than that derived from sating an instinct that has been tamed. The irresistibility of perverse instinct, and perhaps the attraction in general of forbidden things, finds an economic explanation here" (p. 79).

This conceptualization, drawing from a drive reduction model of psychic function to explain libidinal gratification, does not account sufficiently for a variety of other influences that range from the role of object relations to the effects of conscious and unconscious fantasy. It also begs the question of the alleged suffering of an individual who renounces libidinal drive. The fact is that we do not possess sufficient information to assume such suffering; it is perhaps tenable only by evoking the possibility of the "actual neurosis," an entity that enjoys little support today. Moreover, Freud himself, in speaking of St. Francis of Assisi, seems to recognize that at least for some individuals quietism can be successful.

This situation is different from that crudest but "most effective" method of influencing our instincts—intoxication. Stifling the very sensations of pain itself, intoxication remains a powerful, perhaps peerless, weapon against suffering. Looking at the Western world today, it appears that men have taken more than a page from Freud's book because the abuse of intoxicants seems unprecedented. In contrast to the use of hallucinogens in some primitive societies where they played a vital social, psychological, and religious role, the use of intoxicants in the West today has no important relationship to institutions except in two paradoxical situations. The first is that millions of people are introduced to the systematic use of intoxicating drugs by physicians, a practice that is legal and ethical. The other situation is the cultural acceptance of intoxicants, often in the face of criminal sanctions. This may represent divergent attitudes in a given society, but it brings to mind soldiers in combat areas who are tacitly permitted to use illegal intoxicants, suggesting a subtle form of encouragement. It does seem that the use of alcohol and drugs is more prevalent today in the Western world than at any previous time. Is society offering this form of salvation and solace to man in imitation of Huxley's "Soma"? Is opium becoming the religion of the people?

Work as sublimation and as gratification was surely experienced by Freud as much as by any other human being: His life was packed with productive, passionate labor. He recognized its paramount importance for the very few for whom it could be more than just a grinding necessity; unfortunately, it remains so for most individuals. Aside from a tiny minority, most workers are alienated from the productive process, its purpose, and its product. These conditions in the relations of production have not changed since Freud wrote *Civilization and Its Discontents.* That work may represent more than a mere sublimation has been suggested by Hendrick and Hartmann, among others, and it is generally accepted today that if man has a "natural aversion to work," as Freud observed, he can derive pleasure from it that is not purely derivative of drive impulses; for a few, civilization offers contentment. Although people work fewer hours today than in Freud's lifetime, and enjoy more leisure time, more and more individuals are retiring at an earlier age, if they can afford to do so. The small number of individuals who continue to work late in life are either found among professional people, artists, craftspeople, and the like, or those who must continue to labor out of sheer need. The postindustrial society's organization of work holds little promise that work can ever be more for most people than what it represents today. Marcuse's (1955) concept of a de-alienation of work in some form of socialist society must remain an intriguing but Utopian concept until it is demonstrated as a reality in a given society. Moreover, as Freud already saw in 1930, each technological advance, which makes life more reasonable, exacts a price. In our society this concept is frighteningly epitomized by nuclear power.

Has society improved the mutual relations between individuals in the past 50 years? It is not possible to answer in the affirmative. As I noted in regard to nations, where aggression has not abated, there does not seem to be a more effective control of individual aggression.

If the increase in violent crime, terrorism, and hijackings constitutes some sort of benchmark, if the anecdotal observations about a "narcissistic" era have any basis in reality, then it is clear that civilization—at least as it exists in many countries today—is barely succeeding in fulfilling its raison d'être.

The central issue Freud advanced in *Civilization and Its Discontents*—that man must suffer because of restrictions placed on the un-trammeled expression of libidinal and aggressive drives—must in today's world, be regarded as either not true or constituting but a small part of man's discontents. The metapsychological principles on which Freud built his hypothesis are being increasingly modified—indeed discarded—in favor of a less biological, more clinically based theory. Most human misery appears to be, usually and for most people, the bitter fruit of object loss, disease, death, war, and poverty—what Freud called the unhappiness of everyday life. Furthermore, it is not certain that any and all restrictions on libidinal and aggressive wishes lead to unhappiness the presence of fantasies does not in itself represent the frustration of desire. Conscious and unconscious fantasies are precipitates of life-long experiences alloyed with instinctual wishes; and as fervently as the fulfillment of desire may be wanted in fantasy, its fulfillment in reality may be even more abhorred and avoided.

The modalities Freud described by which man mitigates suffering from drive frustration are of equal or greater importance in modulating the unhappiness of everyday life, and Freud suggests as much. But perhaps of greater significance is the role that some of these modalities play—at least for some, and therefore in principle, for everyone—in providing the individual with direct gratification. Freud recognized that art, for example, is one of the pre-eminent products of civilization. Even assuming that it is a derivative of sublimation or a way of dealing with unhappiness, it seems to become a force in its own right. To use Hartmann's expression regarding ego defenses, there is, perhaps, a change in function; people as creatures of culture derive an intense pleasure from art without it necessarily serving some other purpose. I use art as an example of merely one among many such aspects of civilization.

It is unnecessary to elaborate further what I believe are important weaknesses in *Civilization and Its Discontents*—and this is to pass over some of Freud's untenable anthropological theories, his biologism, and his Lamarckism. Yet, despite everything, *Civilization and Its Discontents,* remains a revolutionary statement, subversive of any and all fetishization of civilization; perhaps this explains the relatively meager attention it has received since its publication, both within and without the psychoanalytic movement. If the theoretical bases are often wrong, two major conclusions are outstandingly sound: Civilization is a repressive albeit inevitable agency; and man is capable of destroying civilization. It would be as absurd an exercise to condemn civilization for its role as it would be to criticize man's psyche for repressing instinctual wishes. If civilization has given rise to the sublime products of man's imagination it is nonetheless true that civilized man is always ready—and frequently succeeds—in breaking through what Lord Snow (1979) characterized as a "coat of varnish." Freud's adamantine and austere view of humanity—and of civilization—stands in stark polarity to the soft and roseate optimism of society's leaders. The dangerous innocence generally proposed by civilization's stewards denies the reality around us and in us; repeatedly society makes tragic decisions based on a mythology that emanates from wishful thinking and ideology.

Yet, beyond our expectations, Freud offers neither a mindless nihilism nor a simple-minded hedonism. Although he never wrote a single word recommending or exhorting others how to live, his own life demonstrates that man is not ineluctably bound to atavistic regression in the face of this dour reality. Thus, for Freud, neutrality is more than an aspect of psychoanalytic technique: It represents his credo that no human being has the right to coerce another. Hence, *Civilization and Its Discontents* rises above and beyond ideology, nationalism, class, and religious sect. The life Freud himself lived is a superb model of devotion to the individual, to a search for truth, and to the duty of being human. He "aspired to behave honorably, to spare others and to be kind whenever possible." When he wondered why, when he might become "an anvil" for "brutal and unreliable" people, he could offer no explanation. (Freud, E., 1960, p. 308). Although he was cut from a quite different philosophic cloth than St. Francis of Assisi, he grasped how St. Francis could devote his life to others: It was because of his profound, aim-inhibited love for people. This model was to be Freud's response to Einstein's deep pessimism regarding the prevention of war, and it inherently embodies a commitment to the preservation of civilization, that most elegant and most enslaving of human products.

REFERENCES

Freud, E. (1960). *Letters of Sigmund Freud.* New York: Basic Books.
Freud, S. (1920). Beyond the pleasure principle. *Standard Edition* 18:3–64, 1961.

—— (1927). The future *of* an illusion. *Standard Edition*, 21:3–56, 1961.

—— (1930). Civilization and its discontents. *Standard Edition*. 21:59–145.

JONES, E. (1957). *The Life and Work of Sigmund Freud* (Vol. 3). New York: Basic Books.

MARCUSE, H. (1955). *Eros and Civilization*. New York: Vintage Books.

PARIN, P. (1972). Contribution of ethnopsychoanalytic investigation to the theory of aggression. *International Journal of Psycho-Analysis* 53:251–257.

SNOW, C.P. (1979). *A Coat of Varnish*. New York: Scribner's.

STONE, L. (1971). Reflections on the psychoanalytic concepts of aggression. *Psychoanaltyic Quarterly*, 40:195–244.

CHAPTER II

Freud's "Narcissism of Minor Differences": A Review and Reassessment

[Werman, D.S. (1988). *Journal of American Academy of Psychoanalysis*, 16:451–459.]

ABSTRACT:
Freud coined the name and briefly described the narcissism of minor differences. Although he initially regarded it as a form of individual behavior, he later came to see its implications for groups. This paper explores the manifestations of the narcissism of minor differences in psychoanalytic organizations and treatment. In contrast to Freud's observation that the narcissism of minor differences is relatively harmless, I suggest that in the social sphere it harbors the potential for a pernicious escalation into hostile and destructive actions on a widespread scale.

Origin and Development of Narcissism of Minor Differences in the Psycho-analytic Literature

The "narcissism of minor differences," a term coined by Freud, seems to be so ubiquitous a phenomenon that it might well be regarded as another example of the psychopathology of everyday life. But despite its frequent occurrence (perhaps for that reason) allusions to it in the psychoanalytic literature after Freud are almost nonexistent. Although the narcissism of minor differences may be seen in all walks of life, I shall focus on its occurrence in areas of particular interest to psychoanalysts.

Freud wrote on only three occasions about the narcissism of minor differences, and these remarks were brief and seemingly *en passant*. His first comments appear in *The Taboo of Virginity* (Freud, 1917): "Crawley, in language that differs only slightly from the current terminology of psychoanalysis, declares that each individual is separated from others by a 'taboo of personal isolation,' and that it is precisely the minor differences in people who are otherwise alike that form the basis of feelings of strangeness and hostility between them. It would be tempting to pursue this idea and to derive from this 'narcissism of minor differences' the hostility which in every human relation we see fighting successfully against feelings of fellowship and overpowering the commandment that all men should love one another" (p. 199).

An earlier version of this paper was presented at the Mid-Winter Meeting of The American Psychoanalytic Association, December 17, 1983.

Four years later, in his study of group psychology, Freud (1921) again mentioned the narcissism of minor differences. This passage follows a quotation from Schopenhauer, in which the philosopher uses a simile about porcupines freezing to death: they repeatedly move closer for warmth but then are obliged to move apart, until finally they find "a mean distance at which they could most tolerably exist" (p. 101). Freud observed that this aptly conveys that "no one can tolerate a too intimate approach to his neighbor. The evidence of psychoanalysis shows that almost every intimate emotional relationship between two people which lasts for some time—marriage, friendship, the relations between parents and children—contains a sediment of feelings of aversion and hostility, which only escapes perception as a result of repression" (p. 101).

As in the previous reference, Freud does not attempt to advance a general explanation of the narcissism of minor differences other than to suggest that people utilize minor differences as a rationalization for their hostility—a hostility that truly remains without an objective basis.

In *Civilization and its Discontents* (Freud, 1930), he once again touched on this phenomenon now, however, shifting the locus from individual to group psychology:

It is clearly not easy for men to give up the satisfaction of this inclination to aggression. They do not feel comfortable without it.... It is always possible to bind together a considerable number of people in love, so long as there are other people left over to receive the manifestations for their aggressiveness ... [It] is precisely [to] communities with adjoining territories. and related to each other in other ways as well, who are engaged in constant feuds and in ridiculing each other.... [that] I gave this phenomenon the name of 'the narcissism of minor differences,' a name which does not do much to explain it. *We can now see that it is a convenient and relatively harmless satisfaction of the inclination to aggression, by means of which cohesion between the members of the community is made easier*." (p. 114, italics mine)

In this respect, Freud added, in an ironic aside, the Jews, who are scattered everywhere, have "rendered most useful services to the civilizations of the countries that have been their hosts" (p. 114).

In characterizing the narcissism of minor differences as a group phenomenon, Freud regarded it as a process that enhances group cohesion by fostering the discharge of hostility, externally, towards alien groups in whom perceived differences from the dominant group are denigrated. Furthermore, by the nature of the examples Freud cites—the antagonism of the English for the Scots, or the Aryan for the Semite—it appears that he considered that the narcissism of minor differences operates primarily, and perhaps exclusively, on a conscious level.

To my knowledge, after Freud, there is only one reference to the narcissism of minor differences in the psychoanalytic literature, and although it clearly describes the phenomenon, it does not identify it by name. In a contribution on countertransference in the training analyst, Benedek (1954) examined the professional organization of psychoanalysis. In this organization, she observed, the emotional structure of the family, with its psychodynamic constellations, is reproduced. In Vienna, during the early twentieth century, Freud represented the "patriarch" of the psychoanalytic family, with the "siblings" represented by the other analysts.

In that group, of which Freud was the "unquestioned leader," Benedek noted that the members established their membership through their identification with him and, thus, simultaneously, they identified with each other. "But, at the same time, the members of this group were striving to maintain their own identity by emphasizing their small differences. This group, proudly aware of their insight into a new field of knowledge, was a militant minority in a hostile world of medicine and psychology. Hence, the intensification of the group narcissism; hence, the similarity between the organization and that of the patriarchal family" (p. 13). Benedek observed that the need to maintain individual distinctiveness might lead an individual analyst to enhance his position in the group by "creating disciples."

Group Narcissism in the Psychoanalytic Establishment

What is striking about these remarks is their contemporaneousness. If we substitute for the person of Freud, who was then the preëminent object of identification, the psychoanalytic organization itself, along with the analyst's professional identity *vis à vis* the public, we see that in many respects the situation today is not dissimilar from that described by Benedek. The diminished influence of psychoanalysis in academic psychiatry, the increasingly dominant position of "biologic" psychiatry, and the rise of a multitude of competing psychotherapies have led many psychoanalysts to identify more intensely with each other and with their professional organizations. At the same time, similar to the porcupines, one observes behavior which seems to serve, among other aims, to maintain a given analyst's individual identity. Thus, in psychoanalytic organizations, although some debates clearly reflect genuine and even critical differences of opinion, others demonstrate that the motive force—often revealed by an inappropriate intensity of emotion—is only dimly related to substantive issues. Trivial matters, or matters for which little or no firm evidence exists to support one position or another, are invested with an importance far exceeding any they may merit. The subjective factors implicated in such discussions are often betrayed by the reasonable compromise which competing factors ultimately reach—a compromise that frequently might have been effected much earlier.

Illustrative of this phenomenon are discussions relating to the qualifications for admission to and graduation from psychoanalytic training programs, and for appointment to supervising and training analyst status. Not uncharacteristically, such debates frequently focus on numbers: numbers of hours, cases, supervision and so forth. Now, a decision to establish quantitative criteria is, in itself, reasonable. But when a debate focuses on small differences in the numbers, it is likely that subjective factors are, to a significant extent, influencing the discussants. Throughout such affect laden discussions a disinterested observer has the impression that the very self-esteem of the debaters is at stake. However, once a potential humiliation has been avoided, and one's identity and worth have been publicly and unambiguously demonstrated, the elusive compromise can be reached.

In addition to matters of self-esteem, such discussions are often colored by a subtle aura of hostility, although in psychoanalytic organizations it is usually controlled by reaction formation, intellectualization, and rationalization, if not by simple courtesy. It is often difficult to tease out whether narcissism or aggression is the primary motivation in such behavior; it is likely that in most situations both are present but to different degrees.

In its most benign form, the narcissism of minor differences functions, as Freud observed in the social domain, as a relatively harmless means of discharging aggression. When the aggression is aimed outside of the group, there is a tendency to enhance group cohesion; however, when the target consists of other members of the group, the tendency is towards the creation of factionalism, cronyism and schisms. The history of psychoanalysis bears eloquent witness to such developments.

A related area in which the narcissism of minor differences can be observed, is in some theoretical debates. Extrapolating from the concepts of Kuhn in respect to the evolution of scientific paradigms to psychoanalysis, Rothstein (1980) noted that the narcissistic investment by the "creators" of new psychoanalytic paradigms, fosters "irrational polemics." It is of interest that although some theoretical debates begin over relatively discrete differences, these may later develop into deep and broadly differentiated points of view. When the narcissism of minor differences occurs in theoretical discussions, it commonly takes such forms as a penchant for coining neologisms, new complexes and syndromes; an insistence on specificity—especially in respect to etiology, psychogenics or psychodynamics; an intolerance for alternative interpretations; and the depreciation of overdetermination, which may be characterized as nihilistic or anarchic. The narcissism of minor differences may also be manifested by an unshakable faith which declares that a given phenomenon is and forever will remain unknowable.

Narcissism of Minor Differences Expressed During Psychoanalysis

The narcissism of minor differences may be observed in the course of psychoanalysis, where it can serve several functions which are not mutually exclusive, as the following vignette illustrates. A thirty-five-year-old professor in the humanities entered psychoanalysis because of an inability to do research, difficulties in his relations with colleagues (especially those who were senior to him) and concern about the deterioration of his marriage. Relatively early in treatment, Dr. M. described a heated discussion he had had with one of his colleagues. It was evident that the initial disagreement was not of great importance, but both Dr. M. and his colleague rapidly moved from their first difference of opinion to a variety of more or less tangential issues. It was also evident that Dr. M. was not in the least aware of the triviality of the original argument, nor of the intensity of his emotions which he reëxperienced in the course of relating the incident during an analytic hour.

Some months later, a similar situation occurred in the analysis. The analyst had commented that something Dr. M. had just told him was reminiscent of an event Dr. M. had once described, that had occurred when he was in the first grade. Dr. M. scornfully replied that the analyst "had it all wrong," and that the event in question had occurred when he was at least ten years old. The analyst admitted that he might well be mistaken on the date of the occurrence, but that the essential point was that it had taken place, and that it was the impact of the event, on Dr. M., that mattered. Nevertheless, Dr. M. used the occasion to characterize his doctor's mistake as "typical" of his "slipshod thinking," and of the "fuzzy" logic that analysts "always" use.

This type of behavior became a major resistance for Dr. M: he repeatedly seized upon minor aspects of a clarification or an interpretation in order to reject the intervention *in toto*. In some ways this behavior was similar to that described by Abend **(1975)** as a "yes, but ..." form of negation. In the course of Dr. M.'s analysis, his utilization of minor differences between himself and the analyst was seen to have several determinants: he used it as a resistance; it served to enhance his self-esteem; it was a subtle vehicle to express hostility; it derived from Dr. M.'s obsessive/compulsive character; and it was an expression of unresolved aspects of his Oedipal conflict. Ultimately it began to be ego-alien to him and he himself characterized it as his "nit picking"; as he grew to understand its determinants, he struggled, generally with success, to reject it.

But the narcissism of minor differences is not used only by the analysand; the analyst too may utilize it to express his own narcissistic needs, countertransference reactions, competitiveness, or any unresolved conflict. He may not, for example, be able to tolerate any disagreement, and may demand that his patient be sufficiently submissive to him so that he can feel secure in his patriarchal (or matriarchal) omniscience. In educational activities and in supervision, the narcissism of minor differences is not infrequently observed. Generally it arises from the more senior individual, but it rapidly becomes a circular and destructive problem.

Conclusion

I have described some of the effects of the narcissism of minor differences in psychoanalytic activities, but I believe the major significance of this phenomenon lies in the social sphere. Recognizing its ubiquity, and usual benignity, Freud (1930) was inclined to regard the narcissism of minor differences as a "relatively harmless satisfaction of the inclination to aggression" (p. 114). Although it most often does manifest itself in such a manner, i.e., as a banal form of aggression in everyday life, the history of the last half-century, if not of preceding millennia, suggests that the narcissism of minor difference has a malignant potential to erupt in vast bloodbaths which have even reached the level of genocide. One can no longer, for example, regard the antagonism of the Aryan for the Semite as a benign event.

On the other hand, we need not accept the violent expression of aggression as a necessary and ineluctable part of the human condition; to do so would be to foreclose the responsibility to attempt to understand and possibly to tame, at least to some extent, human aggression. We know that just as individuals have different propensities to violence and defend against it in different ways, so some cultures have developed institutional forms to deal more pacifically with intra- and intergroup aggression (Parin, 1972). In the age of nuclear weapons, the paramount concern of mankind must surely be the effective control and sublimation of aggression in its myriad forms—whether it emanates from the individual, from groups, or from the state. Cataclysms can and do ensue from events as fleeting and unsubstantial as fantasies and dreams. The circumstances under which a relatively "harmless" narcissism of minor differences is transformed into overt violence—indeed into a program of genocide—need to be elucidated. Clinical experience suggests that the narcissism of minor differences commonly tends to escalate into active aggression when an individual is frightened or angry, or has undergone (or fears) a narcissistic humiliation. Similar psychodynamic situations seem to prevail as well with groups when intragroup aggression increases or when group cohesion is threatened from without. Volkan (1986) has published an informative article on the narcissism of minor differences in confrontations between nations.

"Men indulge in little injuries who can't afford to be wicked enough for great injustice," wrote Trollope (1870). Were the narcissism of minor differences to remain at the level of "little injuries," it would, at worst, be an irksome intrusion into one's life. Unfortunately, it harbors a potential for pernicious escalation into hostile actions: its effects are not only felt in psychoanalytic organizations and in psychoanalytic treatment, as I have noted here, but are widespread throughout society where they inflame chauvinism, racism, and disorganization. Why this phenomenon is so ubiquitous and deeply entrenched in human relations, is, as Freud observed, probably related, at least in part, to its dual function of enhancing self- (and group) esteem, and in permitting a socially acceptable discharge of aggression. Cloaked, as it is, in a desire for "truth," this phenomenon can be as elusive as it is well defended.

Psychoanalysts have paid insufficient attention to the narcissism of minor differences, perhaps because its very banality makes it appear—if not normal—at least unworthy of serious examination. On the contrary, I believe that precisely because of its banality, it invites further study in those situations in which it occurs, not the least of which is in our own behavior.

REFERENCES

ABEND, S.M. (1975). An analogue of negation, *Psychoanalytic Quarterly* 44: 631–637.

BENEDEK, T. (1954). Countertransference in the training analyst, *Bulletin of the Menninger Clinic.*, 18, 12–16.

FREUD, S. (1917). The taboo of virginity, *Standard Edition* 11:191–208.

——— (192_). Group psychology and the analysis of the ego. *Standard Edition*, pp. 67–144.

——— (1930). Civilization and its discontents. *Standard Edition*, 21:59–148. z

PARIN, P.A. (1972). A contribution of ethno-psychoanalytic investigation to the theory of aggression, *International Journal of Psycho-Analysis* 53:252–257.

ROTHSTEIN, A. (1980). Psychoanalytic paradigms and their narcissistic investment, *Journal of the American Psychoanalytic Assosication* 28:385–395.

TROLLOPE, A (1870). *The Vicar of Bullhampton.* New York: Dover Publications, 1979.

VOLKAN, V. (1986), The narcissism of minor differences in the psychological gap between nations, *Psychoanalytic Inquiry* 6:175–191.

CHAPTER 12

Methodological Problems in the Psychoanalytic Interpretation of Literature: A Review of Studies on Sophocles' *Antigone*

[Werman, D.S. (1979). *Journal of the American Psychoanalytic Association* 27:451–478.]

Ever since Freud discovered psychic function, applied psychoanalysis has been closely related to the main body of psychoanalytic theory. This relationship was a natural consequence of Freud's classical education and his fascination and preoccupation with literature as a derivative of man's mental life. In art and literature Freud found illustrations of the theoretical concepts he was organizing out of his clinical experience; at the same time, art and literature presented a convincing body of data to corroborate and demonstrate his ideas.

Although Freud and others such as Abraham and Rank made extensive and often brilliant excursions into a number of cultural areas, recasting them in the light of psychoanalysis, their efforts were limited by methodological difficulties which were evident to the writers themselves. The inherent problem is that the psychoanalytic interpretation of a cultural phenomenon lies outside of the therapeutic process in which an interpretation can be inserted and become a "mutative" element. Ricoeur (1970) likens applied psychoanalysis to data about the analysand that might be supplied to the analyst by a third party. Despite the claim of some authors, such as Greenacre, that "the study of the works of a prolific artist offers material as usable for psychoanalytic investigation as the dreams and free associations of the patient" (1955, p. 13), this assumption has been disputed.

This essay will present some of the methodological problems encountered in the psychoanalytic study of literature. For my purpose I shall examine selected aspects of a number of psychoanalytic studies of Sophocles' Antigone. I shall also indicate methods of approaching the work based on textual analysis and on subjective response—procedures that appear complementary to the usual methods of psychoanalytic explication of literary works.

It might be appropriate to begin by reviewing the mythological background to the Antigone. Following Oedipus' death, his sons agreed to rule Thebes during alternate years. But at the end of his year on the throne, Eteocles refused to step down. His brother, Polyneices, with his father-in-law, raised an army and attacked Thebes, but their attempt ended in a disastrous rout. At the foot of the walled city the two brothers killed each other, and Creon, the former regent and uncle of the brothers, became king. Although he buried the Theban dead, he denied sepulchre to the enemy, including Polyneices. According to the myth, Antigone managed to bury her proscribed brother. The foregoing is all we possess of the mythological context of the play, and it is presumed that the events occurring in Sophocles' tragedy are largely his invention or that of his contemporaries.

The play opens on the day following the deaths of the brothers and Creon's assumption of the throne. Antigone tells her sister, Ismene, of Creon's edict that Polyneices' body must go unmourned and unburied, "a tasty meal for vultures," and that whoever violates his decree shall be stoned to death. Pleading fraternal love and the laws of the gods, Antigone announces her determination to bury Polyneices even if she must forfeit her life. The more Ismene insists that the idea is madness and bound to fail, that as women they must be obedient, the more hardened does Antigone become in her resolve.

When she attempts to carry out the funeral rites, she is seized and brought before Creon, to whom she avows her act but evokes "unwritten laws"—divine laws—that are timeless and universal, that transcend the edicts of any man. Creon proclaims his rule and law, asserting that enemies must be treated differently from friends, even though they be blood relatives. Antigone responds that she loves both her brothers. The king rejects this view and condemns her to death, absurdly and spitefully including Ismene in this sentence. Although Ismene pleads to be permitted to die with her sister, Antigone spurns her offer, desiring neither help nor a partner to share her sacrifice.

Creon's son, Haemon, appears before him and asks that Antigone be pardoned. Although engaged to marry her, his plea is free of emotion; he is logical and tactful, dealing with issues of justice and what he perceives are his father's profound errors. The scene ends with father and son exploding with rage and pain, and Creon poised to kill Antigone before Haemon's eyes.

Nevertheless, the king decides not to carry out the sacrilegious execution and orders that Antigone be immured in a cave with "enough fodder only to defend the country from the filth of a curse" (Braun, 936–937).[1] In her last appearance Antigone chants of her pain in departing from life, of never having been a bride, and never having nursed a baby.

She is succeeded on stage by the prophet Tiresias who describes a series of strange omens symbolic of the gods[1] anger with Creon's impious decree. It is clear that Polyneices must be buried at once. Creon incredibly accuses the seer of selling him out for money; Tiresias replies that the king is a sick tyrant who is committing a "crime of violence" and will be pursued by the "furies of death and deity." Although he repudiates the prophet, Creon is frightened and turns to the Chorus for counsel; they advise him to immediately release Antigone from the cave and to build a tomb for Polyneices. When he sets off to rescind his edict, the dramatic action rushes toward its ineluctable tragic end: Eurydice, his wife, learns that just before Creon reached the cave, Antigone had hanged herself. Haemon, in a frenzy of rage and anguish, attempts to kill his father, fails, and plunges the sword into himself.

Creon enters, bearing Haemon's shrouded body, lamenting his folly and violence; but his punishments are not yet at an end, for a messenger reveals that Eurydice, cursing her husband, has stabbed herself. Torn with grief and guilt, Creon years for oblivion, and the play ends.

From his studies on "neurotic virginity and old maidenhood," Weissman (1964) sought to demonstrate that Antigone is a typical "old maid" reflecting a specific psychosexual development. He found that the fixation of the old maid is not "truly Oedipal," but a fixation on the pre-oedipal mother—a wish for unification with her; and by displacement these disturbed object relations lead to the wish for unification with other family members—father and siblings—which results in an "indiscriminate devotion and loyalty to various members of the immediate family" (p. 32).

In support of his thesis Weissman cites Antigone's passionate desire to bury her brother as a demonstration of her "irrational devotion to the family unit" (p. 34). Similarly, Antigone's request that Ismene join her in the burial is regarded as an "unconscious motive" to unite all the family

---

[1]Quotations are taken from Braun (1973) unless otherwise indicated. I should like to thank Professor Braun, as well as the Oxford University Press, for their kind permission to quote from his translation. Numbers correspond to lines in this edition.

members in death. Since the pivot of the tragedy consists of Antigone's unrelenting drive to secure Polyneices' burial, Weissman does not lack for quotations to buttress his point of view. But at no point does he suggest an alternative interpretation of these actions, such as the sacred import of burial in ancient (and even modern) times. For the ancient Greeks, failure to bury the dead was an unspeakable crime. Bowra (1944) wrote that, although Sophocles' audience might, at most, have disagreed with Antigone, they would have readily understood her need to bury Polyneices. The dead have undeniable rights: to justice, to vengeance, and especially to proper burial. Without sepulchre the body lies unsanctified and homeless[2] Through powerful images the dramatist makes us see the degradation of Polyneices' corpse: "ripped for food by dogs and vulture," "the body was oozing," "the mangled body lay . . . where the dogs had dragged it," "the eagles ripped him for food," and so on. Clearly, the poet forces us to experience the horror of this uncared-for body. The omission of the issue of burial seriously weakens Weissman's thesis.

He stresses Antigone's "irrationalism," indicating that it comes from her unconscious wish for reunion with her mother; logically, her defiance of Creon's edict is "irrational," since it will lead to the death she unconsciously seeks. Weissman quotes an exchange with Creon wherein she declares that Hades makes no distinction between the brothers. But Creon retorts, "Not even death can metamorphose hate to love." To which Antigone responds: "No, nor decompose a love to hate" (p. 34).[3] To this affirmation of the power of Eros, Creon, the "rational" protagonist, exclaims, "Curse you! Find the outlet for your love down there [in Hades]" (p. 34).

To further establish Antigone's irrationality, Weissman presents Ismene not only as a standard of rationality, but as the "loyal mature mate or daughter," who "gives evidence . . . of a mature oedipally derived love . . . " (p. 40). His evidence for this characterization is that Ismene, unlike Antigone, did not wish to die when their father, Oedipus, died. Furthermore, during Oedipus' lifetime, Ismene did not "become his eyes or his single prop, or his partner in pain" (p. 39). Her maturity is illustrated by her "see[ing] no sense in Antigone's wish to die for her dishonorable brother. Her wish is to live, to be forgiven, and perhaps fulfill

---

[2]Sophocles also dealt with this issue in the Ajax.

[3]This line is usually translated as: "I was born not to hate but to love." See translations of Braun (1973), Fitts and Fitzgerald (1939), and Wyckoff (1973).

her own life" (p. 40). (Goethe described Ismene as a "beautiful standard of the commonplace [Eckermann, 1836, p. 185].)

Finally, Weissman's interpretation of an ambiguous passage is of particular significance. He asserts that the following speech of Antigone gives us a climactic portrayal of [her] psychosexual development toward old maidenhood, her preoedipal attachments, her devaluation and incapacity for a finalizing heterosexual relationship and having her own child. She explains to Creon:

> *On what principle do I assert so much?*
> *Just this: A husband dead, another can be found,*
> *A child, replaced; but a brother lost*
> *(Mother and father buried too)*
> *No other brother can be born or grows again.*
> *That's my principle, which Creon stigmatized*
> *As criminal—my principal for honoring*
> *You my dearest brother. So taken*
> *So I am led away; a spinster still*
> *Uncelebrated, barren and bereft of joys;*
> *No children to my name* [pp. 34–35].

While Weissman's broad interpretation of these verses seems challenged by the last three lines, his choice of this passage is of special interest because these lines (904–920 in the original version) have been the focus of a long-standing, unresolved controversy among scholars regarding their very authenticity. At this point it will be useful to make a detour in order to review another psychoanalytic study which is based entirely on the foregoing speech.

Van der Sterren's (1952) thesis is succinct and his methodology explicitly described: "I have used Freud's views on the psychology of the dream as my starting-point . . . myth and poetical productions come into being in the same way and have the same meaning . . . [except that] the secondary elaboration is much further developed . . . I hold, a priori, that this conception is the correct one, and the close study of these plays of Sophocles has shown me once more that this approach alone is able to solve the various problems and is moreover, a fruitful method" (p. 343). Van der Sterren seeks to demonstrate Antigone's neuroticism by asserting that by the time she speaks these lines (904–920) she has "lost the esteem of everyone." Clearly, if this allegation is correct it would totally undermine our acceptance of Antigone as a heroine. However, the evidence to support it is flimsy: Ismene rejects helping in Polyneices' burial only because it means risking her life; the Chorus, a group of timid old men, indeed at first support Creon's edict, but by the time of Antigone's final confrontation with the king they proclaim to her: "You go with fame and in glory/ to the hidden place of the dead . . . Your doom is worth grand fame; for living and dying, both you share/ the heritage of the gods' equals" (972–973, 988–990). Tiresias flatly calls Creon "stupid" and "criminal." Haemon declares that "the whole nation denies [that Antigone did wrong]" (882). Creon himself, far from disputing these assertions, retorts: "Will the nation tell me what orders I can give?" (883). And the denouement of the tragedy is Creon's destruction, working as a counterpoint to the paean of praise to Antigone.

Van der Sterren castigates critics who have questioned the validity of the speech; they are attempting to cover up its "real motive," he notes, and they "make false translations" (p. 349). In this context, he ambiguously quotes Goethe. Inasmuch as Weissman (1964) and Seidenberg and Papathomopoulos (1962) also refer to Goethe's comments, it would be instructive to examine them. According to Eckermann (1836), Goethe observed that: ". . . Creon by no means acts from political virtue, but from hatred towards the dead. Polynieces . . . did not commit such a monstrous crime against the state that his death was insufficient, and that further punishment of the innocent corpse was required . . . Creon . . . has everybody in the play against him" (p. 177–178; emphasis added). As for the disputed passage, Goethe did regard it as a "blemish," but stated he "would give a great deal for an apt philologist to prove that it is interpolated and spurious." In short, he believed the "passage . . . very far-fetched" (p. 178).

Although Jebb (1898) observed that "Few problems of Greek Tragedy have been more discussed than the question whether those verses, or some of them, are spurious" (p. 164), only Seidenberg and Papathomopoulos utilize this literature. This apparent lack of familiarity with the work carried out by nonanalytic scholars, as well as the not infrequent neglect of primary sources, often justifies the criticism of amateurism leveled against studies in applied psychoanalysis.

One might agree with Weissman's thesis that "neurotic virginity and old maidenhood" may mask a deeper attachment to the preoedipal mother; such a psychological schema may be an important factor in some women's avoidance of marriage; but we have little basis for assuming that Antigone had such an attachment to her mother. In fact, we do know that she is betrothed and deeply in love with Haemon; that she yearns for marriage and children; and that, far from "welcoming" death, she goes toward it with suffering and reluctance. At the end she chants: "No wedding song has been sung for this bride. I never nursed a child; and with those I love gone, I go alone and desolate" (1072–1074). These do not sound like the words of a woman in search of death fleeing from life, love, and men. We are overwhelmed by her death because it is a denial of all she desires. The poet obliges us to perceive Antigone as especially rich with the promise of life, precisely so that we experience the tragedy of her death rather than regard it as senseless, paltry, and banal.

Seidenberg and Papathomopoulos have dealt with Antigone in two communications. The first (1962) presents literary examples of "daughters who tend their fathers"; the second (1974) overlaps the earlier paper, but deals entirely with the "enigma" of Antigone. Their thesis is that Oedipus bound Antigone into caring for him, an "enslavement" which she dutifully accepted. "Although she is unable to fight on the battlefield, she seeks arete [virtue] in the capacity of a rebel, against the humiliation which her uncle demanded" (1962, p. 154); she prefers honor and arete to marriage and motherhood; in agreement with Van der Sterren they believe her defiant act represents an "abandonment of the feminine role," and is perhaps a defense against incestuous wishes toward Polyneices; that her defiance of Creon's edict represents an identification with her brothers; and that she has "at last succeeded in playing a role on the battlefield." They believe that "in the age of misogyny" Sophocles apparently realized the "hidden desires of certain women who did not conform to the general role . . . of homemaking and child rearing" (p. 155). Thus, while Antigone perhaps lamented being deprived of marriage and children she "secretly gives them up in favor of . . . a nobler destiny" (pp. 155–156).

Why Antigone "secretly" means the opposite of what she says is not demonstrated. Indeed, if Sophocles intends her words to be false, the drama would cease to be a tragedy and Antigone a heroine. Their speculation (also made by other writers) of her incestuous yearnings for Polyneices cannot be faulted. But much more prominent is the special role of women, in ancient societies, of attending to the sacred burial rites. If one views Antigone's behavior in terms of the values and mores current in Sophocles' time, one tends to accept this as a motive rather than a desire to shed her enslaved feminine self. Curiously, while Van der Sterren's argument is that Antigone is neurotically unhappy being a woman,

Seidenberg and Papathomopoulos refer to him in support of their position that she is secretly and appropriately unhappy being a woman—because she is oppressed.

Seidenberg and Papathomopoulos demonstrate another methodological error in treating Antigone and other fictional characters re-created by the artist (despite their mythological antecedents), as if they are historical figures, treating Euripides' Antigone to explain Sophocles' Antigone.

In their 1974 paper these authors again "confirm" Weissman's contention that Antigone is "a pre-oedipal old maid whose basic drive is to return to her nurturing mother." Through unification with her mother, Antigone "would make herself and create unto herself all those things which her mother lacked, strength, loyalty, convictions, in order to win mother, to be loved and be united with her. With good authority, Antigone would become irresistible to such a mother, for mother could never resist authority" (p. 202). Seidenberg and Papathomopoulos arrive at these conclusions in the following manner: Robert Graves, they note, "feels" that the name of Antigone in Greek means "in place of a mother";[4] "'in place of mother' . . . might . . . mean identification with mother; it is more likely the name represents the life that a woman might lead apart from motherhood with the confinements and passivity it engenders. The ancient Greeks in their wisdom knew that all women did not submit to the role of inferiority that the culture ruthlessly demanded" (p. 202). Such linguistic "evidence" is unconvincing and, furthermore, does not explain the contradiction between what is described as a "ruthlessly" misogynistic society and the wise ancient Greeks who inhabited it. Through the same need to establish an aura of universal misogyny, they cite, correctly, Creon's depreciation of women. Yet they observe that Antigone was "esteemed" by the "whole" city. Actually, Sophocles seems primarily intent on the aesthetic task of polarizing Antigone and Creon in every plausible way. Undoubtedly, the growing regard for women in fifth-century Greece had some impact on him. But his artistic imperative is to stress the conflict between Creon and Antigone, and this is expressed in their respective imagery, the rhythms of their speech, their age and their sex—in order to make the drama work as theatre. Accordingly, Creon is the only male character who demeans women. Seidenberg and

---

[4]Braun notes: "Sophocles took their [names'] meaning seriously, for he created an Antigone who, 'born to oppose,' relies on innate courage in facing tyranny . . . " (1973, p. 7).

Papathomopoulos, along with the authors reviewed here, minimize aesthetic considerations.

The conclusion of their article reiterates their feminist interpretation of the Antigone through a series of speculations, of which I shall quote but one: "Had Antigone been a male youth and had been similarly disobedient, there would have been at most talk of generational gap, oedipal conflict, primal horde, but not deformity" (p. 204). One cannot disagree with the authors' impassioned denunciation of the oppression of women, but one must challenge the correctness of their interpretation of Antigone, its ahistoric viewpoint, and their concept that the Antigone concerns the subjugation of women.

Along with others, Kanzer (1948), (1950) regards the Oedipus Tyrannus, the Oedipus at Colonus, and the Antigone as an Oedipus Trilogy, which "dramatize[s] three stages in the development and resolution of the oedipus complex" (1950, p. 571). Kanzer's focus is on Oedipus, and his remarks on Antigone for the most part relate to her relation to him. For example, he interprets the blinded Oedipus' dependence on Antigone as her playing the "role of the mother." Similarly, he regards her defiance of Creon's ban on the burial of Polyneices as a displacement of "her loyalty from her father to her brother"; thus, her behavior is seen primarily as a manifestation of her unresolved oedipal conflict. While this interpretation is plausible from the perspective of the total "trilogy," it loses cogency when considered within the reduced frame of the Antigone where the oedipal dynamics do not appear central to the drama and in which more acute and gripping issues occupy the stage.

By maintaining an oedipal interpretation of the Antigone, Kanzer is led to interpret Creon as a figure complementary to Oedipus; as the latter partially identified with his rejecting father, Laius, and hence expelled his sons, so, in the Antigone, Creon is the castrator of the sons: Haemon, Polyneices, and Eteocles. "It is the force of this castration anxiety," Kanzer writes, "effecting the resolution of the oedipus complex, which is the unconscious content of the Antigone" (p. 566). But are the sons Creon's victims? In the first instance it is his niece, Antigone, whom he destroys. His son and wife kill themselves, admittedly because of what Creon has done. But Polyneices and Eteocles destroy each other, and the former is victimized by Creon only by being denied reunion with the other dead in the family. In the broadest sense, Creon's victims are all the citizens of Thebes who quickly found themselves under his yoke. Even Creon's clash with Haemon is unconvincing as an oedipal father-son battle because the element of jealousy is totally lacking. Only by hypothesizing a series of displacements can Creon be plausibly described as essentially a "castrating father." As I shall show later on, his behavior seems more understandable when viewed in terms of narcissistic considerations.

Perhaps because Kanzer was not satisfied with his interpretation of the Antigone, he concludes his essay by focusing on the Athenian society of Sophocles' time, which he presents as a necessary background for understanding the tragedies. He suggests that Antigone's behavior might represent a love of family. But he does not integrate the psychoanalytic and sociologic interpretations beyond noting that "Social forces impinge on and are transmitted into the idiom of individual experience" (Kanzer, 1950, p. 571).

Wolman (1965) has related Antigone's sacrifice of her life to Freud's description of self-sacrificing love: an overflowing of narcissistic libido onto the object. The latter becomes increasingly precious "until at last it gets possession of the entire self-love of the ego, whose self-sacrifice thus follows as a natural consequence" (Freud, 1921, p. 113). Wolman calls such self-sacrificial love the Antigone Principle and describes it in terms of valorous acts in battle, rites of passage, martyrdom, and resistance to religious persecution. Since he makes no distinction between heroism in general, heroism in Greek tragedy, courage, martyrdom and self-sacrifice, he is able to place in his Pantheon of heroes the youth of Sparta, Jan Huss, Londoners under the Blitz, and Israeli soldiers. Wolman concludes that, since "not every suffering is heroic," the true heroes are "men who willingly suffer for others" (p. 193). How one might determine willingness to suffer, the degree of pain endured, and what Wolman means by "a better future for others," is unclear. Antigone, he asserts, was a normal individual, not a masochist; she loved life, but her "love for justice was stronger than the love for herself" (p. 200). This abstract "love for justice," however, is different from Antigone's piety, from her moral imperative, from her powerful sense of family bonds, and from her outrage at Creon's violation of the unwritten laws.

Furthermore, Wolman does not use the meaning of the hero in the specific sense in which it was understood in ancient Greece, particularly in Greek tragedy. What makes Antigone a heroine in the classic mold, what distinguishes her from ordinary mortals, are, it seems to me, superior powers: her burning emotions, her keener insight, her capacity both to give and to experience pain, and her endurance of suffering. The hero may rise above common men by his mastery in battle or statecraft, in athletics, in prophesy, or in dance or song. He demands respect, inspires love, and is recognized as noble—as befits "a strange being neither man nor god but both" (Bowra, 1944, p. 315). This delineation of the classic hero has little in common with many of Wolman's heroes, who are measured by other scales; but it is the very essence of the Antigone of Sophocles, who forges her character precisely so that she becomes a heroine in this sense. To misconstrue Antigone's heroism reduces the Antigone, at best, to a brilliantly constructed tale of martyrdom and a one-dimensional view of Creon-as-villain.

Erich Fromm's remarks on Antigone appear in the context of a general discussion of the Oedipus complex and the Oedipus myth (1949). He asserts that the Oedipus myth is "a symbol not of the incestuous love between mother and son but of the rebellion of the son against the authority of the father in a patriarchal society" (p. 338). Like Kanzer (who has critically reviewed Fromm's essay) he leans heavily on regarding the three Oedipus plays as a unity. Although much of their respective these depends on this hypothesis, the evidence remains inconclusive[5]. In a scholarly discussion of this question, Jebb (1898) presents internal evidence in support of the view that the plays do not constitute a connected trilogy, and that the Antigone was actually part of another trilogy, of which the other two plays are lost (of the over 120 written by Sophocles, only seven remain). He concludes that "In nothing is the art of Sophocles more characteristically seen than in the fact that each of these three masterpieces—with their common thread of fable, and with all their particular affinities—is still, dramatically and morally, an independent-whole" (xlix–l). Disagreement with Jebb—and other likeminded scholars—is hardly a breach of critical rigor, but such differences should be acknowledged even if not evaluated.

Again, like Kanzer, Fromm interprets the conflict between Creon and Haemon as analogous to the clash between Oedipus and Polyneices in the Oedipus at Colonus, where the unforgiven son is cast out. But where Kanzer interprets this conflict as fueled by the son's incestuous strivings in a headlong encounter with the castrating potential of the father, Fromm explains it in terms of a conflict between a matriarchal principle incarnated by Oedipus, Haemon, and Antigone, and a patriarchal

---

[5]The three plays were actually written over a forty-year span, with the Antigone written first, the Oedipus Tyrannus at least thirteen years later, and the Oedipus at Colonus over 22 years after that, when Sophocles was close to 90 years old.

principle represented by Creon. These principles were formulated by J. J. Bachofen, between 1859 and 1870, and emerged from his detailed scholarly work on "mother right." Since Fromm reviews this work, and it is also alluded to by Kanzer, only a brief exposition of it is required here.

Bachofen studied the symbols found in the myths, art, and artifacts of ancient Greece, Rome, Egypt, and other areas of the Mediterranean basin. He conceptualized a nomadic, hetaeristic, primitive world governed by unbridled sexuality, which was slowly replaced by an agricultural, socioreligious culture, in which mother right dominated. Ultimately, this era was superseded by a patriarchal society which brought the "liberation of the spirit from the manifestation of nature, a substitution of human existence over the law of material life . . . " (Bachofen, 1859, p. 109). Bachofen stressed that elements of the old often coexisted with the new, or re-emerged after periods of oblivion.

During the era of mother right, there was an "emphasis on maternal property and the name of the maternal line, the closeness of maternal kinship . . . and the inexpiability of matricide" (p. 71). There was greater love for sisters than for brothers, loyalty to mothers, and ". . . the divine principle of love, of union, of peace" (p. 79). Matriarchal love is more

intense, and unlike the patriarchal principle, which is "inherently restrictive, the matriarchal principle, is universal." It is the basis of freedom, equality, and hospitality. "Devotion, justice, and all the qualities that embellish man's life are known by feminine names . . . " (p. 91). The rise of patriarchy saw the emergence of spiritual over corporeal existence, of the Apollonian over the chthonian-maternal principle. Laws, rationality, monogamy, authority, a hierarchical order in society, and inequality became the hallmarks of the new epoch.

Against all objections to Bachofen, Fromm finds the theory of matriarchy "established beyond any doubt," and thus he explicates the Oedipus "trilogy" as a clash between the matriarchal and patriarchal principles. The slow, painful, and often violent passage of matriarchal into patriarchal society, and the continued presence of aspects of the earlier period in the later is represented, according to Fromm, in the conflict in the Antigone. Antigone herself embodies the importance of the human being, of natural law and love, in contrast to Creon who proclaims the state, man-made laws, and obedience. Ismene is the prototype of the woman who accepts patriarchal domination and the defeat of women. For Creon, his son is mere property whose unique purpose is to serve; the king's defeat brings to an end the "principle of authoritarianism, of man's domination over the people" (p. 353).

Fromm thus projects onto the Antigone his social ideology, but, despite undoubted relevances, his formulation seems strangely external to the passions of the drama itself; its approach to the play is with an ideological yardstick that reductively interprets this (or any) work of art, in which the protagonists are in conflict over such issues as authority, law, conscience, and religious standards, as representing a conflict between the matriarchal and patriarchal principles.

Fromm appends to the foregoing interpretation of the Antigone an auxiliary but unintegrated view which attempts to relate the drama to the "specific political and cultural situation of Sophocles' time." He identifies Sophocles as an adversary of the Sophists, whom he describes as seeking to establish a despotism of the intellectual elite and "upholding unrestricted selfishness as a moral principle" (p. 354), and he equates Creon with the Sophists, a view shared by Kanzer. While both authors urge us to accept Sophocles' straightforward antagonism to Sophism, Fromm interprets the trilogy as specifically expressing not only Sophocles' opposition to the Sophists, but his sympathy for the old, nonolympian, religious traditions of the matriarchy, when love, equality, and justice were valued. These assertions are questionable if we look at Sophocles' place in Athenian society. Bowra (1944), Kirkwood (1958), Kitto (1956), Whitman (1951), and other scholars mentioned here, have made authoritative contributions in this area. I shall only touch on some of the sociologic issues raised by Fromm and Kanzer.

There is, in fact, little difficulty in identifying aspects of the Antigone with matters that were prominent in Sophocles' lifetime. That he himself was totally a part of his era, if not an active partisan of positions, is attested to by even the scant knowledge we have of him: a total of perhaps four pages of uncertain biographic data. Letters (1953) sums up some of this material: "Sophocles was not only one of Athens' 'lofty, grave tragedians,' he was an active citizen, man about town, lover of food, wine and company, musician, conversationalist, wit, homosexual, actor, literary dictator, juror, admiral, priest and copious writer of Rabelaisian farces . . ." (p. 2). It is not then surprising that the play brilliantly reflects issues such as divine and human justice, the nature of the unwritten laws, the position of women in society, the individual vis-a-vis the state, the role of the king, and fate versus free will. Much of the critical literature seeks to establish which of these questions is what the Antigone "is about." And yet, the only certain conclusion one can reach is that the drama is as remarkably free of open partisanship on these issues as it is thoroughly penetrated with the social, philosophical, political, and religious issues of its day.

The Antigone, on one level, demonstrates that unreason, impiety (even if religion is only a projection made by man—as the Sophists averred), and pride (hubris) are among the greatest dangers for man. These themes are characteristic of that "impact of society" on the drama to which Kanzer alluded, and they reach us on conscious and preconscious levels of apprehension. But there exists another dimension to the poet's work, of which he himself may have been unaware, and which we may deeply experience even if without intellectual understanding: the resonance of the drama with our unconscious, which has only the most intricate, indirect, and long-term relation to society.

If we seek a psychoanalytic understanding of the Antigone, or any other work of art, we must turn to the text, with as few a priori ideas about it as possible, as the source best embodying the data to be studied (the analogy of listening to the patient, rather than studying documents from other people, seems valid). It is my impression that the first and most striking observation about the drama, as an aesthetic entity, is that it is a tissue of contrasts. The structure is built up through a series of confrontations: of Antigone and Ismene, of Creon and the sentry, then with Ismene, Haemon, Antigone, and Tiresias. Light and dark episodes alternate, as do life and death, hope and despair, authority and revolt, justice and injustice, man's law and divine law, piety and impiety, free will and fate, democracy and autocracy, the individual and the state, reason and passion, flexibility and rigidity—the list of antinomies could be continued. And affectively, as scene follows scene, we swing between states of tension and relaxation, until we are finally swept to the horrifying denouement.

The poet uses all his craft to suggest contrast. As mentioned earlier, the very language used by each character, the cadences of their speech, their imagery—everything builds the atmosphere of conflict. The details of how this is done, e.g., Creon's repeated use of animal images, has been elucidated by Goheen (1951).

Although the superstructure of the tragedy consists of contrasting elements welded into an aesthetic whole, and the chief polarities of that conflict are represented by Antigone and Creon, these characters are not simple conduits for contrasting beliefs; on the contrary, they are concrete as well as generic individuals, whose personalities reverberate in our unconscious. It is because Creon and Antigone are not mere standard-bearers, engaged in abstract verbal exchanges, but are plausible flesh-and-blood individuals, that the drama "works" on the affective as well as cognitive levels. The poet engages us in a powerful enterprise of empathy.

To experience the play is also to recognize that Antigone and Creon transcend simple opposition, for each serves to define the other. If "Antigone is the balance in which Creon is weighed and found wanting" (Whitman, 1951, p. 80), then Creon must be the crucible in which Antigone becomes tempered so that she may achieve the grandeur that death bestows upon her. Creon's behavior leads Antigone to heroism. To experience the Antigone obliges us to enter Creon's inner world.

What manner of man is this ruler? Some authors, such as Kitto (1956), assert that he is the central character in the Antigone; in fact, a third of the drama takes place after Antigone's final appearance. For the Athenian audience, to whom Sophocles spoke, Creon is a tyrant. He first appears with homage to the gods on his lips, asserting that the worst ruler is one who "fails to embrace the best man's counsels" (218). But he swiftly reveals his duplicity, and by the end of his first speech his authoritarianism is revealed in his decree that brutally violates all tradition. Each succeeding confrontation of his power progressively exposes him as stubborn, arrogant, violent, and irrational. At one point his sense of reality is so overwhelmed by rage that he forgets that it is only Antigone, and not Ismene as well, whom he has condemned to death! The more his authority is challenged or even questioned, the more his self-esteem is threatened and the more are ignoble qualities brought to light. His piety is a sham; he courts the gods only when they serve him and denigrates them when they no longer meet his needs. When he fears their anger at his decree of death for Antigone he changes only the letter of his command by ordering that she be permitted to die of starvation. From wherever the source, whatever the validity, he intemperately rejects all criticism—even the timid questions of the old men in the Chorus.

Repeatedly, Sophocles shows us that Creon values individuals only as possessions to be utilized and manipulated for his own aggrandizement. His view of love is mostly limited to its physical aspect: when Ismene asks him if he means to "kill the girl you promised your own son would marry" (701–702) he crassly responds that "There are other fields to furrow" (703). Of utmost importance are the growing distortions in his thinking: he levels totally unjustified accusations of corruption by bribery against those who oppose him: the unknown individuals who first attempt to bury Polyneices "were seduced by money" (372); the sentry who reports the deed is told that "for money—you sold your soul" (402); even the saintlike Tiresias has it flung in his face that he "and his kind, for a long time now, have been selling me out . . . " (196–197). This almost delusional thinking is scarcely surprising, for early in the play Creon complains of "certain men in the city . . . [who] mutter about me" (366–368). When Tiresias aptly states "you are a sick man" (1216), we concur that Creon indeed exhibits paranoid thoughts. His narcissistic hunger pervades all his behavior, his thoughts and feelings, domestic as well as public, and leads to his resentment of youth and women and to his voracious yearning for power. "Nations," he pronounces, "belong to the men with power. That's common knowledge" (888–889).

And yet, beyond all expectations, at his downfall, after we have witnessed the blood bath he has brought about, we do not cast this prototypical tyrant into darkness, but instead feel, as Bonnard put it (1951), "only tenderness and pity." Creon is a figure of "human error" whom Sophocles has given us, not as a warning, but as a fraternal being; too much a part of us to condemn him from the heights of our own abstract principles. Within his character Creon is "right" and must act he does so that the drama will confront us with our divided self and the real world in which it must act. Through Creon the poet awakens sleeping aspects of ourselves, illuminating our complexity. His childlike tyranny acts not only on the people around him but on himself because he is in bondage to his instinctual impulses and primitive modes of response. In contrast, Antigone is more autonomous and object-seeking, and through her death she escapes the very solitude that finally descends on Creon. His need for power becomes impotence; he fears and despises Eros for it would make him vulnerable to the world, and with the loss of narcissistic objects his world collapses. But his late-learned wisdom echoes our yearning to be free from the imperious reign of our own infantilism—thus we rejoice in his tragic growth as we do in Antigone's tragic and heroic death.

This brings us to consider the feelings we experience at the conclusion of the drama. I believe that this subjective dimension, the experience of the spectator, is a critical aspect of the psychoanalytic investigation of literature, and yet, more frequently than not, it is neglected in favor of more "objective" criteria. The "evenly suspended attention" of the analyst in the analytic situation, his brief identifications with the patient, the scrutiny and analysis of his own fantasies, dreams, and feelings are processes that do not often occur in applied psychoanalysis. Paradoxically, the Antigone leaves us with a special sense of pleasure, which suffuses us at the conclusion of the tragedy. The universality of this experience may be open to question, but its widespread occurrence is readily observed. "Tragic pleasure" is more than a simple experience of evasion and disengagement, or a vicarious brush with Antigone's pain from which we escape unscathed. Bonnard (1951) described it as "the price of our active participation in the poet's work. It manifests our commitment to this enterprise of recreation of the world" (p. 71). The tragic poet's classical vocation was educative and formative, and his drama, in which we participate, becomes an apprenticeship in pain that leads to a mastery of the human condition through a process of self-elucidation—a process reminiscent of psychoanalysis.

The contradiction between our pain and our pleasure is only apparent once we recognize that Creon and Antigone represent profound aspects of our self. As Creon acts out before us his infantile wishes for omnipotence, omniscience, approval and admiration, and total license, we cannot reject him because too much of him resonates with elements that once were in us—and may still reside in only relative silence; we see in him our "negative ego ideal"; he incarnates all that we would project on to the other. Antigone, on the other hand, embodies what we would become. Her tragic end represents the expression of our yearnings of our ideal ego; with her we triumph over blind fate, over our infantile self, and we identify with her victory.

Antigone might be perceived as embodying many facets of our ego ideal: courageous, passionate, loyal to her kin, eloquent, loved and loving, generous, competent, and possessing "superior powers"; in short, the qualities described by Bibring (1953) as constituting our narcissistic aspirations. Although we are aware of her arrogance, irrationality, and stubbornness, it is her positive characteristics that engage us. On the other hand, while Creon is stubborn, increasingly irrational, arrogant, misogynistic, unloved, and not truly loving, he feels pain, bereavement, fear, shame, and in some manner he loves his wife, his children, and his subjects, and yearns to be approved of by the city. His downfall brings us no pleasure, for we experience his despair.

Somewhat analogous to the two levels of experiencing the Antigone which I have described, Holland (1968) hypothesized two paths of experiencing a work of art: one tests reality, is intellectual, is generally characterized by other aspects of secondary-process thinking, and is in connection with the "central theme" of the work; the other is characterized by the introjection of the work, the experience of the nuclear fantasy and the formal management of that fantasy as if it were our own. We analogize the work to our own fantasies which become more acceptable to us, and the work itself takes on an intellectual meaning. Our identification with a character would be due to a complicated mixture of the introjection of that character's drives and defenses and our projection onto him of elements within ourself. We can identify with certain characters chiefly on the basis of their instinctual drives, and with others mostly because of their defenses. From this perspective, some of the pleasure of literature would derive from various combinations of limited gratification of drive and other fantasies, and the defensive management of those fantasies, leading to pleasure in the totality of the work. Holland's conceptualization further explains the pleasure we experience from the Antigone.

This dimension of aesthetic pleasure appears to promise much in furthering a psychoanalytic view of literature. Despite studies by Freud (1905), Kris (1952), Lesser (1957), Rose (1964), Waelder (1965), Coltrera (1965), Within (1969), and Ricoeur (1970), among others, the subject remains far from resolved. The analysis of the aesthetic response offers the advantage of obliging us to consider the work as an artistic unity, rather than as a collection of isolated characters and events. It becomes a part of the task of viewing the work as the creation of a given poet in a particular culture, which is being experienced by concrete

individuals at the same and other times and places. Such a holistic view necessarily leads to interdisciplinary studies.

Regarding the expression I have used here, "the psychoanalytic interpretation of literature," it must be avowed that the term is imprecise because interpretations made in the analytic situation cannot be equated with those made in applied psychoanalysis. Loewenstein (1951) succinctly defined interpretation: "In psychoanalysis this term is applied to those explanations, given to patients by their analyst, which add to their knowledge about themselves" (p. 4); these explanations are given piecemeal and ultimately encompass ego and id elements. This definition applies specifically to the clinical psychoanalytic situation. A number of authors have discussed the differences between interpretation in analysis compared with other settings. Kohut (1960) observed that in applied psychoanalysis there is no free association, no therapeutic alliance, no emotional tie to the therapist, no reverbatory dreams that might follow an interpretation, and no motivation (and, one might add, there is no patient). Ricoeur (1970) noted that "the psychoanalytic interpretation of art is fragmentary because it is analogical" (p. 164). What is lacking is the process of interchange, on many levels, between patient and analyst, involving fluctuating levels and varieties of resistance, the vicissitudes of transference and the integration of insight—in a word, the flux of a human relationship in the analytic setting.

CONCLUSIONS

The problems inherent in the psychoanalytic interpretation of literature, not to speak of other areas of applied psychoanalysis, have led at times to skepticism that scholarly work can be accomplished in a field so fraught with pitfalls. Such a position is counterproductive because it is only through many efforts and repeated critiques that more rigorous approaches will be developed.

Great works of art, such as the Antigone, offer different levels of meaning. They are ambiguous in that the elements within them are highly overdetermined—a concept explored by Kris and Kaplan (Kris, 1952). It is natural that exclusive attention to selected aspects, or levels of meaning, of a literary work, can be carried out for research purposes, but these must ultimately be integrated into the work as a whole lest serious distortions occur. Similarly, while it may be useful to isolate a character from a work, to explore him "independently," that character must be reinserted into the network of his dynamic relations with the other characters and with the writer's overarching aesthetic conception. Perhaps the greatest weakness in the psychoanalytic studies of literature is that they rarely acknowledge that several interpretations may all plausibly reveal something about a work of art.

It must be stressed that psychoanalytic interpretations of literature, just as interpretations in the analytic situation, must not only be logical and internally consistent, but must be supported by the text. The more of the work that can be reasonably explained and the fewer the exceptions and contradictions, the sturdier will be the interpretation. The text itself is the final arbiter: other data—such as information about the author and his motives—can at best be used to support and confirm interpretations based on the text, its style, form, and content.

To seek to understand some literature through a purely "psychological" approach appears as untenable as the reverse of that coin—a purely "sociological" approach. It has become increasingly apparent, especially for certain literary works, that it is not possible to understand them unless the web of relations of the work to society are carefully explored.

Similarly, certain works will remain an enigma unless brought into relation with the author's life if useful data about it are available. In still other works, biographical data and information about the social setting may be relatively unimportant for our understanding, and the text itself remains the crucial datum.

Despite the hazards that confront psychoanalysis when it attempts to understand literature, despite the shortcomings and the reductionism, there is little doubt that psychoanalysis has made valuable and unique contributions. Psychoanalysis, of all disciplines, remains the only one able to explore the unconscious and all its derivatives. The cultural products of man are therefore a most fitting subject for psychoanalytic investigation, and if the difficulties are vast, the process itself is its own reward.

SUMMARY

Through a critical review of several studies dealing with Sophocles' drama, the Antigone, I have explored some of the prominent methodological problems encountered in the psychoanalytic interpretation of literature. Foremost among these is the inherent difficulty that the interpretation of literature is unable to benefit from the process of the analytic situation. Divorced from the realities of the therapeutic process, the drama itself is often used to corroborate an author's theoretical bias or to advance some special interest, with consequent distortion or blurring of the text. Although data about the artist's life and sociocultural environment may be of crucial significance, it is the text itself that must be the ultimate object of study. Through a re-examination of the Antigone as an aesthetic totality I have sketched out what appears to be an alternative manner of approaching the drama, and suggested that works of art reach us on both unconscious and conscious levels. I have stressed the need to analyze our emotional response to a work as affording a valuable source of insight into the work itself.

Throughout, I have drawn attention to the need for greater scholarly rigor and the value of interdisciplinary collaboration. An open recognition of the problems in the psychoanalytic study of literature should serve to minimize dilettantism and raise the level of scholarship.

REFERENCES

BACHOFEN, J.J. (1859–1870). *Myth, Religion and Mother Right.* Transl. R. Manheim. Princeton: Princeton University Press, 1967.

BIBRING, E. (1953). The mechanism of depression. In: *Affective Disorders,* ed. P. Greenacre. New York: International Universities Press, pp. 13–48.

BOWRA, C.M. (1944). Sophoclean Tragedy New York: Oxford University Press.

BONNARD, A. (1951). *La Tragdie et l'Homme* Paris: A la Baconnire.

BRAUN, R.E., transl. (1973). *Sophochles Antigone* New York: Oxford University Press.

COLTRERA, J.T. (1965). On the creation of beauty and thought: The unique as vicissitude. *American Psychoanalytic Association.* 13:634–703.

ECKERMANN, J.P. (1836). *Conversations with Goethe.* Transl. J. Oxenford. London: Dent, 1930.

EISSLER, K.R. (1959). The function of details in the interpretation of works of literature. *Psychoanalytic Quarterly* 28:1–20.

——— (1968). The relation of explaining and understanding in psycho-analysis: Demonstrated by one aspect of Freud's approach to literature The *Psychoanalytic Study Child* 23:141–177 New York: International Universities Press.

FITTS, D. & FITZGERALD, R., transl. 1939 *Sophocles The Oedipus Cycle.* New York: Harcourt, Brace & World.

FREUD, S. (1905) Psychopathic characters on the stage. *Standard Edition* 7:305–310.

——— (1921). Group psychology and the analysis of the ego. *Standard Edition* 18:67–143.

FROMM, E. (1949). The Oedipus complex and the Oedipus myth. In: *The Family: Its Function and Destiny.* ed. R. N. Anshen. New York: Harper, pp. 334–358.

GEDO, J.E. (1970). Thoughts on art in the age of Freud *Journal of the American Psychoanalytic Association* 18:219–245.

GOHEEN, R.E. (1951). *The Imagery of Sophocles' Antigone.* Princeton: Princeton University Press.

Greenacre, P. (1955). *Swift and Carroll: A Psychoanalytic Study of Two Lives.* New York: International Universities Press.

HOLLAND, N. (1968). *The Dynamics of Literary Response.* New York: Oxford University Press.

Jebb, R. (1898). *Sophocles: The Plays and Fragments Part III The Antigone* Cambridge: Cambridge University Press, 1972.

KANZER, M. (1948). The passing of the oedipus complex in Greek drama. *International Journal of Psychoanalysis* 29:131–134.

——— (1950). The Oedipus trilogy. *Psychoanalytic Quarterly* 19:561–573.

KIRKWOOD, G.M. (1958). *A Study of Sophoclean Drama.* Ithaca: Cornell University Press.

KITTO, H.D.F. (1956). *Form and Meaning in Drama: A Study of Six Greek Plays and of Hamlet.* London: Methuen.

KOHUT, H. (1960). Beyond the bounds of the basic rule *Journal of the American Psychoanalytic Association* 8:567–586.

KRIS, E. (1952). *Psychoanalytic Explorations in Art.* New York: International Universities Press.

LESSER, S.O. (1957). *Fiction and the Unconscious.* Boston: Beacon Hill Press.

LETTERS, F.J.H. (1953). *The Life and Work of Sophocles.* London: Sheed & Ward.

LOEWENSTEIN R.M. (1951). The problem of interpretation *Psychoanalytic Quarterly* 20:1–14.

RICOEUR, P. (1970). *Freud and Philosophy.* New Haven: Yale University Press.

ROSE, G.J. (1964). Creative imagination in terms of ego "care" and boundaries *International Journal of Psychoanalysis* 45:75–85.

SEIDENBERG, R. & PAPATHOMOPOULOS, E. (1962). Daughters who tend their fathers. A literary survey. *The Psychoanalytic Study of Society* 2:135–160 New York: International Universities Press.

———— ———— (1974). The enigma of Antigone *International Review of Psychoanalysis* 1:197–205.

Van der Sterren, H.A. 1952 The "King Oedipus" of Sophocles. *International Journal of Psychoanalysis* 33:343–350.

WAELDER, R. (1965). *Psychoanalytic Avenues to Art.* New York: International Universities Press.

WEISSMAN, P. (1964) Antigone—a preoedipal old maid *J. Hillside Hosp.* 13 32–42.

WHITMAN, C. H. (1951). *Sophocles: A Study of Heroic Humans.* Cambridge: Harvard University Press.

WITHIN, P. (1969). The psychodynamics of literature. *Psychoanalytic Review* 56:556–585.

WOLMAN, B. (1965). The Antigone principle. *American Imago* 22:186–201.

WYCKOFF, E., transl. (1973). *Sophocles Antigone* ed. D. Greene & R. Lattimore. New York: Washington Square Press.

CHAPTER 13

Thomas Hardy's *'The Well-Beloved'* and the Nature of Infatuation

[Werman, D.S. & Jacobs, T.J. (1983). *International Review of Psycho-Analysis* 10:447–457.]

'Who Ever Loved That Loved Not At First Sight?'
—Christopher Marlowe, *Hero and Leander*

Freud frequently observed that the differences between healthy, neurotic and psychotic individuals are quantitative. Perhaps nothing better illustrates this axiom than the madness that seizes individuals when they come under the dominion of an infatuation. If this virtually ineffable experience is not universal, it surely enjoys an extraordinary ubiquity among people of many cultures and historic epochs; and although most frequently seen during adolescence, it can occur at any age. However, despite the growing psychoanalytic literature pertaining to love, relatively little attention has been paid to the phenomenon of infatuation.

Freud (1914a) declared that *all* adult love formed a continuum. Representing it schematically, he identified two major roots as constituting the origins of 'falling in love' (his expression, which is close to or equivalent to infatuation). The first is an 'anaclitic' form in which the care-taking mother, or in later years her substitute, becomes the love object; and the other is a narcissistic type. In his often quoted schema Freud described three forms that this kind of love may take. A person may love what he himself is, i.e. himself; what he himself once was or would like to be; or he may love someone who represents what once was a part of himself.

Indeed, the narcissistic aspect of infatuation is well-encompassed in the word itself, which is derived from *infatuare*, from *fatuus*, or foolish, and originally referred to a foolish admiration and overvaluation of *oneself*, a meaning still maintained in modern French (Robert, 1970).

Presented in a modified form at the Annual Meeting of the American Psychoanalytic Association, 8 May 1981, in San Juan, P.R.

Note: The style and use of quotation marks and italics witin this article's text is retained from the original journal publication.

In discussing transference love, Freud (1914b) observed that it 'consists of old traits and that it repeats infantile reactions. *But this is the essential character of every state of being in love. There is no such state which does not reproduce infantile prototypes.* It is precisely from this infantile determinism that it receives its compulsive character, verging as it does on the pathological. Transference love has perhaps a degree less of freedom than the love which appears in ordinary life and is called normal; it displays its dependence on the infantile pattern more clearly and is less adaptable and capable of modification; *but that is all, and not what is essential'* (p. 168, our italics).

In his discussion of transference love, which, in many respects resembles infatuation, Freud described other of its characteristics: it is 'lacking to a high degree in a regard for reality, is less sensible, less concerned about consequences and more blind to its valuation of the loved person than we are prepared to admit in the case of normal love. We should not forget, however, that these departures from the norm constitute precisely what is essential about being in love' (pp. 168–169).

Binstock (1973) regarded infatuation, in contrast to a 'gratifying love relationship', as an 'exercise in identity formation' (p. 104). His concepts are succinctly condensed in an epigram: 'Infatuation . . . is an identification wrapped in the appurtenances of a search for gratification' (p. 103). He specifically related infatuation to disturbances in the symbiotic phase of infant life.

In describing infatuation, Miller & Siegel (1972) stressed as a central feature the strong sexual attraction mainly based on resemblance to a fantasy which, for both sexes, derives from the 'original love object'—the mother. The beloved is seen as 'possessing physical and behavioral traits of the caretaking person who first engendered love' (p. 68). Cultural influences further define one's idea of the ideal beauty. Bak (1973) asserted that falling in love represents an attempt to undo the original separation from mother, as well as subsequent separations. Kernberg (1974) wrote that people who become infatuated have an incapacity for establishing object relations; infatuation is a repetition compulsion whose origins are in developmental failures. Men who have such difficulties usually demonstrate intense envy and hatred of women because of early, chronic, frustration by a mother who withheld all that was lovable and admirable.

Arlow (1980) criticized the view which regards the vicissitudes of object relations as the specific determinant of later patterns of loving.

He discerned many diverse patterns, each multiply determined. 'Loving involves identification, but identification at many levels and at many different times with different objects. It is not necessarily a regressive reactivation of the primitive fusion with a love object or regression to a phase where there is no distinction between self and object world' (p. 123).

Furthermore, Arlow saw some pre-oedipal residues in all love relations: 'the loving relationship is a bit of unreality set aside from the world of reality' (p. 128). He broadened the issue in refusing to identify love *only* with object relations, or regressions, or development, and suggested that cultural factors are also important in influencing our ideas of love. In that regard he has pointed out that 'The fusion of the tender and the sensuous streams of libidinal impulse and the idealization of the love object is a notion that was canonized during the romantic period' (p. 179).

Bergmann (1980) stressed the mother imago behind the loved one and analogized falling in love to the dream in which the unconscious wish is the prohibited oedipal desire. In contrast to infatuation he advanced five functions characteristic of a 'felicitous' falling in love: (1) Adequate reality testing to recognize the 'real' qualities of the love object. (2) Integration of several part love objects with the current one. (3) Counteraction of the superego so that the love object is not eliminated by the incest taboo. (4) Counteraction of id demands for the impossible replica of the longed-for symbiosis. (5) Avoidance of the repetition compulsion which forces the love object to conform to the original love object. We believe that it is evident that to a marked degree some or all of these functions fail when infatuation occurs.

Although psychoanalysts have paid relatively little attention to infatuation, poets and novelists have often shown a deep interest in it. Among those who have attempted to express the nature of infatuation, Thomas Hardy is notable because he devoted an entire novel to a character whose life is 'dedicated to Aphrodite' by his pursuit of the Beloved and his attempts to capture her essence in sculpture. His unquenchable propensity to become infatuated-a painful, repetitive, and finally absurd ritual–ceases only toward the end of his life. '*The Well-Beloved,*' we believe, not only provides us with a phenomenology of infatuation, but even suggests something about its psychodynamic underpinnings.

'*The Well-Beloved*' is the least read of Hardy's novels; its implausible plot has been, perhaps excessively, described as a clumsy and ludicrous oddity meriting only derision. Its failure cannot be excused as befitting a piece of juvenilia because the novel just precedes Hardy's masterpiece. *Jude the Obscure*, and the large body of brilliant lyric poetry he was to go on to write.

The bizarre plot of '*The Well-Beloved*' may be briefly summarized. Jocelyn Pierston, a young sculptor of 'budding fame', who has inhabited the cities of the Continent and who has recently been in London, returns after several years of absence to his birthplace, the rocky Isle of Slingers, to visit his widowed father. The Isle is noted for its quarries whose stone is not only widely used in buildings throughout London, but is also the material used by Jocelyn when in his sculptures, he strives to 'give shape to his fancies'. Significantly nowhere in the novel is mention ever made of Pierston's mother.

Shortly after his arrival Pierston meets a distant cousin, Avice Caro, whom he courts and whose hand he quickly asks in marriage. Later he is filled with misgivings because he had mistakenly thought that he had finally rid himself of the 'mad assumption' that the ideal woman of his fantasy was actually the person with whom he was infatuated. At the end of the summer, Pierston must return to London; *en route* he encounters Marcia Bencomb, and, in less than an hour, he finds himself adoring her; Avice has completely vanished from his mind. Jocelyn proposes marriage and is accepted before the train reaches London. But before they can marry, Marcia grows weary of her lover's scoldings, and returns to her father.

Twenty years later, now highly successful, Pierston learns of Avice's death and returns to the Isle of Slingers to visit her grave. He is remorseful over the way he had treated her and his visit becomes a means of restitution. He becomes infatuated with her daughter, also called Avice Caro, who, having married a cousin, carries the same surname as her mother. An intermingling of blood on the island is quite common. Although the second Avice is an uneducated laundress, Pierston cannot shake her from his mind. When he proposes, she reveals not only that she is already married–although separated from her husband—but that she is 'fickle', having had a long succession of lovers. Pierston bitterly realizes that he is 'emotionally not much older than she'. For her mother's sake he manages to reconcile Avice with her husband, who is also called Pierston. When she later gives birth to a daughter, he asks her to christen the child Avice.

The third section of the novel is appropriately entitled 'A Young Man of Sixty'. Pierston learns that Marcia has returned to Europe after having lived abroad for many years. He also discovers that the second Avice's husband had died and that she herself is quite ill. She is living in Pierston's old home and her daughter occupies his old room, a detail which tacitly establishes the maternal symbolism of the three Avice Caros. Pierston once again begins to believe that his attitude towards women had changed, but to his dismay he discovers the third Avice to be a delightful, elegant, and well-educated young woman. As he glimpses her through a window, he feels as though he were an actor in a dream; this Avice is almost a double of the one he knew forty years before. Her mother urges Pierston to marry her, and to her daughter she extols his wealth and prestige. Avice is torn between the desire to please her mother and her repugnance for the ageing Pierston. Moreover, neither Pierston nor her mother know that she is in love with a young man who, we learn, is Marcia's stepson! Avice finally resolves the dilemma by eloping with her lover.

Pierston falls dangerously ill. Upon emerging from a state of delirium he realizes that it is Marcia who has been nursing him. Although in the half-light of the sick room she still seems to retain her beauty, she admits it is merely artful make-up. The next day she reveals herself as the old woman she is: pale and shrivelled. After his convalescence, Pierston abandons his lifelong 'pursuit of Aphrodite', through women and sculpture, and returns to the Isle of Slingers to live quietly with Marcia. Symbolic of his need for reparation, he devotes his final years to community work, initially closing the island's contaminated fountains and undertaking to supply fresh, pure water. From being a dapper man who had always appeared much younger than his age, this man of 62 now could pass for 75.

This is the narrative of the final edition of '*The Well Beloved*'. The first edition differs in a number of respects, of which we shall only mention the ending. In contrast to the tone of reasonable resignation and the renunciation of Pierston's life-long fantasy in the later version, when, in the original, Pierston recognizes that it is Marcia who has been nursing him and that she has become a 'wrinkled crone', he compares her with a photograph of the third Avice. 'The contrast . . . brought into his brain a sudden sense of the grotesqueness of things. His wife was—not Avice, but that parchment-covered skull . . . [he was seized by] an irresistible fit of laughter, so violent as to be in agony . . . He laughed and laughed, till he was almost too weak to draw breath.' Marcia thinks he is 'hysterical', but Pierston responds: 'O—no, no!–I—I—it is too too droll—this end to my would-be romantic history! . . .' (p. 249)[1]. We may assume that this bitter and cynical finale is probably closer to Hardy's intentions than the more conventional ending of the later edition.

Despite the awkwardness of '*The Well-Beloved*', it shares the themes common to many of Hardy's novels and poems: 'Betrayal, grotesque incongruity in clashing desires . . . perpetual dissatisfaction in love, [and] the suffering love causes . . . each case [is] associated with the theme of repetition. All of Hardy's novels in one way or another pose the question: Why is it that most human beings go through life somnambulistically, compelled to repeat the same mistakes in love, so inflicting on themselves and

on others the same sufferings, again and again? *The Well-Beloved* brings to an end the series of novels exploring this question by providing something so close to a definitive answer that the tension of the question dissolves, and novelwriting becomes impossible . . .' Jocelyn 'knows, half-ironically, that in his infatuation with his elusive Well-Beloved he is bewitched by a fantasy. By the end of the novel he is fully demystified. Against the final self-judgements of the other late protagonists one may set the deeper disillusionment of Jocelyn's hysterical laughter—bitterer than any tears, which ends the first version, or his "Thank heaven I am old at last. The curse [of compulsive infatuations] is removed", of the final version' (J. Miller, 1975, p. 14).

The infatuations that lay hold of Pierston long precede the events narrated in the novel. The young sculptor relates to his closest friend, Somers, that his first beloved appeared when he was 9: '. . . A little blue-eyed girl of about eight or so' (p. 54). However, and it is of critical significance in the nature of infatuation, that from the first he noticed that this girl's flaxen hair, coming down her shoulders, attempted to curl 'but ignominously failed, hanging like chimney-crooks only' (p. 54). Pierston had been troubled by this 'defect' and it was one of the main reasons why this embodiment of the beloved was evicted from her place as the boy's ideal. She was, however, to be followed by many other loved ones.

The Beloved took many forms: Actresses, shop girls, authors, musicians, and dancers, but with each one he quickly discovered reasons to discard her. Although each of these women possessed her individuality,

---

[1]All page references without attribution are from Hardy, T. (1897).

they had all been merely a 'transient condition' of Pierston's *Well-Beloved*. 'Essentially she was perhaps of no tangible substance; a spirit, a dream, a frenzy, a conception, an aroma, an epitomized sex, a light of the eye, a parting of the lips. God only knew what she really was . . .' (p. 134). The stress on the part object reappears again and again.

Hardy provides other crucial additional elements to describe infatuation. For one, Pierston is painfully aware of the *repetitive, and compulsive nature* of his infatuations, clearly rising from the unconscious conflict between impulses and prohibitions. The compulsive quality of Pierston's infatuations is brought out by their irresistible nature and his inability to stop this behaviour which inflicts so much suffering on him. Infatuation, in itself, only becomes a compulsion when it becomes driven, repetitive and ritualistic.

When he was courting the second Avice, Hardy introduces—almost casually—a significant fantasy of Pierston which illuminates the aspect of narcissistic object-choice inherent in infatuation. 'To use a practical eye, it appeared that, as [Pierston] had once thought, this Caro family—though it might not for centuries, or ever, furbish up an individual nature which would *exactly, ideally, supplement his own imperfect one and round it with the perfect whole* [our italics]—was yet the only family he had ever met, or was likely to meet, which possessed the materials for her making' (p. 111). Pierston's narcissism thus extends to the wish to idealize his family tree.

Hardy repeatedly describes Pierston's infatuations as 'madness', 'insanity', and 'folly' implying a sense of unreality—of a dreamworld dominated by primary process thinking. This oneiric aura surrounding his infatuations is neatly captured in a passage which finds Pierston attending an elegant soirée. Even before he arrives he is tingling with a presentiment that he will, that evening, once again encounter the Beloved. When he glimpses the woman who will become the Beloved she keeps appearing and disappearing in the dense crowd. As he crosses the vast, crowded salon his progress is continually checked: 'Pierston was as he had sometimes seemed in a dream, unable to advance towards the object of pursuit unless he could have gathered up his feet into the air' (p. 78). This pursuit of the Beloved, and Pierston's inability—actually his superego prohibition—to reach her, well represents his conflict, which resembles the compromise formation of the dream. In fact, in his description, Hardy emphasizes the dream-like quality of Pierston's state of mind as he views the loved one from a distance.

In summary, '*The Well-Beloved*' reveals the following characteristics of infatuation: (1) The experience is intense, irrational, and dream-like. The lover feels himself to be in a state of ecstasy—that is, in a state of consciousness in which he is in the grip of intense, pleasurable feelings or sensations, while his cognitive and perceptual functions are markedly diminished (2) The Beloved is appealing, alluring, beautiful, and cool. (3) The fantasy of the idealized love-object exists as a mental representation long before the object is encountered. (4) The infatuation is typically precipitated by some discrete, usually physical, trait of the object which is experienced as a part object. (5) The infatuation is fundamentally ambivalent, carrying within it the seeds of its own negation in the form of the unconscious, frequently hostile, search for, and inevitable discovery of, the intolerable 'flaw' in the Beloved. This ambivalence is revealed in the pattern of infatuation, followed by disappointment, feelings of betrayal, hostility, and the wish for revenge; then ensue feelings of remorse and a wish to repent and restore the disrupted relationship. It seems that his guilt over the abandonment of the first Avice leads Pierston to repair the damage he has wrought by wooing the daughter and granddaughter of the woman he had wounded and betrayed. An additional facet of his ambivalence is reflected in the vagueness surrounding the sexual nature of Pierston's infatuations—Hardy is more specific about sexual behaviour in his other novels. (6) The experience of infatuation is both intoxicating and painful. It tends to fulfil a fantasy and yet it seeks to avoid that fulfilment; these conflicting trends give rise to inchoate feelings of exhilaration, anxiety, sadness, and a 'sense of something abnormal'. But beyond the foregoing phenomenology of infatuation Hardy suggests something about the underlying fantasy, which may be conscious or unconscious: through a union with the Beloved the subject will either fulfil himself, become rejuvenated, or complement himself in some significant way.

Although the form of infatuation from which Pierston suffered represents a life-long, characterologic compulsion, infatuation can occur at some point in an individual's life, contingent on various psychodynamic, precipitating factors. The following clinical vignette illustrates such an event.

Rather abruptly, about six months after the death of his father, and shortly after being disappointed in his efforts to adopt an infant girl, a 40-year-old business man found himself desperately in love with a young woman who had worked for him briefly. Raised in a different, and more limited, social and economic background, this woman was in financial and emotional difficulty and had appealed to the patient for his help. Readily, almost gratefully, he accepted the proffered role and became her advisor, mentor and guide—in short, a surrogate father.

Within a short time he was totally obsessed with his new love and came within a hair's-breadth of leaving his wife and family for her. In the analysis it became clear that he had been suffering from strong feelings of guilt and depression. He had had bitter battles with his father from whom he had finally wrested the business. He had also, at times, wished that his father was dead, and upon his actual death, suffered pangs of guilt and remorse. He grew angry with his wife, whose new interest in a career he experienced as an emotional desertion. He also experienced her intense involvement with their sons as a desertion of him, a response that was based in large measure on the reactivation of oedipal struggles and feelings of abandonment by his mother. In short, old conflicts, in which unconscious aggression played a central role, had erupted just prior to his falling in love. The clinical result was a feeling of depression, guilt and a sense of futility. The appearance at this time of new love—an idealized and perfect woman who was part mother, part child—and in whom he could find a strong, vital and renewed self, provided a temporary, if unstable, solution.

It was not, however, a new solution. As a child the patient had responded to repeated frustrations in his relationship with his mother by turning for comfort to a young and beautiful aunt. She became the stimulus for the development of romantic fantasies in which a warm, responsive and idealized mother-figure played the central role. This fantasy, which acted dynamically much like the family romance creations of the latency child, contained elements relating to images of a perfect self as well as the perfect mother and, in this way, provided a temporary solution to a variety of conflicts. A feeling of elation mixed with anxiety accompanied these fantasies of childhood just as they did in later life. And the feeling of living in a dream from which one dreaded to awake was common to the infatuations of both periods. Following a tempestuous period in which the patient was desperately in love, the infatuation ended as suddenly as it came. Disillusionment and disappointment developed as the ideal ultimately did not provide the desired satisfactions. Fortunately, in this case, it was possible for the patient to work through enough of the underlying conflicts so that he did not have to wait until old age before being able to dispel the search for the Beloved.

Unlike this patient's single episode of infatuation, and more akin to Pierston's long series of infatuations, a 35-year-old teacher, obsessed by his 'negative self-image', entered analysis after yet another unsuccessful love affair. Although unable to pursue a woman who interested him, chiefly by her physical appearance, unless she seemed receptive to him, once he felt such a responsiveness in her, he was swept off his feet. However, once he saw that she was in love with him his infatuation waned and he grew frightened and angry with her for persisting in her desire to further the relationship. What ostensibly precipitated his loss of interest was some physical trait or aspect of personality in the woman which he found distasteful. Curiously, he invariably observed this trait at his first encounter with the woman who was to become the loved one, but put it to the side at the moment, only to focus on it later when he used it as a rationale for breaking off the relationship. At one point, he worried that a woman whom he had only seen wearing slacks had 'heavy' legs—the 'worst' physical defect, in his eyes. When he discovered that her legs were shapely he could not avoid realizing that behind his pleasure was chagrin.

Until he entered analysis he had not realized that in every relationship with a woman not only did *he* suffer from the break-up, but he also caused the woman to suffer. He dealt with his unconscious guilt by attempts to avoid women altogether, and especially grew more assiduous in his religious activities. His unconscious hostility toward women merged with fear that the woman would control, mutilate, and engulf him.

It became clear that these attitudes towards women were displacements from early struggles with his domineering, coercive, but very attractive mother; at the same time he sought the 'perfect' woman who would resemble his mother and sister, the latter being the person upon whom he had originally displaced many of his oedipal desires.

In the light of Hardy's perceptive insights into the nature of infatuation, we might ask if Pierston reflects Hardy's inner life to any important extent. Unfortunately for the psychobiographer, Hardy carefully covered his tracks, destroying letters and altering his official biography, which in any event was written by his second wife (Hardy, F. E., 1928, 1930). Although many critics have discerned aspects of Hardy's life in his novels (including one psychoanalytical study: Hofling, 1968) the data is more suggestive than conclusive.[2] Still, Hardy seemed to give himself away when he asserted that his novels contained *nothing whatsoever* of his life (Rutland, 1938) ; surely an extravagant claim. Hawkins (1976) believes that 'it is difficult not to consider that *The Well-Beloved* is in some measure a fable of one aspect of Hardy's inner life' (p. 140), at the time of his fiftieth year when he, like Pierston, made the rounds of London music halls studying the beauties with 'lustrous eyes and pearly countenances'. We do know that at that time the life was irrevocably going out of his marriage.

Hardy's birth was markedly traumatic: His mother almost died in childbirth and he was believed to be dead; he was thrown aside until a nurse realized that he was actually breathing. Although fragile for several years, he was fundamentally normal despite this 'miraculous' birth experience. This 'special' quality is evoked in a family story dating from early childhood: On a hot day his mother entered the house and found a large snake coiled on the boy's breast, as comfortably asleep as he.

Thomas's mother suffered from 'brain fever' after his birth and he was entrusted to the care of an aunt. Despite her illness, Mrs Hardy gave birth to another child, a daughter, within a year. These events suggest that the infant Thomas received less than optimal attention from his mother. Notwithstanding (or perhaps as a result of) these possible deprivations in his earliest years, he was kept at home and tutored by his

mother until he was 8. His first teacher outside the home was one Julie Martin, with whom he developed an intense relationship, and he was to think about her throughout his life. Perhaps out of jealousy his mother removed him from that school after a year.

He soon became attached to an older woman, who lived at a nearby manor. She was about 40 and grew deeply invested in Thomas's education. In return he gave her his drawings and sang for her. Intellectually he was precocious and possessed an 'ecstatic temper'; he would often be moved to tears by the tunes his father played and to which he danced by himself. His mother was a well-read woman and took Thomas on many excursions with her; she seems to have favoured him over his three younger siblings—none of whom ever married. During his adolescence there were a few documented infatuations of which one exactly duplicates

---

[2]James Hamilton, in his discussion of this paper, presented an intriguing argument, based on Hardy's life and his novels, to support the view that Pierston represents Hardy.

one that Pierston experienced as a boy. In his adult life he wrote: 'I was a child until I was sixteen, a youth until I was twenty-five, a young man until I was forty or fifty' (Hawkins, 1976, p. 15). Like Pierston he looked remarkably youthful until old age.

Hardy's married life eventually led him to believe that marriage was an 'impossible code' and his views on the 'contractual' restraints of marriage grew more bitter and outspoken. One of the fruits of his success as a writer was to find himself lionized by admiring ladies of fashion. Despite a propensity to flirtatiousness, it is not known if he actually had any love affairs outside of his marriage. His wife became an evangelist and a recluse, and when she died, in 1912, Hardy immediately telegraphed Florence Emily Dugdale (later his biographer) who had been his private secretary and research assistant; fifteen months later they married; she was then 35 and he was 73.

These sketchy details do not make a psychobiography, but they do suggest that Thomas was regarded as a special child because of his 'miraculous' rescue at birth, his frailness, and his precocity. For whatever reason (guilt or restitution) his mother lavished attention on him which, among other effects, led to Hardy's interest in art and literature. The bachelorhood of his siblings makes one wonder how close Hardy also came to becoming unable to commit himself to one woman. That he never mentions Pierston's mother in '*The Well-Beloved*' can hardly be regarded as accidental. We believe that she is not spoken about because she is omnipresent as the epitome of Pierston's ideal woman: Desired, sought-after, and unattainable in this real world of imperfect people. She is symbolized in the three Avice Caros.

A further inferential observation relates to the artistic failure of '*The Well-Beloved*'. Hardy recognized the weakness of the novel, and in his preface to a 1912 edition noted that 'As for the story itself, it may be worth while to remark that, differing from all or most of the series [of his books] in that the interest aimed at is of an ideal or subjective nature, and frankly imaginative, verisimilitude in the sequence of events has been subordinated to the said aim' (p. 26). We would contend that these 'subjective' aspects represent regressive trends which the writer's aesthetic ego was unable to master fully.

The strongest case, however, to support the view that Pierston represents an important aspect of Hardy, lies in the correctness of Hardy's delineation of infatuation, which so closely approximates what one discovers in clinical experience and in life generally. And if Hardy never lived out infatuations such as Pierston experienced, his deep understanding of such states suggests that he had much experience with them in fantasy.

DISCUSSION

It is clear that the characterologic form of infatuation has its principal roots in the earliest years of life. The very essence of the phenomenon, its shifting and inconstant nature, reflects the experience of the child prior to the formation of object constancy, a time when the child's libidinal needs and wishes, as well as his tendency towards primitive idealization, may be projected on to various objects in the environment. It is then that the mother may still be substituted for, and caretakers in various shapes and forms may be the objects of intense desire. The infant's perceptions are at first directed only towards aspects of the mothering figure: a face, a profile, a particular combination of physical traits rather than to a person. Hardy writes of Pierston's powerful attraction to the second Avice: 'he regarded the charm of her bending profile, the well-characterized though softly lined nose, the round chin with, as it were, a second leap in its curve to the throat, and the sweep of the eyelashes over the rose cheek during the sedulously lowered glance' (p. 130). Concealed within this description of a man in love, who is smitten by the sight of his Beloved, one can, perhaps, detect the perceptions of a child focused on the image of the original Beloved, the mother of infancy whose face and form create an arresting gestalt for the child.

In a similar way, Hardy emphasizes the importance to Pierston of the Beloved's voice—the pitch, tone and rhythms of speech: 'she attracted him', he writes of Avice the second, 'by the *cadences of her voice* . . . The charm lay in the intervals, using that word in its musical sense. She would say a few syllables in one note and end her sentence in a soft modulation upwards, then downwards, then into her own note again. The curve of sound was as artistic as any line of beauty ever struck by his pencil—as satisfying as the curves of her who was the World's Desire . . . He took special pains that in catching her voice he might not comprehend her words . . . By degrees he could not exist long without this sound' (p. 107).

Most likely, residues of this early period of interchangeable and shifting objects, as well as the later period when romantic feelings are focused on the person of the mother, play some role in the phenomenon of infatuation as it is experienced under all conditions, but it would seem to play a role of particular importance in individuals like Pierston whose lives become an endless series of compulsive, short-lived infatuations.

Hardy gives us some hints as to why this is so. Pierston is always struggling against his impulse to hurt and reject women, as well as to idealize them. In short, he suffers from the deepest and most pervasive ambivalence towards the object of his desires. The fact that he cannot love one woman in any enduring way, but experiences, rather, repeated episodes of infatuation that end in disillusionment, highlights the likelihood that he has not developed a stable, reliable capacity for object constancy—or that, if developed, that this capacity is easily disrupted under conditions of stress or anxiety.

This particular defect in object relations, as we know from infant observation research, suggests the existence of difficulties in the mother-infant relationship that contribute to the development of critically important aggressive conflicts in the child. These, in turn, lead to difficulties in the youngster's capacity to traverse, without undue anxiety, the separation-individuation phase of development and to establish a firm sense of object constancy. Individuals like Pierston are subject to repeated episodes of infatuation which would seem to have as one of their unconscious aims, the establishment, intrapsychically, of an idealized self-object which can combat the feelings of guilt and depression which accompany the ever-present conflicts over aggression.

For such men, their rejection of women, which comes about as a consequence of this unconscious aggression, is as painful and threatening as the experience of being rejected. Unconsciously they are strongly identified, via their own experiences and fantasies concerning rejection, with the rejected object, and when their own actions lead to rejection of this object, they experience a sense of anxiety and discomfort that can only be removed by undoing the action and repairing the object relationship. This aspect of the oedipal conflict, the rejection of his mother by a youngster with strong unconscious aggressive feelings towards her, is little commented on, but is often a vitally important aspect of the oedipal drama.

Such a configuration is suggested by Proust, in his own life, as well as in that of Marcel, his protagonist in '*Remembrance of Things Past*'. Marcel was destined to go from one love object to another, vainly seeking to realize his incestuous yearnings for his mother. (However, Proust himself, as M. L. Miller (1956) observed, loved a brother image in his male lovers, as his mother had loved him.) Marcel's love is possessive and suffocates the beloved as it does himself; it is riddled with jealousy and humiliation. For example, as long as Marcel lives in the ecstasy of falling in love with Albertine, and believes her to be inaccessible, he desires total possession of her and dreams of marriage. However, once he is assured of her love for him he loses interest in her, grows bored, and begins to cast about for a new love object. Repeatedly he seeks, through his lovers, to re-establish the sweet delight of mother's bedtime kisses and caresses through this repetition compulsion.

The high degree of narcissism involved in the phenomenon of infatuation has been commented on (Bak, 1973) ; (Binstock, 1973). Certainly, the infatuated lover is seeking an idealized self as well as an ideal mother. While narcissistic needs undoubtedly play an important role whenever infatuation occurs, they are of particular importance in those individuals given to repeated and compulsive episodes of infatuation. In such individuals early mother–infant problems lead also to the development of increased narcissistic pathology. The inability to develop mature object relations leads to the incapacity to love in an enduring and stable way.

Infatuation may occur at any age. It may come about when an individual is in a crisis of defensive regression subsequent to severe stress, intense anxiety, or during times of depression. The first clinical vignette illustrates this, with its multiple precipitating factors. At such times the latent narcissistic wishes become accentuated. Stresses may arise from object loss, organic brain disease, waning professional or sexual potency, life-threatening illness, or even when there are fantasies about the imminence of such conditions.

The life crisis is illustrated in Thomas Mann's novella, '*Death in Venice*' (Mann, 1912), which has certain features in common with '*The Well-Beloved*'. The Mann story describes the passion of a celebrated and ageing author, Gustave von Aschenbach, for a young boy of about 13, and the emotional disintegration that accompanies this infatuation. The story opens with Aschenbach unable to work. A highly disciplined individual of rigid character structure who has been able to utilize the process of writing as a channel to sublimate his libidinal and aggressive wishes, he is fatigued and depressed. The sublimatory process has broken down and Aschenbach seeks a new release and channel for the powerful forbidden impulses which are threatening to break into consciousness. He travels to Venice, a corrupted city, and there falls in love with Tadzio, the frail golden-haired youth of his dreams.

Tadzio is the pampered darling of his mother, a vain and aristocratic woman, and it is clear that Aschenbach has fallen in love with an idealized version of himself as a child. He loves Tadzio as he himself yearns to be loved by a mother. The old narcissistic wishes, partially gratified through his art, are reactivated in a regressive way and he is hopelessly, foolishly infatuated. Throughout the story, Aschenbach's conflicts over powerful aggressive strivings are depicted. His aggression, previously under control, can no longer be restrained. At one point he has the fantasy that Tadzio will die at an early age and at this thought he experiences a strange thrill. By not reporting that Venice has been contaminated by a plague he not only puts Tadzio at grave risk, but endangers others as well. He identifies with the hatred that he sees in Tadzio and in the end he himself dies. He cannot survive the emergence and expression of his own forbidden wishes.

Tadzio's mother is prototypical of the beautiful, enticing and rejecting mother. Although she extravagantly indulges her child, she experiences him as part of herself and makes him her work of art. It is, perhaps, mothers who are highly narcissistically invested in their sons, who unconsciously treat them as self-objects, and whose strong wishes for artistic success are to be gratified through their children who foster the development of both the artist and the infatuated lover. The search for the beautiful, ideal motherself image goes on, but in such men the original experiences of disappointment, disillusionment and rejection are endlessly renewed.

For some talented individuals like Pierston and Aschenbach, art and the creative process may provide important vehicles for the objectivication and living out of their conflicts. Through their art both men not only seek, but create, the ideal in line, image and form. They woo ideal beauty in their art and having created the perfect form then must leave it only to start over again. In the case of Aschenbach, until his creative powers waned, sublimation proved effective and his romance was with his art. For Pierston it was less sustaining. While for years the images of the women that he sculpted were of great beauty—perfect in their own way—he still searched in life for the beauteous and perfect woman and thus in each decade fell victim to new and compelling infatuations.

Thus we would suggest that infatuation is a phenomenon which represents a fusion of the ideal self and the ideal mother (or father) imago. The more that falling in love constitutes an infatuation, the more its narcissistic and incestuous elements are close to the surface, and the more does the primary process aspect of the phenomenon dominate. In this way, infatuation has a strong parallelism with dreams and neurotic symptoms, constituting a compromise formation. At its most extreme distance from reality it takes the form of delusional erotomania (Freud, 1911).

Reflection on the underlying dynamics makes clear why the infatuated individual is exhilarated yet anxious and depressed: the relatively unmodified archaic wishes are breaking into awareness; the individual is excited because the unconscious wish seems to be about to reach fulfilment, but this is prohibited by the incest taboo and so must come to nothing. Similarly, the imminent gratification of the narcissistic wishes may make the individual feel elated, but they conflict with the adult ego which recognizes that the self cannot be truly enriched by a merger with another.

It is understandable that adolescence is so frequently a time of infatuation since it is a period of resurgence of instinctual drives and of the oedipal conflict. It is also a time in which the struggle for identity as well as efforts to develop intimacy and autonomy are of central importance. Infatuation seems to provide, at least in imagination, a means of immediate gratification as well as the fantasied resolution of these tasks. Abetted by a lack of experience in human relationships, the adolescent frequently finds himself in a state of infatuation. However, when an individual compulsively and repetitively continues to become infatuated, like Jocelyn Pierston, one is led to postulate important difficulties both in self-development and, inevitably, in oedipal conflict resolution.

The range, then, of the meanings and uses of infatuation is broad: It may occur normatively as in adolescence; neurotically, when it constitutes a repetition compulsion; psychotically in erotomania, and defensively when it denies some reality or serves as a fantasy to inhibit destructive behaviour. As many other such aspects of human behaviour, infatuation is a final common pathway, arising from multiple sources and consequently having different aims.

SUMMARY

Despite the ubiquity of infatuation the psychoanalytic literature pertaining to it is relatively limited.

However, the nature of infatuation is described in almost clinical detail in Thomas Hardy's novel '*The Well-Beloved*'. Not only does he delineate its phenomenology but the novel provides important clues to the psychodynamic underpinnings of the principal character's repetitive and compulsive falling in love. Utilizing Hardy's descriptions, this communication formulates some general statements about infatuation, considering it as a phenomenon that ranges from the normative to the frankly psychopathological, from contingent to characterological forms. We suggest that infatuation typically condenses both narcissistic and oedipal wishes.

A brief exploration of the relationships of Hardy's novel to his own life is made, and two vignettes illustrate some of these concepts in clinical practice. The relevant literature is reviewed.

REFERENCES

ARLOW, J. (1980). Object concept and object choice. *Psychoanalytic Quarterly* 49:109–133

BAK, R.C. (1973). Being in love and object loss. *International Journal of Psychoanalysis* 54:1–8.

BERGMAN, M.S. (1980). The intrapsychic function of falling in love. *Psychoanalytic Quarterly* 49:56–77.

BINSTOCK, W.A. (1973). On the two forms of intimacy. *Journal of the American. Psychoanalytic Association* 21:93–107.

FREUD, S. (1911). Notes on a case of paranoia. *Standard Edition* 12.

———— (1914a). On narcissism: an introduction. *Standard Edition* 14.

———— (1914b). Observations on transference love. *Standard Edition* 12.

HARDY, F.E. (1928). *The Early Life of Thomas Hardy 1840–1891.* New York: Macmillan.

———— (1980). *The Later Years of Thomas Hardy 1892–1928.* New York: Macmillan.

HARDY, T. (1897). *The Well-Beloved.* New York: Macmillan, 1975.

HAWKINS, D. (1976). *Hardy: Novelist and Poet.* London: David and Charles.

HOFLING, C.K (1968). Thomas Hardy and The Mayor of Casterbridge. *Comprehen. Psychiat.* 9:428–439.

KERNBERG, O K. (1974). Barriers to falling and remaining in love. *Journal of the American Psychoanalytic Association* 22:486–511.

MANN, T. (1912). *Death in Venice.* In *Stories of Three Decades.* London: Martin Secker & Warburg, 1936.

MILLER, H.L. & Siegel, P.S. (1972). *Loving: A Psychological Approach.* New York John Wiley.

MILLER, J.H. (1975). *Introduction to "The Well-Beloved."* New York: Macmillan.

MILLER, M.L. (1956). *Nostalgia: A Psychoanalytic Study of Marcel Proust.* Boston: Houghton Mifflin.

ROBERT, P. (1970). *Dictionnaire Aphabtique et Analogique de la Langue Franaise.* Paris: Socit du Nouveau Littr.

RUTLAND, W.R. (1938). *Thomas Hardy: A Study of His Writings and Their Background.* London: Blackwell.

CHAPTER 14

James Jackson Putnam: Philosophy and Psychoanalysis

[Werman, D.S. (1977). *American Imago* 34:72–85]

Perhaps the most direct and persistent attempt to attach a particular philosophical and ethical viewpoint to psychoanalytic theory was that undertaken by James Jackson Putnam. Since Putnam's biography has been amply related elsewhere, I shall simply bring forward some facts which bear on this communication.

He was born in Boston, in 1846, to a distinguished family which counted among its members noted physicians and a grandfather who sat as judge of the Supreme Court of Massachusetts. Putnam was educated at Harvard and after studies in Europe with Rokitansky, Meynert, and Hughlings Jackson, among others, he returned to Harvard and remained on its faculty until retirement. One of the first Americans to specialize in neurology, he was the first professor of Diseases of the Nervous System at Harvard and established the Neurological Clinic at the Massachusetts General Hospital. After a career, rich in practice and clinical research, he developed a passionate interest in clinical psychology.

Putnam became intensely drawn towards psychoanalysis after talking with Freud during the latter's visit to the United States in 1909. He soon began to practice analysis and became one of the leading exponents of psychoanalytic ideas in American medical circles. This was often a thankless undertaking, but for the most part, he bore the attacks on analysis, as well as on his person, with equanimity. Without exception, he was regarded as a man of "lofty standards and moral rectitude" (Freud, S., 1921, iii), tolerant, kindly, and deeply empathic with his patients. His philosophic ideas were a curious mdlange of Emerson, Kant, Hegel, his friend Josiah Royce, and Bergson; although personally close to William James, he was never attracted to Jamesian pragmatism.

Putnam had no difficulty in accepting Freud's views on human sexuality. Putnam was no prim, Puritanical naysayer,and his objections were not with what psychoanalysis said but with what he felt it did not say; in a word, the issue of morality. However, as I will show, despite his warm support of psychoanalytic concepts, and his courageous defense of them in scientific circles, there were areas of disagreement on fundamental issues.

At first blush, it would appear that Putnam's philosophic stance was dualistic, that he wanted to attach ethics, religion and idealist notions about free will to materialist psychoanalysis. Actually, he was a throughgoing idealist who did not accept an objective reality outside of the mind. "Philosophy and metaphysics are the only means through which the essential nature of many tendencies can be studied of which psychoanalysis describes only the transformations . . . [the former deal] with real existence, while nature science and the genetic psychology (of which psychoanalysis, strictly speaking, is a branch) deal rather with appearance and with structure." (Putnam, 1921, pp. 297–298).

This almost solipsistic statement was extended by Putnam's criticisms of the limitations of science in general and of psychoanalysis in particular. Thus, while "psychologic observation of ourselves teaches us much . . . it teaches us nothing with regard to the essential nature of the universe or of ourselves." (Hale, 1971, p. 95). Hence without philosophy, "it is impossible to really know the human mind." (Putnam, 1921, p. 94).

It is likely that Putnam espoused such beliefs before he became a psychoanalyst. An early paper on mental illness (Putnam, 1899) discussed the educative role of the physician quite empirically without philosophical allusions. "Intuition," is used as a psychological notion, and he favorably quoted Janet that psychology does not aspire to set up a system of metaphysics or religion. By 1906, he was attempting to pull together brain, self and community stating that "consciousness is our ultimate reality." (Putnam, 1906, p. 1023).

Throughout his writings on philosophy, the impact of New England Transcendentalism is evident. Against what they felt was the stifling conformity of Unitarianism, the Transcendentalists sang the praises of the spirit, an expression, as Perry Miller (1950) put it, "of religious radicalism in revolt against a rational conservation." (p. 8). Their need for an ideology was filled by German idealism, Victor Cousin, Carlyle, Wordsworth and Coleridge and oriental philosophy. They took over the Kantian concepts of epistemology and existence that transcended the experience of an objective world; although knowledge begins with experience, it does not come from experience.

Although, by the end of the 19th century, Transcendentalism had ceased being a potent force and had become a "harmless exhortation to self-reliance and optimism" (Miller, 1950, p. 13), Putnam still held to many of the now rather threadbare ideas. "How do we know," he asked, about the "repressed devils within us?". . . Because we possess standards of the good, and while at first we may think these are imposed on us by society we can trace them back to one of the most real of all our intuitions." (Putnam, 1921, p. 82). In the most primitive men and even in the newborn are "dim unconscious visions in which the logical formulas of philosophical reason are foreshadowed and the scheme of the universe is intimately perceived; and with these feelings comes a deep sense of obligation." (Putnam, 1921, p. 88).

Putnam was much influenced by F. W. A. Froebel (1782–1852), a student of Fichte and Schelling, and founder of the kindergarten system, which he brought to America. Through creative play and an emphasis on cooperation, Froebel hoped to instill in children a sense of the unity of all human beings, their oneness with all of nature and the universe (God). Susan Blow (1843–1916), a former patient of Putnam's, William Torrey Harris (1835–1909), and others, carried forward Froebel's ideas and Putnam was impressed by their pedagogic views as well as by their underlying philosophy. They appear to have shaped his notions on the goals of psychoanalytic treatment, which he was to develop.

Not surprisingly, Putnam's idealist philosophy led him toward more specifically religious ends. Since all men share the same innate ideas, (the only real, permanent elements) they are all parts of the same eternal universe. We are, then, bound to people not only for themselves, but more because they represent the forces that make them what they are—forces represented by the ties of family, church, and state. These bonds reach out and ultimately bind all parts of the universe into one. Finally, the harmony and the utter order of the universe is God: He is all and is all that is good in ourselves and in others.

Bergson's philosophy appealed to Putnam for it possessed a scientific patina, containing references to the "subconscious," energy, intellect, instinct, dreams, evolution and even an endorsement of psychoanalysis. His *poussée vitale*, the life force, was a form of libido similar to that which Jung advocated (Putnam, 1913), and writing to Freud in 1910, Putnam admiringly described it as a "self-active principal of life" found in the plant and animal world—in man in a higher form, and whose "highest and most throughly unified form is universe—al." (Hale, 1971, pp. 106–107). In another letter to Freud, he declared that "what we call experiences in analysis are really symbols or expressions of an energetic process, call it 'Libido' or what you will." (Hale, 1971, p. 196). Here, as in other statements, it would seem that Putnam simultaneously held to two views of libido, the first as instinctual drive, the other as a phenomenon similar to Bergson's creative energy. He tied consciousness to this form of energy by putting forward the idea that man's awareness of his acts is "inferentially based on a recognition of the bonds that connect him as a moral being, with every other man, and with the source of energy which underlies the universe." (Putnam, 1921, p. 94). Mind then comes to represent a typical form of "unpicturable energy." The picturable world is temporal, merely a "symbolic" representation of the unpictured life—the only "true life." "The mind (or what corresponds to it) makes and modifies the body and not the body the mind, at least not directly." (Hale, 1971, pp. 178–179).

Undoubtedly the most powerful, direct impact on Putnam came from Josiah Royce, whose concept of loyalty so closely mirrored Putnam's own high ethical standards. Royce carried forward Kant's "ethics of the Good Will" making morality the keystone of his philosophy, which in turn was the basis for his overriding concern with the community and the state.

Before Putnam had had any significant contact with psychoanalytic ideas, he had urged that the treatment of psychasthenia should include a reworking of the patient's outlook, based on Royce's principles of social loyalty, and the primary and essential nature of social bonds. (Putnam, 1908).

Despite his personal loyalty to Freud and to psychoanalysis, Putnam was unable to prevent his religio-philosophic outlook from affecting his scientific thinking: The source of our instincts he asserted, is the self-active energy of the universe and all its parts; Freud and Darwin were only "partially successful" because they neglected the influence of human consciousness and will ("the unpicturable")—hence, psychoanalysis "fails to recognize that mind, consciousness, reason, emotion, will are not merely *products* of evolution but *causes* of evolution." (Hale, 1971, p. 118). And finally, his virtually monolithic view of the social imperative: "Social bonds are stronger than the sexual bonds though not exclusive of it." (Hale, 1971, p. 193).

The ramifications of these thoughts are too numerous to trace out here, but, characteristic of them is Putnam's belief in the "deeper causes" at work in making myths reside in the constitution of the mind. Beyond men's personal experiences and special cravings, which merely determine the forms of art, religion and literature, is the *essential motive* underlying them: Men's "dim recognition of their relation to the creative spirit of the universe." (Putnam, 1921, p. 298). Even ceremonial rituals, though they seem to be elaborated from superstitions are an acknowledgement of "something better" in us.

But Putnam leveled more specific criticisms against psychoanalytic theory. He contended that neurotic conflicts arise from the schism between the sense of our infinite origin and the necessity which we are under of attempting to express ourselves, at each moment, in a finite form. The conflict between our infantile instincts and the demands of convention are only superficial. The normal man is moral and social. Putnam was thus only partially able to accept the pleasure principle, and instead put forward a "goal of positive perfection of which our nearer goals are nothing but shadows." (Putnam, 1921, p. 309). If all conflicts are basically ethical, children must be taught that they do not just belong to themselves but to the community; many neuroses might thus be avoided. Although recognizing that analysts "cannot talk of duties and ethical issues," he advocates that they must deal with ethical obligations because these were neglected when the patients were children. Finally, since the unconscious contains what is bad it must also contain the better elements of mental life, which remain unconscious "because they cannot be expressed in words." (Putnam, 1921, p. 87).

A number of Putnam's formulations seem to be interesting adumbrations of later developments in ego psychology. He noted that Freud had only a secondary interest in sociological matters and gave little attention to non-instinctual influences, attributing this to the fact that he had not yet intensively studied the "ego complexes." For the most part, however, Putnam's ego-oriented views are derived not experienially but from his idealist philosophy.

Still, he was in conflict about his ideas and in 1913, wrote Freud that he was aware of the danger of "obscuring truths by mixing in ethical and aesthetical considerations" and vowed not to do so "if I can help it." (Hale, 1971, pp. 167–168). This raises the question of what Putnam actually proposed and carried out in psychoanalytic practice. Here the record is less clear. He frequently maintained that helping the patient to explore his complexes was "not enough," that in almost every patient there were moral issues. While psychoanalytic investigation can approach the ground on which the moral status of the patient rests, this "can be better understood if the patient is willing to make that kind of mental analysis which will lead him to seize obligations in the light of the recognition of his origin and destiny. . . we can and should help him to unravel that portion of his unconscious yearnings which point, not only towards his earthly genesis, but also towards his spiritual genesis." (Putnam, 1921, pp. 90–91). Psychoanalysis cannot be content with a "relative freedom from subjective distress"—there must also be a recovery of a "full sense of one's highest destiny . . . and meanings of one's life." (Putnam, 1921, p. 307).

In 1915, Putnam wrote Freud that he believed it may be unwise for analysts to bring out the "necessary [ethical] influences and presuppositions" in patients—that it "should be done only under special precautions and with the recognition that special forms of self-deception and transference are liable to come into play." (Hale, 1970, p. 183). But he had previously professed to Jones that he was more and more insisting with his patients "that to get well from a psychoneurosis means not only losing symptoms but becoming broader and more reasonable and more moral persons." (Hale, 1970, p. 262). His conflicted position was again evident in another letter to Jones where he observed that he is "root and branch [for psychoanalysis] but only wish and intend to find its place and meaning in terms of the marvelous Auseinandersetzungen [explanations] of Hegel." (Hale, 1970, p. 290). It was inevitable that sublimation become a central concept for Putnam and he commented that "the only logical place of a complete psycho-analytic treatment is a complete sublimation." (Putnam, 1921, p. 204). He lamented that analysts do not strive towards this goal and attributed this to their lack of training in philosophy, and to their one-sided concern with science.

Putnam's ethical and philosophical preoccupations, and his emphasis on sublimation, were surely not without crucial determinants in his own psychological make up. Freud alluded to this in a letter he wrote him in 1911 responding to a statement of Putnam's describing himself as "a very bad character." He suggests that Putnam suffered from "a too early and too strongly repressed sadism expressed in over-goodness and self-torture." (Hale, 1970, p. 112). (Putnam had previously discussed some of his dreams with Freud.) His deep hunger for some religious explanation of human behavior was poignantly expressed in a letter to William James, when the philosopher was traveling in Europe: "I wish you could bring home a clear philosophy and a justified religion . . . Somewhere, somehow, there must be a being wiser and better than ourselves . . . May we not regard the necessarily assumed existence of such a being as a warrant that our existence is in some sense *worth while?*" He wrote of his "longing to get all that metaphysics has to offer . . . (as) an indirect expression of a sort of hope and belief that his [Freud's] terribly searching psycho-genetic explanations correspond to only one part of human life. . . ." (Hale, 1971, p. 79). Three months later, he wrote Freud that he found "many of my patients, and I myself need *all the motive* that can be secured." (Hale, 1971, p. 106). Notwithstanding, in none of his clinical reports does he describe attempts to guide his patients towards ethical or social goals; indeed, in his "Sketch for a Study of New England Character," he deplores the patient's excessive sense of social obligation.

The psychoanalysts of Putnam's time responded to his views with friendliness but they definitely rejected them. In 1909, when Freud spoke at Clark University, Putnam asked him whether men are merely products of biological evolution, personal experience and social education, and if that were so would it not rule out all moral estimates as to whether one person was better than another. Freud replied that "it was not moral estimates that were needed for solving the problems of human life and motives, but more knowledge." (Putnam, 1921, p. 450). In later letters to Putnam, Freud readily agreed with his moral standards, but refused to link them to psychoanalysis. In 1914, he wrote Putnam that the aim of psychoanalysis is indeed "to bring about the highest ethical and intellectual development of the individual," but that on practical grounds he refused to entrust that task to the psychoanalyst: "The great ethical element in psychoanalytic work is truth and again truth and this should suffice for most people. Courage and truth are of what they are mostly deficient." (Hale, 1970, p. 171). Subsequently, Freud insisted that" analysis makes for integration but does not of itself make for goodness." (Hale, 1970, p. 188). Still more sharply, he wrote Putnam, after reading his *Human Motives*, "sexual morality— as society—at its most extreme, American society—defines it, seems very despicable to me. I stand for a much freer sexual life." (Hale, 1970, p. 189).

A few years later, referring to Putnam's proposal to "urge a particular philosophical outlook . . . on the patient for the purpose of enobling his mind," Freud commented: "In my opinion, this is after all only to use violence, even though it is overlaid with the most honorable motives." (Freud, 1919, p. 165).

His preface to Putnam's collected psychoanalytic papers—the first volume published in the International Psycho-Analytical Library—is a warm tribute but unambiguously rejects Putnam's proposals to bring his philosophy into psychoanalysis. (Putnam, 1921, iv). In the same volume, Jones writes that despite Putnam's intense desire to fuse philosophy with analysis "he had no difficulty in keeping them apart." (p. 464). This does not agree with the foregoing material, but may be accurate in respect to Putnam's clinical practice.

In 1911, Putnam presented a communication at the Weimar Congress of the International Psycho-Analytical Association setting forth his ideas. He was highly esteemed for his courageous struggle on behalf of psychoanalysis in the United States, and those attending the congress were eager to meet him; however, his paper on the need to incorporate philosophy into psychoanalysis did not meet with success. Freud later commented to Jones that "Putnam's philosophy reminds me of a decorative centerpiece: everyone admires it but no one touches it." (Jones, 1959, Vol. 2, p. 189).

A resumé of the address, presented and commented on by Theodor Reik, appeared in the Zentralblatt. He identified Putnam's Kantian idealism, and stressed the impossibility of equating metaphysics with science. He disagreed with Putnam's contention that psychoanalysts have a negative attitude toward philosophy; rather, they are neutral—each person is free to adopt his own philosophy which "depends ultimately on the sort of person one is." (Reik, 1912, p. 44). Eventually psychoanalysis should be able to explain the genesis of philosophy rather than vice versa.

Putnam wrote a lengthy rejoinder to Reik stating that he was more "deeply convinced of the justification and practical value of [his] argument," than ever before, and felt that the complexities of metaphysics had led to its neglect. If psychoanalysis is to strive for "sublimation as its ultimate goal," the analyst, "in his role as educator," must have a formal background in ethics and philosophy. He attacked the view that "the mind is the ultimate result of a pure physical evolution," and protested that ethics had been demoted to the level of a pure and narrow utilitarianism. His central idea, he affirmed, is that mental activity derives not only from experience but from innate processes such as man's concepts of motion and causality. By claiming to be neutral (vis à vis philosophy), psychoanalysis is taking a negative attitude. He concluded his rebuttal with the wish that Jung's concept of libido be further extended to where it merges with Bergson's *poussée vitale*. (Putnam, 1913).

The discussion was continued by Ferenczi who observed that it was premature for psychoanalysis to lock itself into any given philosophic system—psychoanalysis has the right, and duty, to investigate all products of the mind, including philosophy. "There is only one science, but there are as many philosophers and religions as there are human beings, each endowed with their own mental and temperamental evolution." (Ferenczi, 1912, p. 521). He characterized "spontaneous energy" and "divine power"—which for Putnam are the ultimate realities from which the material world is derived— as among the oldest "creation myths." He was particularly sensitive to Putnam's "attack on psychic determinism"— which he believed was the most decisive advance of psychoanalysis. To Putnam's allegation that psychoanalysis leaves no room for free will, he responded that psychoanalysis is not content merely to trace out the consecutive events of a preordained course, but attempts to evolve a dynamic explanation of mental events. Although we manifest our subjective will we cannot avoid the force of the determinants within us. Our acts are not the simple expression of a "laissez-faire" principle, because by actively taking into our own hands the steering of our fate we observe not an act of free will "but the result of phylogenetic and ontogenetic determinants that protect us from falling into an inactivity leading to self and species destruction." (Ferenczi, 1912, p. 524). Determinism, he observed, must not be confused with fatalism. He concluded by emphasizing the central role of unconscious mental processes, pointing to their neglect by psychology prior to Freud's discoveries; should the flow of knowledge from the unconscious ever become exhausted, then perhaps, research related to consciousness, or physical determinants, would be taken up more vigorously.

Putnam's rebuttal to Ferenczi reviewed his earlier positions and once again affirmed his belief that science must subordinate itself to philosophy because it alone "deals with the essence of the mind." (Putnam, 1912, p. 528). He rejected Ferenczi's view of philosophy as a derivative of mental life basing himself on Royce's neo-Kantian views.

In 1915, he expressed some regret about the Weimar paper, attributing its weakness to his lack of clinical experience, and suggested that philosophical speculation is a camp of refuge for those who are limited by "temperament and infantile fixations." (Putnam, 1921, p. 297). Nevertheless, he continued to profess the same opinions. His last paper, "Elements of Strength and Elements of Weakness in Psychoanalytic Doctrines," which he was revising at the time of his death in 1918, reiterated his earlier arguments; and after ascribing many complimentary traits to Freud, he suggested that these are "neither solely a by-product of 'libido', nor due solely to the combined action of that influence and of the influence of social pressure . . . but . . . to the coming to light of powers . . . which exist essentially in their own right . . ." (Putnam, 1921, p. 451).

DISCUSSION

Putnam was not merely a genteel product of 19th century New England who was unable to stomach Freud's views on sexuality. Quite the contrary, his courageous defense of psychoanalysis has earned him a secure place in its history. I have sought to demonstrate that despite his intellectual allegiance to science, he was unable to transcend his religious, ethical, and philosophical positions. It is not unusual nor contradictory, for scientists to maintain superstitions, mystical or religious beliefs, or to adhere to an idealist philosophy; it is exceptional, however, for them to introduce these ideas into their workshop. Like Schrödinger, Eddington, Jeans, and others, they may deploy their scientific knowledge to buttress a philosophic or religious point of view, but they do not attempt to derive the latter from the former. For example, despite Oscar Pfister's deep piety, he never sought to link religion to psychoanalytic theory. Indeed, he complained that Freud's pupils were too metapsychological for his taste. He attached Jung's "high-falutin interpretations which proclaim every kind of muck to be spiritual jam . . . and [attempts] to smuggle a minor Apollo or Christ into every worked-up little mind . . . it is Hegelianism transferred to psychology." (Meng, 1967, pp. 86–87). Later, he was critical of Putnam's "haughty" attempts to influence the direction of empirical science. (Pfister, 1923).

In presenting this communication, I have wished not only to offer a backwards glance, of some historic interest, but to draw attention to contemporary incursions of culture into science. While we are now witnessing an apparent vogue of anti-reason which is as blatant as it is destructive, less obvious are those points of view that represent the intertwining of value-systems with observational methods. In psychiatry, this has frequently taken the form of populism and relativism. Some of this activity is reminiscent, but without the philosophic basis, of Putnam's ethical goals; however, he never suggested that his position was based on scientific data.

Accordingly, it has become a shibboleth to ascribe mental illness to a "sick" ("permissive" or "constrictive") society, without offering evidence to support such hypotheses. Similarly, in the past few decades, it has become an unquestionable tenet that the "Judaeo-Christian" tradition represents a universally accepted code of morality and conduct, ignoring that most of the world population adheres to other, no less valid, and often more ancient, principles of behavior.

During the 1960's, in the psychological discussions about student dissent, it often appeared that those who approved of the events regarded them as the responsible acts of selfless, socially-minded youth; those who disapproved stamped the students as neurotic. In a like manner, the once useful concept of "acting out" has become a victim of cultural mayhem. From a fairly precise term regarding the behavioral representation of neurotic conflict, most particularly related to transference phenomena in the analytic situation, it has evolved into a catch-all label applied to any conduct which the user regards as reprehensible. Obviously, psychoanalysts alone did not bring about this transformation, but they did participate in it. That analysts and most of their patients are in a fairly narrow socio-economic and cultural range creates an additional complicating and challenging difficulty.

The other side of the cultural coin is a dogged allegiance to a concept of "science" that is a caricature of scientific thinking—such as an infatuation with numbers, a compulsion to ape techniques from the natural sciences, and a disdain for intuition. C. P. Snow (1974) recently commented that "Reason is not everything, but for many purposes it is our best working tool. Often we require insights other than those of reason to ally themselves with the insight of reason. . . what we never require, and what is always dangerous, and can be calamitous, are the instincts of anti-reason." (p. 2).

It appears that the farther away an inference is from the clinical datum, the more likely is it to reflect a cultural bias. The present reexamination of certain psychoanalytic concepts, such as sexual devlopment, energy, and the nature of the instinctual drives, is a tacit recognition, I believe, of the cultural penetration of psychoanalysis. Since the phenomenon is undoubtedly inevitable, it would appear that its influence on theory and methods of practice can only be limited by a constant awareness of its presence.

SUMMARY

James Jackson Putnam played a significant role in establishing psychoanalysis in the United States. A philosophical idealist, he sought to attach his ethical and religious ideas to psychoanalysis. This communication describes the sources of his neo-Kantian philosophy, and the reaction of psychoanalysts to his endeavors. It is suggested that the incursion of cultural influence into science, not excepting psychoanalysis, is inevitable, but awareness of the phenomenon creates the possibility of containing it.

REFERENCES

FERENCZI, S. (1912). Philosophic und psychoanalyse. *Imago* 1:519–526.

FREUD, S. (1919). Advances in psycho-analytic therapy. *Standard Edition* 17:165 London: Hogarth Press, 1955.

HALE, N.J., JR., Ed. (1971). *James Jackson Putnam and Psychoanalysis.* Cambridge, MA: Harvard University Press.

JONES, E. (1959). *Free Associations.* New York: Basic Books Inc.

MENG, H. & FREUD, E., Eds. (1967). E. Mosbacher (transl.). *Psychoanalysis and Faith: The Letters of Sigmund Freud and Oskar Pfister.* New York: Basic Books.

MILLER, P. (1950). *The Transcendentalists.* Cambridge, MA: Harvard University Press.

PFISTER, O. (1923). *Some Applications of Psychoanalysis.* New York: Dodd, Mead.

PUTNAM, J. (1899). Not the disease only but also man. *Boston Medical and Surgical Journal* 141:53–57; 77–81.

——— (1906). The bearing of philosophy on psychiatry, with special reference to the treatment of psychasthenia. *British Medical Journal* 2:1021–1023.

——— (1908): The treatment of psychasthenia from the standpoint of the social consciousness. *Am. J. Ment. Sci.* 135:77–94.

——— (1912). Antwort auf die Erwiderung des Herrn Dr. Ferenczi. *Imago,* 1:527–530.

——— (1913). Psychoanalyse and Philosophic eine Erwiderung auf die Kritik von Dr. Otto (sic) Reik. *Zentr. f. Psychan.* 3:265–269.

——— (1915). *Human Motives.* Boston: Little, Brown & Co.

——— (1921). *Addresses on Psycho-Analysis.* Vienna: The International Psycho-Analytic Press.

REIK, T. (1912). James J. Putnam, Über die Bedeutung philosophischer Anschauungen und Ausbildung für die weitere Entwickelung der psycho-analystischen Bewegung. *Zent. f. Psychan.,* 3:43–44.

SLOCHOWER, H. (1975): Philosophical principles in Freudian psychoanalytic theory; ontology and the quest for matrem. In: *American Imago,* vol. 33, no. 1. Also in Snow, C. P. (1974): *Medical Possibilities and Human Conscience.* Chapel Hill, NC: University of North Carolina.

CHAPTER 15

The Faust Legend Seen in the Light of an Analytic Case

[Werman, D.S. & Rhoads, J.M. (1976). *Journal of the American Psychoanalytic Association* 24:101–121.]

> O, what a world of profit and delight
> Of power, of honor, of omnipotence,
> Is promis'd . .
> —Christopher Marlowe, *Hero and Leander*

Legend and literature are rich in Faustlike characters—men so dominated by a wish for omnipotence, omniscience, and boundless sexual experience that they are willing to enmesh themselves in a pact with the devil, usually through magical means, to achieve their ends. A patient, a 40-year-old physician, after eight months of analysis, reported an episode of acute anxiety while watching a televised performance of Marlowe's The Tragical History of Dr. Faustus. He found he had identified with the eternally damned hero of the play. While recognizing that the psychological configuration of the Faust complex (as we shall call it) is but a "final common pathway" from many different psychodynamic mechanisms, we believe an understanding of this patient's personality development enhances an understanding of the Faust character and the persistent appeal of the Faust legend. The Faust complex, in common with other psychopathologic formulations, is but a distorted and maladaptive hypertrophy of the more normative and ubiquitous strivings of human beings for strength, knowledge, wisdom, and gratification of the sexual drive. Our patient's yearnings were perhaps more banal than those of the heroic Fausts created by Marlowe and Goethe, and his commitments perhaps more meager. He nevertheless believed himself to have confronted "eternal damnation," and if his stature does not bring to mind the Marlovian and Goethian Fausts, we should remember that these promethean figures are dramatic prototypes of man.

FAUST IN LEGEND, LITERATURE, AND HISTORY

The Faust legend goes back to ancient times and seems to derive from seasonal and kingship rites. Man's yearning for omnipotence is found in such diverse sources as Persian legends, the Hebrew Kabbalah, Arab mysticism, Neo-Platonism and Saint Augustine. Perhaps the earliest description of such an individual was that of Solomon, who was given a magic ring with four stones, endowing him with power over nature, men, and all spirits. In this way he was transformed into a potent wizard representing the wish of the primitive medicine man (Butler, 1948), (1949). Simon Magus (magician), mentioned in Acts VIII: 9–13, 18–24, who gave his name to one of the great vices of the church, simony, the selling of ecclesiastical offices and indulgences, was a magician by profession and wanted to place himself above God. He claimed to be able to make himself invisible, to pass through mountains, and to fly (this latter feat occurs frequently among Faustlike figures).

A curious legend concerned Gerbert, a magus who was presumed to have become Pope Sylvester II and to have served as Pontiff from 999 to 1003, despite having signed his soul away to the devil. As Pope, he shockingly abused his power, giving himself up to a wicked and luxurious life. Although he was assured that he had nothing to fear so long as he abstained from celebrating high mass in Jerusalem, he one day, without premeditation, found himself breaking his oath by doing just that. Despite an open confession of his guilt, he was drawn and quartered by horses, and "laid to rest." The actual Gerbert was an eminent philosopher and mathematician. But because learning and science were suspect in the Middle Ages, he was believed to have had "carnal intercourse" with the devil and was described as having been accompanied by a familiar spirit in the form of a shaggy, black dog. (The black dog recurs repeatedly, in these stories, as a minion of the devil.)

Gilles de Rais (1404–1440), popularly known as Bluebeard, was also denounced for having entered into an agreement with the devil. Although the accusation was never proven at his trial, it was clear that he had employed magicians who probably made such satanic contracts, and he had participated in the black masses and other magical ceremonies that were carried out by these men on his behalf. Although the erotic-sadistic nature of de Rais's interests is well known, he was also dominated by a thirst for the acquisition of knowledge, riches, and power.

The fifteenth century was notable for the emergence of what can now be recognized as elements of the modern world. Slow, patient assimilation of the knowledge of the ancients, the steady accretion of improvements in agriculture, transportation, architecture, and the beginnings of modern chemistry, joined with the growth of urban centers and the greater accumulations of capital and led to the Italian Renaissance, the discovery of America, and to the greater spread of learning throughout Europe. While for the most part the Church idealized tradition, custom, and obedience, certain elements within it, such as the universities, offered an outlet to the creative energies of the populace and encouraged speculation and experimentation, which ultimately led to the development of modern science. Inevitably, these forces collided, and humanism, individualism, scientism, and sensualism were opposed by authoritarian, pietistic, ascetic, and superstitious traditions. These conflicting forces are exemplified in the Faust legends, just as, later on, the more personal and individual aspects of the struggle between sin and rectitude, between man and the repressive elements of culture, are depicted in the legend.

Men such as Paracelsus (1493–1541) and Agrippa (1486–1535) probably served as models for the Faust figure of the period (Pachter, 1951). Although such alchemists, philosophers, and scholars as these were often publicly damned, they were also praised and envied. Sexual themes crept into the legends, and many writers of the era of the Borgias, Erasmus, Luther, Leonardo, and Columbus depicted Faust not only as seeking illicit knowledge, but also as a carnal sinner.

The actual Faust, born, it is believed, in Wurtemberg, about 1480, studied magic at the University of Cracow (Palmer & More, 1936). There are reports that he disparaged the miracles Jesus had wrought and boasted that whatever Jesus had done he could repeat. Although Luther and Melanchthon regarded Faust with horror, others induced this pundit to teach school. It was said that he molested the boys entrusted to his care, and when discovered, fled to escape punishment. A Franciscan monk admonished him to return to God and threatened him with eternal damnation, but Faust replied: "I have gone further than you think and have pledged myself to the devil with my own blood, to be his in eternity, body and soul" (Kaufmann, 1961).

The records of the city of Nürnberg contain a refusal for a safe conduct to Dr. Faust, and a description of him as "the great Sodomite and necromancer"—it seems he publicly called the devil his "brother-in-law."

The first literary work to deal with the Faust legend was Johann Spies's Faustbuch, published in Frankfurt-am-Main, in 1587. Numerous editions of this book, many pirated, were to appear during the next several decades, including a rhymed edition in 1588. The last of these Faustbuchs appeared in the early 1700's and was translated into English, Dutch, and French. Although the English Faustbuch is reputed to be a grossly inaccurate translation, it is important because it was the source from which Christopher Marlowe drew his materials and inspiration to write *The Tragedy of Dr. Faustus*. In his drama, the details of Faust's contract with Mephistophilis (sic) consist of promising his body and soul to the devil after 24 years, by which time all his desires shall have been fulfilled. Marlowe's Faust conjures up a fantasy of the beautiful Helen of Troy for a group of scholars, and then asks Mephistophiles if he can have her as his paramour. Ultimately he must pay the price, and at the end of 24 years he is taken to hell by the devils.

During the late seventeenth century, at least 150 versions of the Faust story were cast into some literary or theatrical form. One can readily understand the popularity of the Faust theme with the audiences of the day; they could identify with Faust's evil desires, while at the same time assuaging their superegos with the assurance that justice and virtue would ultimately triumph.

Characteristically, these plays are about Faust's desires for omnipotence, wisdom, and voluptuous experience, which he secures through compacts with the devil. The central idea in all these plays is the test to which a noble man's virtue is put: can the devil destroy Faust's soul, or will this trial purge and purify the Lord's servants? This is the view Goethe adopted in renouncing the Marlovian conception of satanic greatness. And it was Goethe, in the second part of his Faust (completed at the close of his life) who permitted Faust to enjoy an eventual salvation.

Lessing (1729–1781) was the first prominent writer, after Marlowe, to deal with the Faust legend, introducing a change in attitude toward the pursuit of knowledge. Whereas in

Marlowe and in the puppet plays Faust's intellectual curiosity was regarded as sinful, Lessing held the thirst for knowledge and truth to be one of the highest of ideals and therefore his Faust could not be cast into darkness. Although he worked on his version for twenty years, it is questionable whether he actually completed his drama.

Goethe's Faust, as befitting a work universally acknowledged to be a supreme masterpiece, has been the subject of an enormous number of studies (for example, Lukacs, 1969). This drama is not only a precipitate of several thousands of years of legend, history, and superstition, but embodies much of the historical and cultural ferment that was present from the Renaissance through the eighteenth century.[1]

Goethe was able to incarnate the great social struggles of his time through powerful, concrete characters who were symbolic of his own personality. The problems of understanding nature, and the relations between thoughts and action had already existed in the earlier Faust legends. The Lutheran influence, however, regarded the strivings for knowledge, experience, and pleasure as sinful, and Faust as an example to be abhorred. As Goethe deals with the legend, the struggle becomes one between man's creative and human qualities and the destructive potential within him. This view is similar to Eissler's, who notes that Faust is basically a play about the rescue of man's soul from Hell. Goethe's Satan reveals his essence as naked greed for gold and sexuality in these lines uttered by Faust (in Lukacs, 1969, p. 214):

> *And I have neither land nor money,*
> *Nor worldly honor nor glory.*
> *No dog would continue to live like this!*
> *This is why I have taken to magic.*

Goethe's Faust lamented the presence of these yearnings—both insatiable: one for limitless gratification of the senses, the other for knowledge. But ultimately there is salvation for him, as there had been for such earlier magicians as Cyprian and Theophilus. Far from remaining a magician who with a little luck might escape eternal damnation, Faust becomes a symbol of man's incorruptibility; though he may sin over and over, he will finally find the pure light.

The most recent literary Faust is Thomas Mann's Dr. Faustus (1948). Whereas Goethe sought to represent the essential impotence of evil, which he held up to ridicule in its most grotesque and repellent aspect, Mann emphasized its sinister power. There is a wider dimension to Dr. Faustus in Mann's premise that compromise with evil is difficult if not impossible, inasmuch as Adrian Leverkühn, the Faust figure of the novel, is generally regarded as a symbol of Nazi Germany and its

---

[1] We do not attempt to survey the literature that relates Faust to Goethe's own personality, background, and development, for this is not germane to our present purposes. Undoubtedly the most complete treatment of the subject is K. R. Eissler's two-volume study (1965).

antihumanistic regime. Congruent with the earlier Faust stories, Leverkühn, too, makes a pact with the devil, who grants him 24 years of musical creativity in return for his soul; again, eternal damnation, preceded by a syphilitic infection, which he punitively brings upon himself, does not have treated, and which progresses to a tertiary stage and his final deterioration. Although Mann's hero fled from the sociocultural madness that surrounded him, the resolution of his internal crises led him to a pact with the devil so that he could unblock the inhibitions that had settled over his creative activity (Mann, 1961).

THE CASE OF DR. B.

The patient, as we said earlier, was a 40-year-old physician who complained of attacks of anxiety, often without any evident cause; "homosexual thoughts" in the form of intrusive ideas that he must perform fellatio on certain men; difficulties in developing reasonable relations with men; frequent feelings of anger and fears of retaliation; and an unsatisfactory marriage. Although he felt that he had been helped by previous psychotherapy, after much procrastination he decided to undergo analysis.

Dr. B. came from a working-class family that had been badly affected by the depression. He grew up in a house, half of which was occupied by his parents, his sister (ten years his senior), and himself; the other half by an aunt, uncle, and other members of the family. Two sisters had died in infancy before the patient was born, and the family frequently spoke of their beauty. The two families had their own rooms and periodically changed kitchens in order to "equalize" the arrangements. The patient always had the choice of where to eat, depending on what was being prepared and with whom he wished to dine.

Until he was three or four, he slept in his parent's bedroom and had vague memories of them "moving around." He was enuretic until age twelve; his mother nagged him about it, but he felt no one else cared. After wetting his bed, he would go to his parents' room to have his mother change the sheets.

His mother had worked since his infancy. She was a pious, ambitious woman, who wanted her children to be socially successful and hovered over their religious and secular education, pushed them to take music lessons, and saw to it that they were involved in church activities. She doted on her son, frequently buying him gifts and preparing dishes that he alone enjoyed. But he chafed under her intrusiveness and control, and recalled his feelings of intense loneliness on coming home for lunch when she was at work—he felt abandoned and uncared for.

His father moved from one menial job to another. He was a vituperative man who constantly talked about what he "was going to do" to his alleged enemies and delighted in relating gruesome stories about dismemberment and mutilation. The patient was afraid of him and felt that his father didn't care "a rat's ass" about him.

The parents fought constantly: the mother disparaged her husband for his inadequacy as a breadwinner, and he attacked her for alleged flirtations with other men. The patient felt his father was really talking about him at these times and was frightened, but at the same time felt he "could do better" for mother than did his father. He was both excited and frightened when his father threatened to leave home.

His exquisite sense of specialness came not only from his mother's seductiveness and her demeaning of his father, but also from his opportunity to go to his "alternate family" whenever he wished. In effect, he had a "family romance" in permanence, which was enhanced by the loving attention his aunt and uncle lavished on him.

Excessively stimulated by witnessing his parents' sexual activities, he began to masturbate, alone and with other boys, from about the age of five. He occasionally engaged in fellatio and attempted anal intercourse. Masturbation became loaded with special meanings and fantasies, and ultimately became a complicated mechanism that was used to deal with libidinal impulses, loneliness, fear of castration, anxieties about abandonment, self-punitive needs, and, still later, his "obligation" to maintain a passive posture as a "homosexual" (he believed masturbation to be a symptom of homosexuality). Masturbation also permitted him to introduce a fantasied love object into his "empty" home. The same pattern continued into adult life: whenever he felt lonely during his wife's absences, he either ran to his mistress or masturbated.

His feelings of omnipotence and his dread of castration were given a powerful impetus when he was about four years old. He and his sister had scuffled, and he had stumbled down a flight of stairs. The patient told his father, who spanked her severely, something he almost never did. That night she developed abdominal pain and was operated on for appendicitis. The patient felt he had caused this to happen. When she brought home her appendix in a bottle of formalin, he believed "her penis had been taken from her." He was subsequently haunted by the thought that his father could just as easily inflict this mutilation on him.

His castration anxiety was increased by his mother's intrusiveness, her dressing him in "sissy" clothes, and having him sing in public. When he was about four and a half years old, he took a little girl into his parents' bedroom, undressed her, and played with her on his parents' bed in a symbolic dramatization of possession of his mother. His mother discovered them and paddled him. She had been ironing at the time, and the patient was afraid that she would "iron out his penis." These incidents became lodestones of oedipal strivings and castration fears, and frequently came to mind in similar situations.

During his adolescence, the patient contemplated either becoming the devil or selling his soul to him, "if I could have intercourse with a woman—have sexual freedom." His pacts were for great power, knowledge, and freedom from sexual anxiety and guilt. "Power" encompassed a number of profound needs: to dispense with his castration anxiety, to achieve victory in his repetitive confrontations with the oedipal father, to achieve greater narcissistic gratification and freedom from the galling feelings of powerlessness, and to gratify his insatiable oral incorporative needs.

He gradually became deeply involved in church activities and, by thirteen, had become a youth leader. He believed that to become a minister would delight his mother. At the same time it became the master fantasy and major restitutional maneuver through which he would put an end to his sins and atone to God for all his broken promises (masturbation, incestuous thoughts, murderous fantasies about his father, "homosexuality," and the like).

The patient's shift from the devil to God calls to mind Freud's (1922) observation that "God and the devil were originally identical—were a single figure which was later split into two figures with opposite attributes. In the earliest ages of religion God himself still possessed all the terrifying features which were afterwards combined to form the counterpart of him" (p. 86).

By his mid-teens he was permitted to conduct religious services and had begun to feel like Christ. He became an outstanding athlete in several sports. The periods before games were extremely anxious ones for him because he was torn between taking his teammates for prayer or masturbating. The former route led to winning, whereas the latter, by displeasing God, meant losing.

His mother's inculcation of his specialness led to fantasies of playing David to his father's Goliath. At times he experienced a sense of "kinship" with God who, he believed, would give him special powers if only he "knew the right combination, used some special incantation, or whatever."

He won a scholarship to a prestigious university where he pursued a predivinity program, but by the time of graduation he felt impelled to break his "contract" with God: to be a clergyman would inhibit sexual activity too much and would not allow for the counterphobic activities he engaged in to attenuate his unrelenting castration anxiety. Accordingly, he accepted a commission in the armed forces, where he spent several years performing at a superior level and volunteered for high-risk activities. During this period, he ruminated at length about his broken pact, anticipating various sorts of punishments. He developed backaches, "paraesthesias," pylorospasms, and episodes of acute anxiety. He believed he was going mad. He feared God would "strike him down," that his "appendages would burn."

Casting around for a suitable career, he struck on medicine: it would appease God, would permit him to live well, would allow for greater sexual license, and at the same time, he could be helping others. He recalled his mother's once speaking warmly of an intern who had attended her during an early hospitalization, and he felt some pangs of jealousy.

In medical school, dissection of the cadaver precipitated anxiety attacks. He sought psychiatric help and underwent psychotherapy for about a year and a half. He successfully continued his career with no further difficulties except some depression following his mother's death about six years prior to his beginning analysis.

After graduation from college, he married a woman who was bright, successful, assertive, and competitive, and whom he likened to his mother and sister. The patient felt she controlled their relationship, citing the fact that she had never failed to assume the superior position during sexual intercourse. He was enraged by this, but was unable to deal with it, or with his fear that she might "twist off" his penis during foreplay. Their marriage degenerated into an abrasive, loveless relationship which had a sufficiently bad effect on their children to necessitate psychotherapy for them.

His intense, preconscious oedipal conflict was pervasive. Deriving from this, as well as from his mother's intrusive, controlling behavior, was his almost crippling castration anxiety, which extended into virtually every area of his life. This anxiety was the spur for a vast array of counter-phobic acts which involved either literally or symbolically dangerous deeds. He carried an almost paralyzing load of guilt, built up from his oedipal wishes, his extramarital affairs, his early and continuing masturbation fantasies and his intrusive "homosexual" thoughts.

The first hours of analysis quickly introduced his widespread use of magical thinking. He described his "contracts" and "deals" with God and the recurring pattern of breaking his agreement, seeking restitution by promising something still more difficult to adhere to, then in turn breaking his new contract, and so on, until his life was filled with the massive debris of broken promises and he himself was deeply "in debt."

Probably influenced by his previous psychotherapy, he rapidly developed both an intense oedipal transference to his analyst and an effective therapeutic relationship. He expected his analyst to make decisions for him, as had his previous therapist. He inquired whether he should be having an affair (his previous therapist advised him not to—advice he had ignored, though not without a great deal of guilt). He wondered whether the analyst was "queer" and had designs on him; he asked for a rule about whether he should use profanity or not, and feared that he might harm the doctor. Later he recognized a great desire to please the analyst-father-God, and associated him with an uncle of whom he had been very fond and who had been like a father to him. By the 100th hour he was treating the analyst like a god. Coincident with this, his castration anxiety peaked, he became afraid of both the analyst and his wife, and feared that sexual relations led to cancer. An amusing displacement of this transference occurred when he was called for jury duty, but was excused by the judge. He was so anxious that the bailiff had to tap him on the shoulder to step down, for he thought the judge had said, "Guilty of adultery and incest as charged!"

In the early months of treatment he made a series of contracts with God, mostly concerning promises to stop seeing his mistress; each of these pacts was in exchange for something he wanted. His need to continually reassure himself of his genital intactness, however, drove him to visit her; each visit resulted in the need for a new contract. It became evident that these "contracts with God" were attempts to make a pact with the analyst, who would confer omnipotence on him. Being a "good patient" was in exchange for extramarital sex without guilt, for the creative energy to do momentous research with minimal effort, and for unlimited sexual potency. Working in analysis or not seeing his mistress were payments in order that he not be castrated.

By the 140th hour while he reported continued guilt feelings when having sex with his mistress, a feeling he counteracted "by silent prayer and incantations," he also described a somewhat decreased need to placate God, and coincidentally a greater feeling of security with the analyst. There followed a period of attempted bribes of the analyst by various means, interpreted in light of his needs to bribe God and his father, most of all by being a "good little boy." He strongly believed in "an all-powerful God who can inflict punishment, deliver you to Heaven or Hell, depending on what you do." Although he believed he had "fulfilled at least part of the bargain by becoming a physician," he was plagued by doubts that it was not a sufficient restitution. In analysis, he ruminated about whether Christ had had a penis, and if not, how did He urinate, how did He defecate, etc. On the one hand, he felt that "sooner or later God would catch up" with him and, on the other, he felt "selected to do God's work; perhaps I felt I could be like Christ."

He thought that, despite everything, God had been good to him by making him "talented." But as he looked back over his life, he realized that "everything seems to have centered around my penis and my fears of losing it. And yet [although this was the greatest fear], to be sexless would be to be like Christ," and that, in turn, meant possession of his mother because he then would be perfect and omnipotent. Constantly stimulated, he was unable to resolve this dilemma. Everything good that came his way was a gift from God; all that was bad was a punishment; the greatest punishment was to be prevented from having sexual intercourse.

Although he often felt in combat with the devil, he felt he had "sold" himself to him when he did not become a minister, for he had (and still) felt that "God had set me aside to do something great . . . I've had the idea that I can do anything I want, as well as any other man. It's in this way that I think of my work as having omnipotent power." Being a physician confirmed his omnipotence by the life-and-death power he felt he exerted over his patients. At the same time, his sense of guilt was greatly increased when one of his patients died. He asked his analyst if they were to meet on the next day, which was Good Friday; told that the hour would take place, he avowed that at that moment he had the thought: "Hallelujah, I am born again!" Although he had renounced the cloth, he had not relinquished the ministry in his speech, for he used orotund

figures of speech and polysyllabic words wherever possible, sounding like a caricature of a pretentious
preacher. This allowed him to cling to the idea of being a pastor and, at the same time, to ridicule the ministry.

One of his principal concerns throughout analysis was the intrusive thought of wanting to suck a certain man's penis. This overdetermined obsession ritualistically brought together many of his magical thoughts: the need to reassure the oedipal father (or substitutes) that he had nothing to fear from him, inasmuch as he was passive, submissive, and feminine; to reassure the projectively perceived aggressor that he was not enraged and threatening; that by ingesting their semen he could simultaneously drain the virility and strength of "powerful" men and disarm them and steal it for himself. Assuming a feminine role was a means of castrating himself, thereby ending the frightful, recurrent fears of castration (he frequently said that it would be better to have no penis than to live with the constant threat of mutilation). It was self-punitive: through an attack on the guilty organ ("if thy [right] eye offend thee, pluck it out . . ."). And by becoming a woman he could achieve an identification with the adored, dead sister-angels about whom the family, and especially his father, rhapsodized.

At times he felt like a "fallen angel" because of his "adultery." He pleaded that he had "tried to be good but didn't quite make it . . . I thought of being the devil or signing my soul over to him, when I was twelve or thirteen, if I could have intercourse with a woman and have total sexual freedom. The most satisfying thing in life seemed to be sex, which I saw as the supreme feeling. But it has always felt bad, even with my wife. I guess I feel like the devil's disciple when I commit adultery." He often thought that if he could "endure enough hell on earth, I won't go to Hell ultimately. . . I don't understand why I want to be bad or see myself as evil; on the one hand, I see myself as a disciple of God, like Christ, and yet I come across as wanting to be bad. Goodness has always been so futile, it doesn't fit my sexual needs, and yet I feel like a dog when I'm having intercourse."

In the final months of analysis, as his magical thinking abated, he became mildly depressed when he was unable to deal with conflicts through his usual contracts with God. However, together with the integration of other insights, most particularly those arising from the analysis of his Oedipus conflict and his castration anxiety, he was able, a little at a time, to renounce his Faustian posture.

He struggled to accept his sexual drives as natural phenomena and was amazed to realize that all the people he saw around him "must have sexual feelings and genital organs, and have sexual relations." Increasingly, he realized how his mother had treated him as a special person, and he recalled his bittersweet elation over "having won the battle with father." He was able to see the absurdity of his omnipotent posture and was able to verbalize fantasies relating to his omniverous needs for power and gratification. Ultimately, he was able to recognize his own identification with Christ (his ideal expectations), was able to joke about his magical prayers, and remarked that, "It's been nice to have found the father I never had. Now I must revert to reality again." Termination was characterized by sadness at leaving, but with appreciation of the analyst's role.

DISCUSSION

We have described the essential aspects of the Faust figure as consisting of an intense desire for omnipotence, omniscience, and boundless sexual gratification; traditionally, in legend and literature, these goals are obtained through a contract with a supernatural being, god or devil. We have characterized this process as magical because it is an attempt to manipulate the objective world by wishful thinking. Although one accepts magical thinking as developmentally appropriate in the small child, it is usually abnormal in the adult. Undoubtedly, the goals of a Faust are not dissimilar to those of all men; but where most people seek to control their destiny, gain knowledge and wisdom, and enjoy the gratifications of love and sexual pleasure, the Faustian's strivings have hypertrophied into a grotesque, grandiose caricature of these desires.

What most requires clarification is the employment of magic by a person with a scientific training. Ferenczi (1913) outlines the steps that lead from the newborn baby's achievement of its wishes through positive and negative hallucinations to fully established secondary-process thinking. The epitome of wish-fulfillment is the intrauterine existence when "one has nothing to wish for." The mother's nurturance of the infant re-enacts many aspects of intrauterine life, which the child experiences as due to his magical powers. Later, he begins to emit signals to make his wishes known. The child "passes through an animistic period in the apprehension of reality, in which every object appears to him to be endowed with life, and in which he seeks to find again in every object his own organs and their activities" (p. 227). The child's wishes are "magically" fulfilled because the adults easily read his mimicry; later, his words (thoughts) are also understood. Ferenczi notes that magical thinking in adults is a reaction to feelings of omnipotence fixed in childhood and represents a "'return of the repressed,' a hopeless attempt to reach once more, by means of changing the outer world, the omnipotence that originally was enjoyed without effort" (p. 231).

Dr. B. had ample grounds for his fixation to a magical mode of thinking for, in addition to having an overgratifying mother, he also enjoyed the curious circumstances of the double household that permitted him to misuse his possibilities of fulfillment through this additional "romance family," all of which was enhanced by his mother's derogation of his father.

His excessive early sexual stimulation through repeated observation of the primal scene led to overt masturbatory activity whereby again he was able to maintain his feelings of (sexual) omnipotence through fantasy. But this premature stimulation led to the development of a precocious and menacing superego constantly demanding that he be punished, by castration in the first instance; and this in turn led to the need to appease his father and propitiate God; hence, the pacts and deals ad infinitum. However, as Ferenczi points out, the omnipotent "ego" is ultimately confronted with the experiences of "the bitterest disappointment after every disregarding of reality." In this light, Dr. B.'s feelings of powerlessness at being abandoned by his mother, who left him to go to work, made his adaptation to the reality of the world more difficult. He was led to obtain gratification through the "next best" means, mainly through magical contracts which involved pacts aimed at gratifying his libidinal and narcissistic needs. Contract-making of this sort was a lifelong trait, with regression to a stage of magical thinking occurring whenever he could not shape reality to his wishes. We suggest that this is typical of the Faust figure in general.

Dr. B. attempted to solve his neurosis in many ways. He sought possession of his mother symbolically by undressing the little girl in his parents' bed; he gratified his desire for mother (sexually) through masturbation and its associated fantasies, and in the same way brought her into his fantasy world when he felt lonely. He dealt with his desires through sexual "games" with other boys, and each time had to promise something (to God) to diminish his mounting guilt. The more he denied his erotic desires, the more he was exposed to them. The ultimate contract was to become a minister (a euphemism for God or Jesus Christ), and on the strength of this pact he was able to do well in many areas. However, when it had become clear that the ministry would interfere with his erotic desires, he broke the pact, precipitating his neurosis. Until then, the contract had served well enough to deal with his guilt and anxiety.

Piaget (1926), in his outline of cognitive development, has delineated another view of the magical phase of childhood Ferenczi described. In the stage of "preoperational thought" the child begins to use symbols in simple ways. This period is characterized by egocentric thinking in which the child relates everything to himself and his subjective experiences, and includes a "preconceptual" stage, from one and a half to four years, which seems to parallel Ferenczi's period of magic thoughts and magic words.

Dr. B.'s lifelong feelings of omnipotence—and strivings for still greater power—raise the question of whether we are dealing with a neurosis whose roots (despite important pregenital influences) arose from his Oedipus complex, or whether we are dealing with a narcissistic personality disturbance. Kohut (1971) postulates a form of grandiosity resulting from the child's attempt to save an "originally all-embracing narcissism by concentrating affection and power upon the self—here called the grandiose self—and by turning away disdainfully from an outside to which all imperfections have been assigned" (p. 106). "Under favorable circumstances (appropriately selective parental response to the child's demands for an echo to and a participation in the narcissistic-exhibitionistic manifestations of his grandiose fantasies) the child learns to accept his realistic limitations, the grandiose fantasies and the crude exhibitionistic demands are given up, and are pari passu replaced by ego-syntonic goals and purposes, by pleasure in his functions and activities and by realistic self-esteem" (p. 107). Ultimately, then, the child recognizes his own imperfections and limitations, and the grandiose fantasy diminishes. Acrophobia may thus be less a psychoneurotic symptom than a manifestation of the infantile, grandiose urge to fly, which is modified by an ego recognizing such wishes as destructive. Dr. B.'s father was phobic about flying, whereas Dr. B. himself enjoyed it (typically, like other Faust figures such as Simon Magus), although he was acrophobic about buildings. His complicated attitude to heights seemed to be a reflection of his counterphobic behavior, his oedipal rivalry, and his unmodified infantile grandiosity.

His inability to give up his grandiose fantasies seems to stem not only from his continued magical thinking, but from his mother's treatment of him as her favorite. Freud (1917), discussing a childhood memory of Goethe's, states, "I have, however, already remarked elsewhere [*The Interpretation of Dreams,* p. 398n] that if a man has been his mother's undisputed darling, he retains throughout life the triumphant feeling, the confidence in success, which not seldom brings actual success along with it" (p. 156). (Jones [1957] tells us that this idea is basically autobiographical.)

Kohut (1971) points out that the narcissistic personality predominantly fears the loss of reality of the self either by merger with the idealized parent imago, or through "quasireligious regressions toward a merger with God . . . fear of loss of contact with reality . . . frightening experiences of shame . . . and hypochondriacal worries" (p. 153). Although some of these features were noted in Dr. B., what emerged within the first months of his analysis and was strikingly evident throughout the next two years (until analysis was terminated because of his transfer to another area) was a classical transference neurosis. This bore the marks of conflict arising from his oedipal complex and was characterized by powerful castration anxiety, constant triangular fantasies, fears of punishment, rivalry with the analyst (as well as other males), and fears of retribution. Thus, in contrast to the hypochondriacal worries of the narcissistic patient who fears "autoerotic fragmentation," Dr. B.'s castration anxiety was expressed in terms of a variety of physical illnesses and accident proneness. As Kohut states, the longer the analysis goes on, the clearer the source of the danger becomes. This led to the conclusion that Dr. B.'s primary problem was an unresolved Oedipus complex, with consequent regression to more primitive modes of thought and action.

SUMMARY

The Faust legend has an ancient history and has formed the basis of folktales, myths, poems, plays, and novels. We have characterized the Faust figure as one who strives intensely for omnipotence, omniscience, and boundless sexual gratification, and magically seeks to fulfill these goals through contracts, or pacts, that he makes with a god or a devil. Whereas the psychogenetic background of such individuals may be very different and the complex described here is but a "final common pathway" through which various psychodynamic mechanisms are represented and expressed, we believe at least one of these psychodynamic configurations has been delineated and some additional light cast on the Faust figure.

REFERENCES

BUTLER, E.M. (1948). *Myth of the Magus.* Cambridge: Cambridge University Press.

——— (1949). *Ritual Magic.* Cambridge: Cambridge University Press.

——— (1952). *Fortunes of Faust.* London: Cambridge University Press.

EISSLER, K.R. (1965). *Goethe: A Psychoanalytic Study.* Detroit: Wayne State University.

FERENCZI, S. (1913). Stages in the development of the sense of reality In: *Sex in Psychoanalysis.* New York: Basic Books/Robert Brunner, 1950, pp. 213–239.

FREUD, S. (1917). A childhood recollection from Dichtung und Wahrheit. *Standard Edition* 17:145–156. London: Hogarth Press, 1961.

——— (1922). A seventeenth century demonological neurosis. *Standard Edition* 19:72–105 (1961).

JONES, E. (1957). *The Life and Work of Sigmund Freud I.* New York: Basic Books.

KAUFMANN, W. (1961). Introduction to Faust. In: *Goethe's Faust.* New York: Doubleday and Company.

KOHUT, H. (1971). *The Analysis of the Self.* New York: International Universities Press.

LUKACS, G. (1969). Faust studies In: *Goethe and His Age.* New York: Grosset and Dunlap.

MANN, T. (1948). *Doctor Faustus.* H.T. Lowe-Porter (Trans.) New York: Alfred A. Knopf.

——— (1961). *The Story of a Novel: The Genesis of Doctor Faustus* Winston, R. & Winston, C. (Trans.). New York: Alfred A. Knopf.

MARLOWE, C. (1604). *The Tragical History of Dr. Faustus* In: London: J. M. Dent, 1909.

PACHTER, H.M. (1951). *Magic into Science.* New York: H. Schuman.

PALMER, P.M. & More, R.P. (1936). *The Sources of the Faust Tradition.* New York: Oxford University Press.

PIAGET, J. (1926). *The Language and Thought of the Child.* New York: Harcourt Brace.

www.ingramcontent.com/pod-product-compliance
Lightning Source LLC
Chambersburg PA
CBHW072101020426
42334CB00017B/159